A PRIMER OF
ENGLISH LITERATURE

A PRIMER OF
ENGLISH LITERATURE

by

W. T. YOUNG, M.A.

Lecturer in English Literature in the University of London
Goldsmiths' College. Joint Editor of *The Cambridge Anthologies*

Cambridge:

at the University Press

1914

CAMBRIDGE
UNIVERSITY PRESS

University Printing House, Cambridge CB2 8BS, United Kingdom

Cambridge University Press is part of the University of Cambridge.

It furthers the University's mission by disseminating knowledge in the pursuit of
education, learning and research at the highest international levels of excellence.

www.cambridge.org
Information on this title: www.cambridge.org/9781107505483

© Cambridge University Press 1914

First published 1914
Re-issued 2015

A catalogue record for this publication is available from the British Library

ISBN 978-1-107-50548-3 Paperback

PREFACE

THE study of literature is, rightly, a pursuit in which the faculties are liberated and disciplined by the freshness and variety of imaginative experience, and are made strong and supple so that they learn to enjoy the pleasure of their own activity. The following pages attempt to present the outlines of English literature in accordance with this ideal. The book is offered as a companion to studies, not as a short cut to a superficial and specious knowledge of the classics of our language. It does not seek to pronounce any final criticism, or to dictate on matters of judgment or taste; for these are the greatest disservices a teacher can render to a student. Its intention is, rather, to prospect in company with the reader, to unearth and investigate clues with him, to lure his curiosity, and to challenge him to thought. The student will eventually discover that certain periods or writers are more to his taste than others; he will require,

above all, bibliographical guidance. This he will
find in *The Cambridge History of English Literature,*
to which this *Primer* may serve as an introduction.

I am under a debt of obligation to Professor
Elton, who read through the proofs of the book, and
also to Professor P. G. Thomas, who generously
revised the medieval section in minute detail. But
I must accept the responsibility for the final form
of the statements in the book throughout.

W. T. Y.

August 1913.

CONTENTS

PAGE

BOOK I. OLD ENGLISH LITERATURE TO THE NORMAN CONQUEST 1

BOOK II. THE MIDDLE AGES 14

BOOK III. THE RENASCENCE 46

BOOK IV. THE LITERATURE OF THE MIDDLE CLASSES 112

BOOK V. THE REVIVAL OF ROMANCE . . . 146

BOOK VI. THE VICTORIAN AGE 177

APPENDIX 211

INDEX 214

It may be well to explain that the division into prose and verse in each period is fairly rigidly maintained. If this seems sometimes to disperse the work of one writer under several headings, there are compensations for this disadvantage, and the disadvantage is minimised almost to extinction by the index.

BOOK I

OLD ENGLISH LITERATURE TO THE NORMAN CONQUEST

1. POETRY

THE earliest poem still extant in the English speech is *Widsith*, 'the far-traveller,' recording the
The pagan verse journeyings of an imaginary singer among the Teutonic tribes of the continent in the fourth, fifth and sixth centuries. It gives us an outline, which we may fill in with detail from other poems, such as *Deor's Lament* and *Beowulf*, of the place of the 'scop,' or king's harper and remembrancer, in the social fabric of our ancestors. He appears as the honoured companion of kings, the recorder of heroic exploits, the memoriser of lays and stories of the past, which he chanted in the meadhall after the hunt or the battle. These lays developed, in time, by the passage from mouth to mouth, and, no doubt, by the finer artistic skill of some individual 'scop,' into epic poetry. This may be the evolutionary history of the early English
Beowulf epic *Beowulf*, shaped from pre-Christian lays in Northumberland in the eighth century, though the only MS existing is in a dialect

Y. 1

of king Alfred's time. *Beowulf* may interest us in various ways: as a story; as a picture of a social system; as a repository of fragments of other Teutonic epics; and as an example of heroic style. Its three thousand lines tell, with many digressions, the life story of Beowulf, who sails from his native Gautland in Sweden to the succour of Hrothgar, a king in Zealand, because his hall Heorot is being ravaged by Grendel, such a monster as vivid imaginations might suppose to inhabit the damp and gloomy forests behind the sea-board. Beowulf, who has the strength of thirty men, tears an arm from the monster and drives the fiend to its lair. Attacks are resumed by Grendel's mother, and Beowulf achieves a second hard-won victory in a cave beneath a lake, powerfully described by the poet. Thus, peace is restored to Heorot, and Beowulf returns to Gautland to become, after many years, its trusted and honoured king. He engages, finally, in a third conflict, with a dragon, keeper of a buried treasure (a common feature of Teutonic stories), in defence of his own hall and country. By the aid of his shield-bearer, Wiglaf, he is victorious, but at the cost of his life. The poem ends with a eulogy of his justice and valour by his thegns over the mound where his ashes are buried.

In all probability, these three splendid fights are based on a myth, or on some folktale, adapted to the hero's story. But we can discern behind these events a strongly marked social economy, at its head the king, round him the thegns, and, more dimly seen, the lower ranks or ceorls. It is a life lived, like the Homeric, in the open, with little enough privacy;

and the poetry is a poetry of action, devoid of subtleties of thought and feeling, a record of things done. Hunting, feasting, voyages, warfare, savage, and sometimes treacherous, feud, are the chief concerns. There is much about the ocean and ships, but no feeling of affection for the sea, rather the pride of conquest, as in Beowulf's swimming match. Strength, daring and the instinct for command are the most approved qualities, though the hero himself has many gentler traits, and, in a rugged way, is conscious of the lack of wife and children. There are references to institutions like the king's body companions, were-gild or blood-money, the nightly feast in the meadhall, with the gracious figure of the queen, held in highest reverence, pouring out the mead, and bestowing gifts, collar, armlet and mantle upon the hero. Then, benches are pushed aside, bolsters are spread and the thegns sleep with arms at hand. Many arts have developed; the hall Heorot is finely ornamented with gold, rich in famous swords and trophies of adventure, hung with embroidered tapestry; people are skilled in fashioning war-gear, ringed mail and boar-crested helmets; and the art of song is almost universal. They have no humour except that of grim challenge and competitive boasting— a common national trait, not to be judged by our standards. The religious feeling of the poem is, as it were, in two strata, pagan and Christian. The characters submit unprotestingly to 'wyrd,' or fate; and there is both melancholy and dignity in this fatalism, which never condones dishonour. 'Death is better for every warrior than a life of infamy,' is Beowulf's standard. The customs and rites, too, are

1—2

heathen throughout. But the sentiment and reflection are largely Christian; king Hrothgar, for
instance, speaks warningly of pride of strength and
possessions. We are forced to conclude, therefore,
that the poem was still in the process of making
when it passed to minstrels who had been influenced
by Christianity.

This full, well-ordered life, this grave discourse,
these courtly manners, this long-practised art of
epic poetry—for it must have taken centuries to
perfect the verse-form and establish the current
synonyms for hero, sword, sea, ship and the like—
show us that we are viewing the advanced civilisation of a race with a great and varied history, the
Germania, in fact, of Tacitus. The poem, also, is
the repository of fragments of other sagas. We
hear of Scyld, a Dane; of Sigemund, father of
Sigurd the Volsung; of another Beowulf, a Dane;
of Finn, a Frisian, who has some relation with
another Old English poem, *The Fight at Finnsburh*, describing a typical fierce onset, with the
ringing clash of separate blows, by small bodies
of men in a tight corner. *Beowulf* is evidently but
a fragment of the great northern *corpus* of stories
which includes the *Nibelungenlied*, and the tales
told in magnificent narrative prose in the Icelandic
sagas. The racial tradition, the dignity and valour
of the hero and the style give the poem an epic
rank, which its mere story, as it exists to-day,
would not win for it. It is written in Old English
alliterative measure, in which the rhythm depends
upon accent; the line is divided into two parts,
each containing two main accents. These accents

must fall on the emphatic words in the sentence; as a general, but not quite invariable, rule, two of these accented syllables in the first part, and one in the second part, of the line are alliterated, that is, they begin with the same letter (in the case of vowels, any vowel may be supposed to give alliteration with any other). The number of unaccented syllables is indifferent so long as they do not put too large a strain upon the normal rhythm. A line with so much freedom as this adapts itself readily to the poet's moods and purposes; landscape, battle, description of valiant exploits and elegiac meditation are equally well expressed in this vigorous and flexible measure; the style of the poem, in fact, often seems to be greater than its matter. There are few complete similes in the Homeric manner, but the diction is essentially figurative, and some of these figures become picturesque conventions; the sea is the whale-path; a ship, the foamy-necked one; the king, a gift-bestower; an arrow, a war-adder. Furthermore, there is a tendency to excessive use of apposition, which, together with a deficiency of particles, makes the story, however vigorously told, move slowly.

With this early poetry must be classed some short charms or pagan incantations for such occasions as bewitched land or stolen cattle; and of finer quality are five elegiac lyrics, the most Lyric original of all Old English poetry. In *The Wanderer*, the person spoken of, bereft by destiny of his chief and comrades, seeks to evade the bitter companionship of sorrow; a dream restores a momentary vision of joy, but, soon, the solitary poet awakens to realise that man is at the mercy of night, storm, winter and mortality. *The Ruin* is a picture of a town (possibly a Roman settlement, such as Bath), laid waste by violence and time; the poet conjures up in imagination its towers, pinnacles, courts, its flowing springs and halls filled with the mirth of warriors; these, he contrasts with the ruined masonry, fallen gates and frost-bespangled lime. *The Seafarer* describes, perhaps in a dialogue, the emotion and fascination of a sailor, lured to the bitter and lonely sea again, in spite of its peril and hardship. *The Lover's Message* and *The Wife's Complaint* are the only Old English verse based on the theme of love; the former is a message carried by a wooden tablet, recalling old affections and bidding the one addressed to join the sender beyond the sea; the latter, the plaint of a woman falsely accused and banished, is full of the despair of separation.

This group of poems, evidently the mere wreckage of a great literature, is decisively pagan in origin; but the Christian elements are intimately fused; there is a kind of compromise between the old and new beliefs. The pagan system of society, art and morals out of which the poems arose suffered three successive shocks from the southern world of Roman culture and religion. The first, at the conversion by St Augustine (though Irish missionaries from Iona had been long at work, and Whitby was a Celtic monastery). The second, at the accession of the scholar-king Alfred. The third, at the Norman conquest. What is left of Old English poetry enables us to mark the encroachment, at first very gradual, of Christianity upon pagan feeling.

Before the Christian spirit was fully manifested in literature, the church had been established a hundred years. Most Old English poetry was written in the dialect of Northumbria, though preserved for us in the dialect of Saxon Wessex; for Northumbrian civilisation, with its libraries at Jarrow, where Bede dwelt, and at Whitby, was the centre of European culture for a century, and Charles the great found there his educational adviser Alcuin, just before it was destroyed by Danish invasions.

The Christianised verse

Only two names (one of them, Cynewulf, doubtfully authentic) can be assigned as authors of the Biblical verse of Northumbria, Caedmon and Cynewulf. There is a well-known story, told by the venerable Bede, of how, at Whitby, Caedmon the neatherd, who had not the gift of song, was suddenly inspired to sing about the creation; the song Bede attributes to him is closely parallel to the opening of the poem *Genesis*, which, with *Exodus, Crist and Satan* and *Daniel*, forms the school of Caedmon. *Genesis*, to which the picture of Satan's torments in *Paradise Lost* may be indebted, has two parts, divergent in style, *A* and *B*. *A* is a paraphrase of the scriptural text, with expansions of the warlike episodes and the flood; *B*, the finer part, records again the fall of the angels. *Exodus* is a forceful description of the disaster of the Egyptians at the Red sea. *Crist and Satan* gives one of several pictures in Old English of the harrowing of hell.

Caedmon

In this way, the Christian religion first found its lodgement in Old English verse; from the Bible

were eagerly taken certain stories, especially those
animated by a spirit akin to the existing heroic
lays; the grim, primitive pugnacity common both
to Hebrews of the Old Testament and to our fore-
fathers makes possible such an association of poetry
with the sacred book of Christianity as we may see
in *Genesis* and *Exodus*.

The later school of Cynewulf, who is supposed
to have signed his name in runic characters in
Cynewulf   *Crist, Juliana, Fates of the Apostles*
                    and *Elene*, is also responsible for
Andreas, The Dream of the Rood, Guthlac and
The Phoenix. The titles of the poems are indi-
cative of the change in the choice of material; in
place of the more ferocious themes of the Old Testament, we find here stories of the New Testament,
of saints' lives and of the martyrology; the mystical
introspective spirit of Christianity is reflected in
them and the pictures of landscape and seascape
are gentler. They have, at the same time, a more
polished art, though this may seem to be at the cost
of the rude vigour of their predecessors. *Andreas,*
the story of a voyage of the apostle Andrew to
rescue St Matthew, contains a sublime description
of storm; *Elene* tells of the finding of the true cross
by Helena, mother of the emperor Constantine; its
descriptions of the sea and of the embarking hosts
close with the poet's conversion and adoration of the
cross, a theme dealt with in the dramatic though
brief *Dream of the Rood*. The cross speaks with
subtle and passionate emotion of the agony it shared
with the young hero Christ. *Guthlac* is a martyr's
conflict with fiends. *The Phoenix* is the most

inventive creation of the school, giving to the legend an allegorical significance and a background of exquisite natural and mystical beauty in the sinless land. Some of the *Riddles*, with their finely descriptive effects, may be by Cynewulf. The remaining verse includes a *Physiologus*, which is concerned with the animal symbolism of the art of the catacombs, and a dialogue *Salomon and Saturn*.

Reviewing the poems of the two schools, all written in the alliterative measure, we may see that religious innovations are more vital in the Cynewulfian group; in the Caedmonian, only the matter —the narrative of the *Pentateuch* and the book of *Daniel*—is given from without: the working up is by a poet similar in temper to the composer of *Beowulf*, and everything is translated into terms of the viking heroic age. The Cynewulfian poets, dealing with the contrasted matter of the gospels, remote from pagan sentiment, bring to its treatment a gentler spirit, though they still use some of the phrases of *Beowulf*. The Caedmonian hero wars with his foes and with the sea for fame, admitting no master but fate, and finding battle the necessary outlet for a natural instinct in him; the instinct did not die out of Old English life, for we find it in full activity in the war poetry of the *Chronicle* in the tenth century. The Cynewulfian hero, whether Christ or the saint, battles with fiends or with persecution or with torments for the sake of his fellows and for the glory of God. Thus is indicated the passage into a new world; from the civilisation which lies at the back of *Beowulf* and Old Norse

10 OLD ENGLISH LITERATURE

verse, the Icelandic sagas and the Old German epic
to the civilisation of Latin Christianity.

2. OLD ENGLISH PROSE

We may first name briefly writers in Latin: Gildas
author of *The Destruction of Britain*; the shadowy
Nennius, a historian; bishop Aldhelm;
Latin Writers the venerable Bede; and Alcuin, who,
in 792, went to serve Charles the great. Bede
lived at Jarrow from 672–735, and wrote numerous
scientific and theological manuals, all over-shadowed
by his *Ecclesiastical History of the English Race* 731.
Its five books cover the period from the invasion of
Caesar to the year 731. Bede was a writer whose
scholarship and discernment entitle him to rank
among the great historians of our literature. This
wide Latin culture, centred both in Northumbria and
at Canterbury, was swept away by the Scandinavian
irruptions, and learning did not raise its head again
King Alfred till, a century later, the idealist Alfred
sought its alliance in consolidating the
kingdom of Wessex. No worker in the cause of education ever faced more disheartening circumstances.
In all the country south of the Thames not a priest
could be found able to read Latin, and only two
north of it. The Latin *Life of Alfred* by the Welsh
cleric Asser, and Alfred's own preface to Gregory's
Pastoral Care, inform us of the enterprises which the
king set on foot in his two periods of comparative
leisure 888–93 and 897–901. He instituted a court
school for the reading of Latin and English, sought
out scholars abroad and translated or instigated the

translation of the chief works of erudition of his day. Bishop Werferth of Worcester translated the *Dialogues of Gregory the Great*. Alfred, with other help, translated the *Cura Pastoralis* of Gregory; the *Universal History* of Orosius was freely adapted and extended, as in the voyages of Ohthere and Wulf-stan, and in the geographical description of Germania. The English versions of Bede's *Ecclesiastical History* and Boethius's *De Consolatione Philosophiae* were other channels by which he brought to his people new streams of knowledge in ethics, philosophy and history. At the same time, he acquired a prose style, remarkable, in the passages which are not merely translations, for an attractive simplicity, which seems the direct reflection of his high-minded and courageous personality. To Alfred we owe in all probability the fuller records of the Old English *Chronicle,* which, in some recensions, dates back to B.C. 60. But, with the exception of a barbaric incident of Cynewulf (not, of course, the poet) and Cyneheard in 755, the monkish annals are bald enough till we come to the reigns of Alfred and his son. From 893–7 and from 911–24, the tale of the Danish wars is full and practised in expression ; and this is true, likewise, of the years 975–1001. Between these two periods comes a barren patch, completely redeemed, however, by the war poetry which ranks with the earlier epic as the finest outcome of the pagan English spirit. Under the date 937 is a verse record of Athelstan's victory at Brunanburh.

War poetry in the *Chronicle*
Tennyson made a poem of his son's prose translation of these lines. Of much finer quality is *The Battle of*

Maldon 991, the story of the raid of Anlaf the Dane
for tribute, in which the noble Byrhtnoth fell. The
insolent demand for gold; the reply that the oppressed will yield only the tribute of sword and
spear; the fierce clamour of hand to hand fighting;
the heroic death of Byrhtnoth at the head of his
band; the maintenance of the battle by Aelfwine,
Offa and Dunnere with their proud, simple talk—
these are set forth in a vigorous narrative which
rings with loyalty and valour and in which we
single out each stroke and fall as we do in the
poems of the heroic tradition, *Beowulf* and *Finnsburh*. *Judith*, once thought to be Caedmon's, is
now dated in the tenth century also.

Judith

The poem is a fragment based on the
Apocrypha, and records with intense dramatic energy
the slaughter of Holofernes, and Judith's summons
to the Israelites. Like the war poems, *Judith* is in
the alliterative measure; and we should have said
that alliteration as the normal form of verse made
a noble ending in these poems, were it not for the
remarkable revival of it in the fourteenth century,
in the western parts of England.

To the religious revival under Dunstan and his
pupils in the middle of the tenth century we owe
other prose in Old English. The nine-

Aelfric

teen *Blickling Homilies* are sermons and
legends, rough prototypes of the more finished
Homilies of Aelfric 990-5, these last some eighty in
all, expounding the mysteries of religion on various
occasions of the church year. Aelfric's writing is
impassioned and symbolical in his later works and
has a loose alliterative rhythm, like a broken down

form of the older verse. He died about 1020 and, for generations, was the most famous of English theologians.

Wulfstan was a contemporary of Aelfric, but more closely in contact with affairs; he, also, wrote *Homilies*, of which the most memorable is *The Address to the English*, which castigates his country, describes the demolition of the villages and the terror of the people and affirms that they are suffering for crimes for which they must now repent. There is mingled gloom and patriotism in the picture of the England over which Danish invasions were encroaching; it is like a late echo of the plaint of Gildas concerning the harrying of Britain by the English themselves.

Henceforth, judging from the records extant, Old English prose ebbs away, leaving insignificant traces, such as the continuation of the *Chronicle* at Peterborough till Stephen's reign, when the cry of a ravaged land is repeated a third time. Some legends of the east are found, which are prophetic of the incoming tide of that fashion of romance. Two hundred years elapse before a prose as accomplished as Aelfric's is evolved again in English.

BOOK II

THE MIDDLE AGES 1066–1500

1. POETRY FROM THE CONQUEST TO CHAUCER

IT is hardly possible to overstate the importance of the Norman conquest in the history of our literature. All the changes which it brought in its train did not become immediately apparent; but they were implicit in the historical fact. By the time of Chaucer, a new nation had been evolved by the crossing of English and Norman stocks. The process, at first slow, was accelerated by the separation from Normandy in 1204, with the result that, in poems such as *Richard Cœur de Lion* and Robert of Gloucester's *Chronicle* c. 1300, a sense of patriotic unity is completely developed. The vital requirement of a new speech was met by the acceptance of the Teutonic trunk, upon which was grafted the vocabulary of the invaders for all the interests and enterprises which the new ruling and leisured class had brought into national life. At the same time, the natural tendency of Old English to shed some of its many inflections was hastened by the Norman, following quickly upon the Danish, invasion. The process

The language

was almost completed by Chaucer's time, and the language thus formed is one of the marvellous accidents of history.

While this formative process was at work, books were written in Latin. Latin was the tongue of the schoolmen and of the vast compendia of theology, philosophy and law which

Latin

are characteristic of the Middle Ages. Anselm, John of Salisbury, Walter Map, Robert Grosseteste, Roger Bacon, William of Ockham, Duns Scotus and Richard of Bury, author of *Philobiblion*, carry the story of scholarship from 1089 to about 1350. Latin chroniclers had great influence on succeeding literature, as, for instance, William of Malmesbury, Giraldus Cambrensis, who describes Wales and Ireland, and Matthew Paris, d. 1259, a historiographer of rare historical sense and fine independence. Geoffrey of Monmouth has no standing among the exact historians; but he has a higher title to fame, for his *History of the Kings of Britain* c. 1136 is the parent-stock, not only of the stories of Lear, Cymbeline and Sabrina, but of the legends of king Arthur as well.

Anglo-French did a greater work in conveying Norman culture to England than in producing literature. The chroniclers Gaimar and Wace followed, in Anglo-French verse,

French

the romantic track of Geoffrey of Monmouth. Marie de France c. 1180, who lived in England, wrote her delightful *lais* of virgin-worship, love and fairy-lore in almost pure French. A *Bestiary* and some saints' lives were also written under the religious impulse which was strong among the Normans.

English was preserved only by the conquered people, much more numerous than its conquerors, English poetry but excluded from all offices of authoto 1250 rity; its writings, therefore, were rather depressed and halting. In the main, they followed the tradition of Old English sacred verse; a rapid review of them, however, will show some of the steps by which was evolved the final form of English verse; syllabic, accentual, rimed, not alliterative by principle, as in Old English, not quantitative, as in Latin, not having a fixed caesura, as in French, though each of these speeches contributed something to the final result.

The *Moral Ode* c. 1170, a religious exhortation, has rimed lines of fourteen syllables with little alliteration. *Ormulum* c. 1200, by one Orm (a homilist and phonetician whose most valuable quality is that he doubled the consonant after every short vowel in a closed syllable, in the 10,000 lines of his poem), has alternate lines of eight and seven syllables, with neither rime nor alliteration. A *Bestiary* c. 1210, an allegorical interpretation of a mythical natural history, ·has, generally, six-syllabled riming lines with some alliteration. The *Orison of our Lady* c. 1210 has riming couplets of uncertain length and occasional alliteration. *Genesis and Exodus* c. 1250, a paraphrase, has riming verse of four beats, an amazing forerunner of the metre of *Christabel*, though it had no immediate followers. The *Proverbs of Hendyng* c. 1270, about twenty years later than the *Proverbs of Alfred*, have six-lined stanzas with a regular rime scheme. From all this we may draw the conclusion that regular metre and rime were gradually ousting the older alliterative verse.

Two poems of this date have intrinsic worth and show how English was coming to its own, though dealing with matter imported from France; these are Layamon's *Brut* (one version of 1200 and one of c. 1250), and *The Owl and the Nightingale* c. 1220.

The age was full of *Bruts*; Layamon's material was derived from one of the copies of Wace's chronicle, and he distils his original into English; in the 32,000 short lines of his poem there are not a hundred French words. Being a priest on the borders of Wales, he incorporated stories and legends from his own country and he probably had sources of which as yet we know nothing. His fame lies in the fact that he was the first Englishman to treat the story of Arthur in English. In Layamon, the elves are concerned in Arthur's birth, the king becomes a more knightly and courteous figure and his mysterious passing is added; we hear more of the Round Table than in Wace; the poet tells, also, with occasional power and poetry, the tales of Lear and Cymbeline and other legendary kings. The shambling measure of his poem, chiefly alliterative but often drifting towards rime, with no certain principle of line division, illustrates afresh the passage from the old to the new romance metres.

The Owl and the Nightingale was the work of a practised writer making use of the Provençal form of the *tençon* known, later, in Scots, as a 'flyting,' that is to say, a heated dispute. In this case, the nightingale states and illustrates the case for the poetry of noble love; the owl replies on behalf of the poetry of religion. The underlying contrast is that between art and morality. The natural background is pleasing, and the poet has command of many resources of characterisation and humorous abuse. Though the poet does not definitely take sides, his work is one of the first pleas in English for gaiety, and, at this period, it comes like an oasis in the dreary waste of homiletic verse; it is written in a perfectly accomplished form of rimed octosyllabic couplets.

The poem of Layamon may serve to introduce us to the vast province of romance, the taste for which, if not of Norman origin, was certainly of Norman importation. The epic temper of *Beowulf*, or of *Le Chanson de Roland* in France, gives way to this new spirit, how completely we may see by a comparison of the enterprises of Beowulf with those of people of his rank in Chaucer's *Knight's Tale*. The ideals of court, battlefield and monastery pervade nearly all the stories which the age gathered from the story-loving east, from late Greek romances, from history and legend and from such prolific soil as that of Wales and Brittany. The transformation may be seen at work in the crusading zeal of Roland, whose anti-Saracenic heroism is far removed from the simple patriotic courage of Byrhtnoth. The Frank is dislodging the Teuton. Upon this type of prowess were brought to bear many influences to which we may give the general name *courtoisie*. The church fostered the chivalric zeal of the crusades; the castles of the feudal system provided a polite and refined audience, largely dominated by women, for whose approval these later *trouvères* and *jongleurs* (makers and singers) sought. Here came into play the softening influence of the troubadours and the Provençal courts of love, and, indirectly, of the amorist poet Ovid. All this was as powerful in England as in Normandy, and the final result was that England became a literary appanage of the Latin nations and looked for its faith and ancestry no longer to Old English mythology and history, but, in common with the rest of Christendom, to the mythical Brutus of Troy and Rome.

Romances were classified by an old French poet, Jean Bodel, under the headings of France, Britain and 'Rome the great'; but, even if we allow Rome to signify all antiquity, there are other ' matters ' (as they were called) not comprehended in his classification. We have little of the Carolingian matter of France in England; the best in this cycle is *Sir Ferumbras*. Of the matter of Britain, the Arthurian stories are discussed separately; but there are other Celtic tales: *Sir Tristrem, Ywain and Gawain* and the alliterative *Awntyrs of Arthur*, which came from Wales or Brittany, as, also, fairy stories such as *Sir Orfeo* (Orpheus), *Sir Gowther* and the riming *Mort Arthur*. There are Old English stories which were put into French romance forms and then back again into English, such as *Havelok* and *Horn*, of which the former retains more of their common Anglo-Danish origin than the latter. *Guy of Warwick*, also, in the first place, was Anglo-Danish. *Bevis of Hampton*, the most lengthy and popular, though not the most distinguished of native romances, similarly belongs to the matter of England. As for the matter of Rome or antiquity, the Troy legends will be discussed in connection with Chaucer's *Troilus and Criseyde*; there exists a romance of *King Alisaunder*; Chaucer used Thebes in *The Knight's Tale* and Lydgate wrote *The Story of Thebes*. Chaucer made some use of the *Aeneid* also. The matter of the east provided *Floris and Blancheflour* and *The Seven Sages of Rome*, and Chaucer found it useful in *The Squire's Tale*. Some are outside these cycles, such as *Cœur de Lion*, and other tales of famous kings; the perfect story of *Amis and Amiloun*, *The Squire of Low Degree* and *Ipomedon* are unattached tales of chivalry. Most of these romances share the same unlocalised, often enchanted, background; they have not any national or patriotic note; they are altogether aristocratic, and do not touch at any point the actual life of their day. They consist, generally, of thousands of lines, mostly in the octosyllabic couplet of their French progenitors; but English stanza forms of the type which Chaucer quizzed unmercifully in *Sir Thopas* developed alongside the couplet.

It is not profitable to discuss whether the Arthur of legend has any historical prototype; he is not

King Arthur mentioned in the Old English *Chronicle*, nor in Bede, nor in Gildas; the first historical reference is in the *Historia Brittonum* of Nennius, where he has miraculous powers, and wars against the Saxons. Early Welsh and Breton lays know him as a wizard and a hero. Through the contact between Breton and Norman he was transformed into a romantic and chivalrous hero and he finds his way prominently into literature in Geoffrey of Monmouth's Latin *History of the Kings of Britain* c. 1136, in which the chronicler's fertile imagination evolved a complete genealogy of British kings from Brute to Cadwalader, including such names as Sabrina, king Lear and Gorboduc. So late as Milton, it was taken for authentic history. In this book are recounted tales of Merlin and of Arthur's miraculous birth, his conquests throughout Europe, the advance upon Rome and his recall to fight a last battle with his faithless nephew Mordred. The book had enormous popularity and, from this time, Arthur became one of the major heroes of European romance. The *Brut* of the Jersey poet Wace developed the hint of the Round Table; many heads and pens, mostly French, busily wove separate legends into this main fabric. Chrestien de Troyes inwove the tale of Lancelot and the faithless Guenever, whose courtly love is worlds apart from the elemental passion of the Celtic lovers, Tristram and Iseult. Robert de Borron is thought to have attached the Graal story, with which are linked up the monastic legends of Joseph of Arimathea. At first, Gawain was the hero of the quest, but he is deprived of this honour in Malory and Tennyson; Sir Percival is also deposed later in favour of the still more ascetic Sir Galahad. From these five main sources, the stories of Merlin, of Lancelot, of Tristram, of the Graal and of the death of Arthur, Malory drew the scenes and motives, the groupings and the colouring, with which he composed the pictures in his enchanted gallery *Le Morte Arthur*.

The Auchinleck MS, which contains a number of these romances, is of about 1320, and romances continue long after Chaucer's death; his pointed satire of them in *Sir Thopas*, if it intended extinction as well as ridicule, was ineffective. The other verse of the period consists largely of homiletic work, the religious impulse being reinforced by the Dominicans and Franciscans about 1221. The poems of William of Shoreham c. 1300, on church rites and the like, are in lyrical stanzas which may faintly remind us of George Herbert. He also made a prose translation of the *Psalter*. Robert of Gloucester wrote saints' lives c. 1300, after he had composed a chronicle from the siege of Troy to his own day, in riming lines of fifteen syllables. Cycles of saints' legends exist in the north and south but they are inferior to the Old English *Andreas*. Akin to these cycles are the didactic poems *Handlynge Sinne* 1303, and *The Pricke of Conscience* 1349?, the former by Robert Mannynge of Brunne, a popular sermon-maker of anecdotical turn, who also wrote a chronicle; the latter either by Richard Rolle of Hampole, some of whose prose works have an impetuous emotionalism, verging at times on mysticism, or by others of his school. Of equal importance in the same school is *Cursor Mundi* 1300, a popular compendium of accredited and apocryphal Christian legend, exalting the Trinity, the Holy Rood and the Virgin Mary; its octosyllabic couplets are lucid and clear, and its numerous stories told with no mean skill. It may well have influenced the analogous material of the miracle plays.

Verse from 1250 to 1400.
1 Religious

Some scraps of social satire, such as *The Land of Cockaigne*, making mock of friars and of cheating professions, presage Chaucer and Langland, as *Dame Siriz* c. 1260 anticipates Chaucer's *Miller's Tale*. *The Fox and the Wolf*, with Chaucer's *Nun's Priest's Tale*, are almost all we have of the great continental beast-epic *Reynard the Fox*. *The Battle of Lewes* 1264 points to the political and patriotic verse, vigorous and scornful, if not highly imaginative, in which Laurence Minot castigated the French and the Scots and celebrated the prowess of Englishmen at the sieges and battles of Edward III from 1332 to 1352.

2 Satire

The solitary *Love-Song* c. 1240 of Thomas de Hales, treating of the passing of earthly beauty, is all that precedes an outburst of lyric, including *Sumer is i-cumen in*, *Alysoun* and *Lenten is come with love to toune*: daintiness of feeling, skilful choice of fitting natural imagery and gaiety of treatment make these songs memorable in the history of English lyric; others have a note of melancholy, not unlike Wyatt's; others are religious and penitential.

3 Lyric

There is a brilliant renascence of the Old English alliterative measure, with marked technical changes, in the fourteenth century. The knowledge and practice of this old prosody presumably survived in the western counties. There are romances, such as *Gawayne and the Grene Knight*, *Morte d'Arthure*, *The Awntyrs of Arthur* and *William of Palerne*; religious and satirical poems, as those of Langland and his followers; homiletic and allegorical poems,

4 The alliterative revival

Cleanness (inculcating purity), *Patience* and *Pearl*; together with other things, such as *The Pistil* (epistle) *of Susan*, which has some rare touches of pathos. *Sir Gawayne* c. 1370, which mixes romance measures, at irregular intervals, with the alliterative, records the coming of the Green knight to challenge the knights of Camelot to an exchange of blows. Sir Gawayne at length accepts and cuts off the stranger's head. The mysterious and adventurous sequel to this deed is told in a narrative, enriched with colour and pageantry, diversified by surprises of enchantment and suggestions of terror, and set in a background of rare scenic beauty. By virtue of its art and its individuality the poem ranks among the major products of medieval romance.

Pearl is an elegiac vision of the spirit of the child of the writer, probably a married priest in minor orders. The poet creates a land of crystal cliffs, magic streams and flowered fields, where he meets his daughter, Pearl, and, after much play upon the name, begins to speak in terms of rebellious grief, to which the child replies with heavenly wisdom. Scriptural imagery and story run through the poem, consummating in a finely imaginative picture of the new Jerusalem and of the brides of the Lamb. It is the climax of English medieval religious poetry. These two poems, together with *Cleanness* and *Patience*, are in one MS and, probably, by one author. The proposal to father these and other alliterative poems of this period on a Scottish poet called Huchowne is still a matter of debate.

There have been recent attempts to dissolve the

shadowy personality of William Langland 1332 ?–

99 ?, into some five unnamed persons;
be this as it may, we shall, for the present, regard him as a poor minor clerk, or priest,
whose wanderings acquainted him with peasants
about the Malvern hills, dwellers in London, professional beggars and, generally, with the classes
most affected by the oppressions of the rich, the
corruption of the church, famine, the black death
and war-taxation. The poem attributed to Langland,
entitled *The Vision of William concerning Piers
the Plowman*, was made public in three forms, now
known as the A-, B- and C-texts, the short A-text
in 1362, the longer (generally printed) B-text in
1377 and the C-text in 1398 (?). The B-text has
a prologue and seven sections followed by the visions
of Do-wel, Do-bet and Do-best. It is rather form-
less and inconsequent, being made up of a series of
abruptly introduced dreams and sermons, such as
those of Holy Church and Reason; allegories melting
into realistic scenes, such as the field full of folk, the
trial of Lady Meed at Westminster, and the gather-
ing of the seven deadly sins; fables, such as the rats
and the mice; and pilgrimages in search of truth.
All these are unified, not by any constructive scheme,
but by the prophetic spirit of the writer, working,
at times, through satire and, again, through exhortation. He is not a Lollard, nor a factionist defying
authority; he is 'a church and king man,' well
content with the organisation of the state, but
distressed that not a single class is fulfilling its
divinely appointed function. Piers, the honest
peasant, is the saviour of the state, affording it

subsistence, leading pilgrimages in search of truth and providing the immediately practicable remedy for social ills by setting all classes to work. The writer pictures the church, as did Chaucer and all other contemporary witnesses, as a nest of hypocrites, but he does not propose its abolition; his wish is that its orders should resist the blandishments of Lady Meed and live well. Realism and allegory meet in the subtly conceived figure of Lady Meed, a woman of wanton graces, fallen from the high estate of just reward to that of dishonest bribery. The later sections, Do-wel, Do-bet and Do-best, are less realistic and more doctrinal. The first is a vision of Activa-Vita, in the main, a picture of Piers the peasant; the second is a vision of faith, hope and charity, closing with Easter bells; the third, in a darker mood, paints anti-Christ and death, and leaves the dreamer setting out anew in search of Piers (or Christ) throughout the world. The un-doubted power of the work lies in its spiritual and mystic ideal, its urgent sincerity, its vivid obser-vation and realistic detail, its hatred of abuses and the plain-spoken earnestness of its teaching. It is the chief product of the alliterative renascence of the fourteenth century. Of the same school are the contemporary poems *Richard the Redeless* and *Piers the Plowman's Creed*.

Geoffrey Chaucer 1340 ?–1400 towers like a peak above the rest of contemporary poets; he was a man of more varied experience than they, being tradesman's son, squire at court, soldier, diplomat, ambassador, keeper of customs, warden of the banks of the Thames, member of

Chaucer

parliament, clerk of the royal works, scholar and scientist. His first training was in French, and he wrote ballades, *virelais* and *roundels* (now partly lost), complaints, *unto Pity* and the like, an *A.B.C.*, a verse-prayer, and *The Book of the Duchess*, on the occasion of the death of John of Gaunt's first wife (Chaucer afterwards married the sister of the duke's third wife). Of lasting import was his translation of part of *Le Roman de la Rose*, the French poem of Guillaume de Lorris and Jean de Meung, of whom the former personified the perils that beset lovers, whilst the latter shrewdly satirised the whole social economy of his day. In this exercise, Chaucer acquired practice in the octosyllabic couplet, and a store of medieval conventions—the dream motive, allegory, the garden with legend-haunted walls and the May morning scene. Much of his learning came from this source, and some of his later characters, as the friar and the prioress, may be discerned in embryo in the French poem.

Chaucer never completely discarded his French training, but he is distinguished from all his fellows by his contact with the Italian renascence; the two influences are seen contending in *Anelida and Arcite*. His first Italian journey in 1372 brought him acquainted with Latin works and, for a time, he turned to church legend and martyrology for themes, writing the tales of St Cecile, of Griselda and of the tragedies of fallen princes, later incorporated in *The Canterbury Tales* as those of the Second Nun, the Clerk of Oxford and the Monk respectively. After his second Italian visit in 1378–9, he tired of this partial attitude to life. He wrote *The Parliament of Fowls* 1382, a dramatic picture of a bustling vivacious crowd of birds, with much humorous observation and fine feeling; in *The House of Fame*, which owes some debt to Dante, he is initiated by the cheerful explanatory eagle into the 'quick forge and working-house' of Lady Fame, and the caprices of rumour. The prologue of *The Legend of Good Women* is Chaucer's last use of the allegorical dream : the legends are Ovid's *Heroides* re-told. Chaucer left it, like many other experiments, unfinished. *Troilus and Criseyde* belongs to the Troy section of the 'matter of antiquity,' which reached Chaucer by devious ways. The forged Latin chronicles of Dictys the Cretan and Dares the Phrygian, supposed eye-witnesses of the fate of Troy, gave rise to extended fabrications, first by Benoît de Ste More c. 1165, in French verse, and then by Guido delle Colonne 1287, in Latin prose, whence *The Geste Historyale of Troy* in English and the *Filostrato* of Boccaccio in Italian. *Filostrato* has a finely studied portrait of Troilus. Chaucer revised and enlarged Boccaccio's tale in his *Troilus*. It is, in fact, a long novel, though written in rime royal. In construction, appropriateness of detail, blending of humour and tragedy, skill in dialogue, sense for the romantic background and historic figures of Troy and, above all, in its characterisation of Pandarus, no mean predecessor of Falstaff, and of the 'graceful mutable soul' of Criseyde, it immeasurably surpasses all other romances of catholic Christendom.

By this time the poet had won—a difficult accomplishment in the Middle Ages—freedom for his own individuality. The years from 1386 to 1400 are often called, only half relevantly, his English period. He had already made collections of stories in *The Monk's Tale* and in *The Legend of Good Women*. The *Canterbury Tales* are far more varied, for Chaucer's art is evident, not only in his choice of the framework of a pilgrimage, but, also, in the vivacity with which the conception is sustained. The initial jest of the host, Harry Bailey, and his efforts to ensure its success, the coercing of the recalcitrant pilgrims, the frank expressions of opinion, the diverse qualities of the travellers' mounts, the incidents in the open lanes and at stopping places, all combine to impart an air of lifelikeness and animation, not attained even by Chaucer's accomplished competitor, Boccaccio, in his *Decameron*. The company numbers thirty-one, of whom a third belong to the church. All men in orders save one are offenders against their vows, as the poet's penetrating, though never violent, satire makes plain. There are gentlefolks, men of professional rank and of the wealthy middle classes, coarse underlings and the ploughman, who, with his brother, the poor parson of a town, does his duty and wins Chaucer's approval. There is no bishop, no noble, no professional soldier (the knight is a crusader) and no beggar, but, these apart, all classes of fourteenth century England are sketched to the life in Chaucer's masterpiece of portraiture, the *Prologue*. The persons in the wonderfully managed crowd are characterised by dress, temperament, manners and pursuits, by the tales they tell, by the links of conversation between them and, once or twice, in

lengthy monologues. Dryden did not overstate the
case when he said 'Here is God's plenty.' The
tales are of every kind and, generally, though not
always, suited to the teller. *The Pardoner's Tale*
is of narrative skill all compact; *The Knight's* and
Squire's show how Chaucer strengthened and refined romance; the coarse *fabliaux* of the Miller
and Reeve have brilliant farcical humour, which
takes a decisively satirical turn in *The Somnour's
Tale*. The religious legend told by the Prioress has
the purest and most sustained melody in Chaucer;
The Nun's Priest's Tale, a fragment of the beast
epic, opens quietly and closes with furious speed.
This variety of material shows the suppleness of his
imagination, shaping, with equal ease, realism, satire,
enchantment, frolic and romance.

Chaucer had the keenest enjoyment of the
panorama of life, focussing his vision on its lighter,
rather than on its more sombre, side; it has been
remarked that, in his poetry, he avoids the large
events of his time; his mental temperament was
unfitted for the supreme themes of tragedy. He
met minor disasters with a buoyant spirit, as in
his genial salute to hard times, *The Complaint to
his Empty Purse*. His truest quality was his
humour; he viewed mankind with tolerant worldly
irony; he loved nothing better than to set rogues
betraying themselves. Upon nature, too, he had a
fresh and joyous outlook; he invests his conventional
landscape with a touch of Botticellian grace; the
May mornings in Chaucer are lit with sunshine and
alive with woodland sounds. There are qualities in
which he differs from the modern poet: we are apt

to resent (forgetting that Chaucer was, in many
things, of his age) the irrelevant learning which
clogs the movement of his narrative; he may con-
done faults which we cannot allow to be venial; his
immovable benignity may not be so stimulating as
the exacting moral challenge of later poets. But
he is our first humanist, our first lover of the life
and mind of man at large, not making any reserves
and bestowing the same zest and sureness and art on
the portrayal of the noble, the tender, the mirthful
and the base. This he did in incomparable narrative verse, and his only rival in English is his poetical
kinsman and disciple, William Morris. For this, he
wrought out for himself a measure, bolder, charged
with a more subtle music and demanding a greater
mastery than French romantic models offered,
namely, the ten-syllabled line, which for centuries
proved the inevitable medium of most English verse,
except lyric. Chaucer used it first in rime royal,
and then in the heroic couplet. Whether Chaucer
derived this from Guillaume de Machault, or detected it among earlier native experiments by his
own prescient ear, or took the suggestion from the
couplets at the close of his rime royal, is uncertain;
in any case, this is the verse in which he achieved
the 'divine liquidness of diction' and 'fluidity
of movement' which charmed the ear of Matthew
Arnold. It is no longer contended that Chaucer
imported French words wholesale into our speech;
Spenser called him the 'well of English undefiled';
and it is proved, now, that Chaucer, like Gower,
employed the normal vocabulary of the London
of his day. No doubt, his practice, together with

many accessory circumstances, established the eastern midland dialect as the standard form of English.

Sir John Gower 1325?–1408 is what Chaucer might have been without genius and without Italy.

Gower

He wrote first in French his *Mirrour de l'Omme*, a book of edification and allegory, which may have provoked Chaucer's reference to him as 'moral Gower,' though this reference may equally have been to some of the less improving of Gower's tales. Next, in Latin verse, he wrote *Vox Clamantis* 1382, much of which deals with the social conditions out of which arose the peasants' rebellion of 1381: the successive versions of the poem indicate his dwindling faith in Richard II, and his Latin *Cronica Tripartita* 1400 records the events preceding Richard's fall and Bolingbroke's triumph. His third poem, *Confessio Amantis* 1390, in English octosyllabic couplets, turns from these disquieting matters to the courtly subject of love, 'somewhat of lust, somewhat of lore.' The lover makes confession to Genius, the priest of Venus, and is instructed by means of some scores of fluently told stories from the classics, the chronicles and medieval collections (though not *Gesta Romanorum*), how to remedy his faults, and atone for his delinquencies. All this resembles *Le Roman de la Rose*, and Gower, in fact, belonged to the *Rose* generation by the make of his mind. He is neglected now, but he was a great collector of stories, and told them well, though not with the iridescent gleams of humour and insight which colour those of Chaucer. He is clear and has some sense of form; his verse and language are sound and regular; it may be that the very regularity of his verse induces the feeling of monotony which causes us to neglect him: there are too few prominences in his landscape.

2. PROSE FROM THE CONQUEST TO 1400

The prose of this period does not show well beside the best prose of Old English; for, following French **Religious** practice, English writers put the most **prose** prosaic subjects into verse. Apart from the Old English *Chronicle*, which closes gloomily in 1154 with the death of Stephen, the existing prose is of the type of homily—as, for instance, part of *The Soul's Ward* c. 1210—or of saints' lives—as, for instance, of *St Margaret* and others, full of crude incitements to the conventual life; these, with *Holy Maidenhood* c. 1210, are in a heavily alliterated prose, very near to verse. One memorable exception to the dullness of this catalogue is the *Ancren Riwle* or *Rule for Anchoresses* c. 1210. Its eight books define the duties and observances for three nuns, settled in a Dorset convent. Its engaging humanity, freedom from pedantry—though its framework is entirely medieval—sympathy and enlightenment have won for it universal recognition as the expression of a fine and delightful religious mind. The *Ayenbite of Inwit* or *Remorse of Conscience*, another collection of sermons, by Dan Michel c. 1340, has not much value as literature or translation, though it is interesting to see the ever-present seven deadly sins (they appear in *Ancren Riwle*, Chaucer, Langland,

Y.   3

Wyclif, Dunbar and, later, in Marlowe) here treated allegorically. Richard Rolle of Hampole has been named elsewhere. Chaucer wrote prose both secular and religious, always competent, and rising to high levels at times in his *Boece*. His religious prose includes this translation of Boethius, his portentous 'littel thing in prose' the tale of *Melibeus and Prudence*, and *The Parson's Tale*, which expounds the whole doctrine of sin, penitence, confession and discipline. But the best religious prose of this age was written by Wyclif and writers belonging to his school.

John Wyclif 1320?-84, like Richard Rolle a Yorkshireman, was closely connected with Balliol college, where an arduous training in the scholastic curriculum put him in the front rank of controversialists. He opposed the church on such doctrines as transubstantiation, the tenure of property and the superiority of scripture over tradition. Political events, in which he was supported by John of Gaunt, his own independent disposition and his growing disbelief in the papacy, accentuated by the existence of two rival popes in 1378, drove him to appeal to the people at large, first by his institution of poor priests, and, secondly, by inspiring (his personal share in the work remains unidentified) the translation of the Vulgate version of the Bible. Of the two versions of the translation, one partly composed by Nicholas of Hereford, and the other revised by John Purvey, the latter is by far the superior. No doubt it had been preceded by many translations of portions of the Bible; but, all things considered, the version known as Wyclif's

Wyclif and the Bible

may be taken as the worthy inauguration of the
great series of translations of the Bible. It has two
of the qualities of the Authorised Version—simplicity
and dignity; it is lacking in the grace and power of
rhythm which the subtler ear of a later generation
added. Whatever part Wyclif took in the version,
he must have credit for the generous intention and
courage of the undertaking. He and his allies
poured out a multitude of tracts and sermons on
the abuses of the age, and the Lollards afterwards
carried these charges and doctrines to extremes.
The pamphlets are awkward in composition, but their
purpose demanded popular qualities, and a keen,
vigorous, democratic speech.

By the year 1400, proceedings in law-courts were
conducted in English, parliament had been opened
Secular in an English speech and boys con-
prose strued their Latin in school into
English instead of French. Nevertheless, all prose,
until the time of Chaucer, was in the form of translation. In 1387 appeared John of Trevisa's version
of Higden's Latin *Polychronicon*, a history of the
world from the creation. It gives the first topo-
graphical description of England in English and
set a long-enduring fashion. In 1397, he completed
a translation of the *De Proprietatibus Rerum* of
Bartolomaeus, the best-known medieval encyclo-
paedia of nature. Trevisa's · style, though not
polished, is robust and colloquial, and gained for
his writings a wide popularity. Chaucer wrote his
Astrolabe, mostly translation, in 1391, for his 'little
son Lewis.'

The first book of entertainment in English prose

3—2

is *The Voyage and Travel of Sir John Mandeville,*
Knight, written originally in French
Mandeville   1371, and put into English by an
unknown translator.   Mystery surrounds the titular
author; we do know that Sir John never existed,
but we do not know whether to attribute his creation
to one D'Outremeuse, or another Jean de Bourgogne.
The book professes to be a manual for pilgrims to
the Holy Land, and, in the first part, describes
Constantinople, Egypt and Palestine.   The second
part, based on the authentic travels of friar Odoric,
ranges afield, introducing Prester John, the great
Cham, the 'islands' of China, growing diamonds,
loadstone mountains and the valley of devils.   By
a process of thorough-going and unacknowledged
filching from all the travellers' books within reach,
the writer gathers a *corpus* of fictions and marvels
and relates them with an air of ingenuous pur-
posefulness and candour that would have left any
but his credulous medieval audience aghast either
at his daring or his humour.   As prose, it is tech-
nically little better than any other of its time; but,
until Berners's *Froissart*, it is the only book which
fascinates a modern reader.   This it does by its
firm resolve to entertain at all costs, and also by
the absence of the deadening sense of anonymity
which renders many medieval books unimpressive
and commonplace.

3. VERSE FROM CHAUCER TO THE RENASCENCE

There were devoted followers of Chaucer—though generally of his immature work—in England, such The Chaucer- as Lydgate and Occleve, but their ian tradition voluminousness does not compensate for their almost invariable flatness and lack of inspiration; Chaucer's mantle did not descend upon them but upon the contemporary lowland Scots. John Lydgate 1370?–1451? wrote a *Troy Book* of 30,000 lines and, at still greater length, *The Falls of Princes*, embodying the same medieval conception of tragedy as *The Monk's Tale* and, later, *The Mirror for Magistrates*; his *Story of Thebes* he proposed to insert in *The Canterbury Tales*. *The Pilgrimage of Man* combines all the medieval forms of allegory, and, in some remote way, may have influenced Bunyan. *London Lickpenny*, a piece of realistic social satire describing the undoing of a countryman by the sharps about Westminster, is not now credited to Lydgate. The chief poem of Occleve c. 1368?–c. 1450? is his *De Regimine Principum*, which gives advice to the prince of Wales, based on 'a blending of Aristotle and Solomon'; in *La Male Règle*, the poet confesses himself a pale kind of wastrel. These writers do not bring anything new in theme or treatment, and their attempts at rime royal and heroic couplet only show how completely they had lost hold of all that Chaucer had won for English prosody. More pleasing are several poems once thought Chaucer's but now detached from his canon. To Clanvowe is assigned *The Cuckoo and the Nightingale* 1403–10; to Lydgate, *The Complaint of the Black Knight*; and to an unknown writer *The Flower and the Leaf* c. 1450, picturing the retinue and livery, green and white, of those who serve the transitory flower and the permanent leaf. Dryden thought it Chaucer's and re-set it in his *Fables*. *The Court of Love*, that is to say, of Venus, instances the prolonging of the Chaucerian tradition of *Le Roman de la Rose* well into the sixteenth century. It was resumed in the reign of Henry VII by Stephen Hawes 1475–1530. The training and practice of the knight in learning and chivalry is the theme of his allegorical *Pastime of Pleasure*; but Hawes's dream has no magic and his personifications are anaemic; the subject awaited its predestined master, Spenser. John Skelton soon turned from the fashion of allegory in rime royal, but not finding any adequate models to hand, took to writing a quick short line, sufficiently superior to doggerel to acquire the label Skeltonic verse; 'ragged, tattered and jagged' he calls it, though it has more music than this description suggests, and it has pith. In this metre he wrote the playful *Book of Philip Sparrow*, on the death of a nun's pet bird, and *Colin Clout*, one of many satires of which the most stinging was his attack on Wolsey, 'Why come ye not to Court?' Skelton came too early; sixty years later, his audacity and learning would have made him a university wit. Alexander Barclay freely translated the *Narrenschiff* of the German Brant into *The Ship of Fools* 1509; he also brought into English, without

adorning it, the form of the eclogue. The feebly
flowing currents of inspiration in fifteenth century
work in England were soon to be refreshed by a
torrent; the renascence was at our shores. Meanwhile, we may turn to the truer disciples of Chaucer
in the north.

The literature of Scotland is written in a northern dialect of English; Barbour, the first consider-
able poet, called it 'our Ynglis.' His
Brus c. 1376 is a heroic presentment
of the national hero Bruce, full of fervid patriotism,
closing with the triumph of Bannockburn. The
same pride of country is in the *Orygynal Cronykyl*
1406 of Andrew of Wyntoun, fabulous in its earlier
parts like the English *Bruts*. Blind Harry (the
minstrel) produced a violently Anglophobe *Wallace*
1470-80, which touched and stirred Burns four
centuries later. None of these felt the influence
of Chaucer, nor, in the next century, did Sir David
Lindsay, whose *Satire of the Three Estates* 1535, a
rough dramatic composition, is bitter and penetrating and does not shrink from any extreme of licence
and indecency. But *The Kingis Quair*, or book of
the king, c. 1423, written, in all probability, by king
James I, during his imprisonment in England, is made
in the image of Chaucer and his school and has resemblances to *The Court of Love*. Its theme is the
tremulous awakening passion of the youthful lover,
and its delicate beauty is in consonance with its
subject; it may be that it represents the king's own
feeling towards the Lady Joan Beaufort whom he
afterwards married. It is in rime royal; the measure may, in fact, derive its name from the kingly

The Scots
poets

composition. Robert Henryson, William Dunbar and
Gavin Douglas are later Chaucerians; the perfervid
Scotticism of the chroniclers is scarcely heard in
them. Henryson's *Fables of Aesop* has many topical
hits and plentiful moralising; *The Testament of
Cressid* completes Chaucer's *Troilus* with a pathetic
relation of Cressida's beggaring and death; *Robene
and Makyne* is a pastoral dialogue of rare freshness
and independence of form, more akin to *The Nut-
Browne Maid* than to the English poet. Dunbar is
the greatest, but the least like Chaucer, of these
poets; his many short poems scarcely admit of
classification. He has an allegory, *The Thistle and
the Rose* 1503, and *The Lament for the Makaris*
(poets) closing with the refrain *Timor mortis con-
turbat me* and exalted by its manifest sincerity.
But most typical are his boisterous satires, *The
Two married Women*, and *The Seven Deadly Sins*;
the sins are bidden by Satan to dance 'as varlets do
in France'; the grotesque orgy is described in verse
astonishing in its brilliance and indelicate humour.
These poems seal Dunbar of the clan of Rabelais
and Burns by bent of mind, though he revered and
is indebted to Chaucer for gentler qualities; he is also,
like Chaucer, a master of metrical effect, though his
music is harsher. Gavin Douglas translated Vergil,
condemning Caxton's romantic *Eneydos* without get-
ting much further away from its medieval temper; to
each book he prefaced a prologue and some of these
present, with real poetic power, Scottish country
scenes. Summing up the matter briefly, we may
say that the narrow pre-Chaucerian patriotism gives
way to qualities more intimately national in the

force of satiric invective and comic phrasing in
Dunbar and Lindsay and in the genuinely observed
landscape of Douglas. It is interesting to note in
these poets a fitful occurrence of alliteration in the
manner of Old English verse; in everything else, they
are the true disciples of Chaucer.

We have little evidence for assigning any date
to British ballads; the first invaluable collection is
The ballads and popular poetry in the MS called the Percy folio, of
1650. Most appear to have been com-
posed between 1100 and 1500; but they
were still being made in the eighteenth century.
Scholars are coming to the conclusion that they
originated, as their refrains seem to indicate, in a
song accompanied by dancing and a chorus, not
unlike the French *Carole*. They are not to be
thought of, for the most part, as degenerate
romances; they are not degenerate at all, but an
elaborate form of art, admirably fitted for a definite type of narrative of a temper more akin to
the epic than the romance. The first short love-
song or nonsense rime gave place to a longer narrative, and this, after a time, came to be sung or
recited by itself; in one case, a number of these
narratives were shaped together, attaining almost
to epic proportions, as in *The Little Geste of Robin
Hood*. Their themes are as numerous and often as
untraceable as those of the romances. Some are
of border warfare, as *The Hunting of the Cheviot*,
some of fairyland, as *Thomas of Ercildoune*, some
of the supernatural, as *The Wife of Usher's Well*,
some of romance, as *Clerk Saunders* and *Fair Annie*,
some of treachery and murder, as *Parcy Reed* and

Childe Maurice, some of outlawry, as *Robin Hood*, who makes a splendid ballad end. Though some, like the romances, end happily, the best of them are tragic, portraying, in stark outline, hot and violent action, barbarously heroic in its sentiment, with a curious untrained art, which gets the most powerful effects out of naïve repetitions and out of economy and purity of speech. One of the most moving of all ballads, *The Nut-Browne Maid*, is almost too elaborate to have the title of ballad at all. It is a dramatic dialogue telling, with a surer touch of pathos than Chaucer has in *Griselda*, of a maid's constancy in face of the almost intolerable exactions of her lover. In addition to ballads there are many contemporary popular songs, carols, drinking-songs, religious songs and love-songs; these are generally of a rather primitive type, but they witness to the universal taste for song and dance. Some of the Latin student songs, such as *Gaudeamus igitur*, date from this century as well.

4. PROSE FROM CHAUCER TO THE RENASCENCE

In the line of chroniclers, Capgrave c. 1450, Fabian c. 1510 and Hall c. 1530 lead on to the Elizabethan chroniclers Holinshed and Stow; here, too, should be mentioned Leland's *Itinerary* c. 1540 and the Paston *Letters* 1424–1506, intimate revelations of fifteenth century life, some of them still warm with the personal feeling of the writers. Pecock's *Repressor of over much Blaming of the Clergy* c. 1455 defended the church against the assaults of the Lollards; but, since he based his argument on reason, in place of authority, the church found him disquietingly progressive and discarded him; he had brilliant gifts both in dialectics and in the adaptation of language. Something of the same modernity is to be found in Sir John Fortescue's *Difference between an Absolute and a Limited Monarchy* 1471, a short plea recommending constitutional relations between king and people. We cannot do more than mention the sermons, c. 1509, of bishop Fisher—who was something of a rhetorician—and of Latimer—the first of a number, Bunyan, Cobbett, Bright, who gain simplicity and force by holding fast to the English stock in the vocabulary. Sir Thomas Elyot's *Governour* 1531 is a treatise from Italian sources on education and politics, which, incidentally, gives the story of Gascoigne and prince Hal. There is also a pious biography of Wolsey by his usher, George Cavendish. But the more captivating works of the time are still concerned with chivalry; the greatest is *Le Morte Arthur* of Sir Thomas Malory. He professed to trans-

Malory

late from a French book which as yet has eluded identification; the five main threads of the romance have already been named (see p. 21). Malory made the search for the Graal the central motive of his story, though it is sometimes obscured by lengthy interludes; the whole is rounded off with marvellous art; the separation and deaths of Lancelot and Guenever move us like a tragedy. 'Here may be seen,' says Caxton, 'noble chivalry, courtesy, humanity, friendliness, hardiness, love, friendship, cowardice, murder, hate, virtue and sin.' Caxton adds, 'Do after the good and leave the evil and it shall bring you to good fame and renown'; a more humane judgment than Ascham's harsh strictures on the book. Malory has the magic control of words and rhythms which makes us grant him the 'willing suspension of disbelief,' while he creates an imaginative world. The natural grace and beauty of his writing are touched with a faint melancholy, which seems to reflect the soft and bewitching tints of twilight; in 1470, the nightfall of extinction was upon the ages of faith and chivalry. We cannot here attempt an estimate of the gain to letters through Caxton's introduction of printing into England in 1476; he printed many translations, including Malory's, making some of them himself; his original prefaces reveal a splendid personality keenly interested in romance and in the transitional world about him. This is true, again, of Lord Berners, the translator of *Froissart's Chronicles* c. 1523. Here are

Froissart　 the trappings of knighthood, 'trumpets blown for wars,' sieges and sea-fights, stratagems and parleys, set down with a persuasive touch of intimacy; it is not the sifted history of the modern scholar, but it is singularly faithful to the speech and life of the fighters and rulers of his time. He uses, for the most part, a simple graphic prose in the chronicles, but he envied those who possessed the 'facundious art of rhethorique,' and, in his version of the Spaniard Guevara's *Dial of Princes*, he anticipated some of the extravagances of Euphuism. It is credited to him, also, that, in his translation of *Huon of Bordeaux*, he enriched the fairy lore of England by the kingly figure of Oberon.

Encouraged by Erasmus's pronouncement for a Bible in the native speech, Tyndale worked devotedly at the New Testament and other parts of the Scriptures until his martyrdom in 1536; his original was not the Vulgate but the Greek New Testament of Erasmus, and, substantially, though with revisions of detail, his translation is the Authorised Version; he conferred upon it that popular but dignified idiom which proved admirably in consonance with the Semitic matter of the Old Testament. Coverdale had a hand in the first Great Bible 1539, Cranmer in the second Great Bible 1540, archbishop Parker in the Bishops' Bible 1568. Forty-seven divines were entrusted with the making of the Authorised Version 1606–11; they retained from the earlier Bible its simplicity, its unaffected archaism, its picturesqueness, its predominantly English wording, with occasional doublets, sin and transgression, and the like, and added some indefinable quality, never again to be attained; it is impossible to degrade the English of the Bible, and, apart from the fact that it is 'the anchor of national seriousness,' it has remained a permanent and undisputed standard of prose, the most powerful plea in our language for the virtues of simplicity and rhythmic grace in writing. *The Book of Common Prayer*, also, is a product of many minds; chief among them ranks archbishop Cranmer, though prayers were added down to 1661.

The Bible

BOOK III

THE RENASCENCE 1500–1660

1. The new forces at work

NOTHING in the past at this date, except the persistently ignored later work of Chaucer, prophesied what was to come. The tired mechanism of medieval existence had almost stopped when history gathered that immense volume of force which we call the renascence and drove it forward with well-nigh ungovernable speed. It is astonishing that literature should have been able to cope with this torrential energy of thought and discovery and conserve it with little loss for later times. But literature faced the task and mounted with its opportunity. Faustus and Bacon took all knowledge for their province, Spenser all ethic and political art, Shakespeare plumbed the profoundest depths of human passion, groping for the point where the endurance of the spirit breaks before accumulated ills, discovering in his quest the unsuspected grandeurs which trials reveal in men. The driving forces were many. First, the revival of learning, in its two-fold aspect, the unfolding of ancient civilisations, and the stimulation of native literary endeavour. The vision of civilisations like those of Greece and Rome, the work of men's hands, based on beauty and harmony, and on law and order, made people question the medieval organisation based on traditions of the church, tyrannous and indisputable. People enquired into the axioms of this philosophy and found them too full of assumptions; they called in the senses to adjust the distortions of the scholastic vision. Hence, in Bacon, the foundations of science and the revolt of the early freethinkers and speculative pioneers, such as Giordano Bruno, Ralegh and Marlowe. Marlowe's *Faustus* is the expression of the desire of the Elizabethan mind for untried fields. Invaluable MSS, sole repositories of the records of older civilisations, were being expounded by Greek doctors in Italian city-states, the magnet of all Europe. An honoured line of English scholars taught the new doctrines in the universities, men like Grocyn, Linacre and Colet at Oxford, Erasmus, Cheke and Ascham at Cambridge. The other power which the renascence exercised as a creative stimulant was due to its coming to us coloured by Italian writers; its wealth of learning, art, story, music, state-policy, philosophy, as well as of vice, was brought over by diplomats, men of the world and courtiers. Adherents of learning, strictly as learning, hated Italianate culture, and there were persistent attempts by rigid classicists to fetter it. Ascham proffered his hard dry Hellenism; Sidney, a drama 'climbing to the height of Seneca his style'; Gabriel Harvey, a metrical scheme borrowed directly from classical exemplars. Through all this, the romantic

impulse, at first fretting, finally burst forth in such
Elizabethan restatements of the classics as Chapman's
Iliad, and Marlowe's *Hero and Leander*; in drama,
untrammelled by any canons (except in the case of
Ben Jonson, who welcomed them); in the wave-like
independence and diversity of Spenser's stanzas; and
in the golden treasure of harmony which Marlowe
conjured from his new blank verse. These writers
flung off the classical tradition; but the debt to
Italy in thought and form grew larger with each
new writer. The second of these rejuvenating
forces was the reformation (coming in by a 'side
door' finally, but inevitable since Wyclif), with
all its conflict and stimulus to freedom, on which
followed the religious compromise of Elizabeth.
Out of this came the eloquence of the Anglican
divines on the one hand, and, on the other, the mili-
tant inarticulate rebelling of nonconformity; for,
though there were pamphlets in plenty in England
—witness the Marprelate campaign—it was abroad
that the new theology was elaborated in Calvin's
Institutes 1536. In 1563 came Foxe's *Book of
Martyrs*, the treasury of anti-papist animus. The
third force was the Tudor monarchy, with its ingenious but effective diplomacy, beginning now to
tell heavily in the councils of Europe. With characteristic astuteness, it established an absolute sove-
reignty, at the same time making an appeal to the
nation's affections which became an almost fevered
and uncontrollable patriotism when Elizabeth turned
to it for support. This was the real bond which
held together the activities of Drake and his free-
booters, Spenser and the poets, Hooker and the

divines; at its bidding, men saddled themselves with tasks like Drayton's *Poly-Olbion*; and the chronicle play, a purely English offshoot of the drama, has no other origin. Fourth, there is the new epoch of adventurous voyaging and world discovery, whose prose epic was written by Hakluyt, and whose effects are plain in Chapman's *De Guiana* and in *The Tempest*. The centre of humanity shifted from the narrow bounds of the Mediterranean (discovery falsified the very name), and England's naval war was fought in the Atlantic, for the prize of the riches of Eldorado, richer, in the sequel, in letters than in treasure. Fifth, science struggled for truth, and, in spite of some early set-backs and envious hostility, contrived to inspect the processes of nature and unravel some of its mystery. Galileo's *E pur si muove* was the motto of the conquering doctrine of Copernicus as against the fated, though picturesque, errors of Ptolemy. Systematised experimental science begins with Bacon. Finally, to serve as bulwark for all that had been won against such an inundation as had swept Greek civilisation from memory, there had come the introduction of printing 1476, and the rapid distribution of books.

The Middle Ages did not, however, disappear in a cataclysm; many things had in them the seeds of evolution and still bear fruit. The Middle Ages and the renascence overlap in Chaucer, who, at his greatest, is a humanist, though not a scholarly one, and was acknowledged by the Elizabethans. There are filaments between medieval Provence and Petrarch, the pervading influence in Elizabethan lyric. Sackville, a true poet,

Medieval survivals

though he deserted the muses for politics, exemplifies the new imagination at work within old forms. His *Induction* and *Complaint of Buckingham* in the otherwise dreary *Mirror for Magistrates* 1559–63 (a continuation in rime royal of Lydgate's *Falls of Princes*), have grandeur and power, especially in portraying the gallery of allegorical shades, to whose abode, Dante-like, he is led by Sorrow. He is a strong sombre genius, with more poetry in reserve than all the fifteenth century poets had ever exercised.   Spenser, too, is an allegorist, and uses for his 'dark conceit' feudal chivalry, like that of Sidney; his pageant of the seven deadly sins (Marlowe has one, too) is archaic like some of the ingredients of his dialect.   He brought over to the new age what has been the perpetual rival of classicism in England, the love of legend. Henry V prays like a medieval churchman, and the pictures of the world of spirits in *Hamlet* and *Macbeth* are formed by popular religious fears and hopes.   The folk-lore and fairy-world and the legendary British history of Shakespeare hark back to these earlier centuries.   Finally, popular tastes in jest, song and drama were formed in the Middle Ages, and traditions as deep-seated as these were bound to shape in some way the practice of those who appealed to this wide audience.

The impetus of the renascence is continuous and fairly homogeneous from Sir Thomas Wyatt to the death of Milton; but we may allow ourselves a breathing space in the survey of this long period at the end of the reign of James I, taking the prose, verse and drama of Elizabeth and James, and then

the prose and verse of the Caroline and commonwealth periods, indicating, on the way, the change
of temper which took place in the early years of the
seventeenth century.

2. POETRY TO THE DEATH OF JAMES I

The age was prolific both in poetry and prose,
but, in excellence and variety, the accomplishment
in poetry is the higher; only outlines of the record
can be given. Sir Thomas Wyatt and the earl of
Surrey, scholars and diplomats, pretending that their
art was but a pastime, were the pioneers of the
Italian fashions in verse; they were called the
'courtly makers.' Wyatt naturalised the sonnet
form, and with it came the necessity for standard-
ising accent, and for settling the question of the
inflectional -e. The subject, ornament and much
of the phrasing of Wyatt's and many following
sonnets come from Petrarch; unrequited passion
and the lover's melancholy are the gist of most of
them. But Wyatt's lyrics for the lute have a more
direct sincerity and a studious art. He was, moreover, one of the few in England who caught the
strain of Horatian satire. Surrey was a lesser man,
but, profiting by the experience of Wyatt, he proved
a more graceful writer; he struck out the sonnet
form of three quatrains and a couplet, but used
only three rimes to Shakespeare's seven; a more
historic innovation was the blank verse measure,
clumsy though it was, in which he translated books
II and IV of the *Aeneid*. Neither Wyatt nor Surrey

published any writings, but an astute bookseller,
Richard Tottel, gathered their work, together with
other courtly poems, into his miscellany, *Songs and
Sonnets* 1557.

The interval between Surrey and Spenser is void
of any great poetical product; but, meanwhile, two
things call for notice: first, the experimenters,
Turbervile, Googe, Churchyard, Whetstone, Tusser,
a versifier of agricultural lore, and Gascoigne, only
the last calling for remark; his versatile experi-
menting included a prose comedy from Ariosto, *The
Supposes* 1566, *Jocasta*, a blank verse Senecan play,
a satire in the same measure, *The Steel Glass* 1576,
and an essay on English verse, *Notes of Instruction*;
secondly, the increasing influence of the *Pléiade*,
the academic poets of the French renascence, Du
Bellay, Desportes, Ronsard, on the development of
the sonnet.

The fashion of the sonnet sequence, derived
from Petrarch's *Laura*, had enormous sway in England as abroad; one of the earliest
disciples was Sir Philip Sidney, whose
Astrophel and Stella 1580–4 was addressed to Pene-
lope Devereux, sister of queen Elizabeth's Essex,
and, afterwards, Lady Rich; in sincerity, Sidney had
few rivals, and he employs the conventional form
with unusual grace, but it is not often that he can
fuse it to the glow of passion. The series, more
than a hundred in number, contains some exalted
religious feeling. Watson, a secondary person, wrote
his *Hekatompathia* or *Passionate Century of Sonnets*
1582, in eighteen-lined stanzas, showing how loosely
the word sonnet was used by the Elizabethans; he

advertises the source of all his material in preliminary prose paragraphs.

Spenser, in his *Amoretti* 1595, possibly addressed to his wife, falls far below the passionate adoration of his *Epithalamium*; his sonnets are mannered and full of conceits; the best of them involve his Platonic doctrine of beauty; he made, characteristically, some metrical innovations. Other poets, Barnes, Constable, Lodge, Fulke Greville, Daniel and Drayton—these last two rising once or twice, in *Delia* and *Idea* respectively, to the heights of inspiration—attempted the form, as did Sir William Alexander and Drummond of Hawthornden in the reign of James. The sonnet came to be used as an introduction to other poetic ventures, and the best in this kind is Ralegh's preface to *The Faerie Queene*. But all these are utterly out-distanced by the sonnets of Shakespeare, written, probably, between 1590 and 1600, though not published till 1609. They raise unsolved problems; how far do they mirror actual events? who are the *dramatis personae*? do they bear any relation to the changed tone of the plays about 1600? Though, to some extent, they draw on the common fund of renascence ornament, they are written with less conscious artifice; the sinister history of twofold treachery and resignation is revealed with stirrings of passion, with subtle shades of emotion, from the deepest shame to exultant triumph, which give it a moving power not found elsewhere. The sequence has some motives common to all; the havoc wrought by time and decay upon beauty, and the vaunt of the eternising power of verse are familiar themes; but, whether in treating of these or of the poignant bitter story, the lines have a wealth of natural imagery, a rich sonorous harmony, a mastery of vowel-sound and alliteration, in short, a variety of music and mood which preserves them alone among all the sonnet sequences from the charges of unreality and monotony.

Lyric, like the sonnet, is apt to draw on French and Italian sources, but its triumphs are vastly more numerous. Some breath laden with the pollen of lyrical fertility swept

Lyric

across the age. There is the graceful trilling of artificial notes by Greene, Dekker, Peele, Breton and Lodge, whose songs are too impersonal to be distinguished from one another; the more closely observed nature, the finer music, the perfect emotional truth of the songs of Shakespeare, deftly modulated in the larger harmony of the plays; the polished classical art, wanting only in spontaneity, of Ben Jonson, whose successor is Thomas Campion, a master, as his *Four Books of Airs* prove, of rime, metre and lyric diction as well as of music; there are also the admonitory stanzas of Dyer, Wotton and Daniel; the lofty insolence of Ralegh; the pastorals of Marlowe and Drayton, who is also the best of the patriotic balladists. Of the numerous lyric miscellanies, only two can be named, *England's Helicon* 1600, and Davison's *Poetical Rhapsody* 1602; of the song-books, only the madrigals of Wilbye and the songs for the lute of Byrd and Dowland, wherein is the keenest rivalry between exquisite words and melodious tunes. The relations between Elizabethan music and lyric poetry await further study.

This brief chronicle of sonnet and lyric has

carried us past the date of Edmund Spenser 1552
–99, whose independently published
Spenser
work begins with *The Shepherd's
Calendar* 1579, by which time he had shaken off the
heresies about classical metres in English propagated
at Cambridge by his pedantic friends, Abraham
Fraunce and Gabriel Harvey. These *Eclogues* of
the months turn back to Theocritus, Vergil, Mantuanus, Sannazaro and Marot; the conventional
pastoral pretence is employed on divers themes,
love-lays, allegorical fables, church-controversy, a
plea for poetry, a verse-contest, love-complaints
(against his first and unresponsive love Rosalind)
and the praise of Elizabeth. But it was chiefly the
metrical versatility and unwonted musical skill of
the idylls that won for him the title 'the new
poet.' The archaic speech was condemned now by
Sidney and afterwards by Ben Jonson, but Spenser
never abandoned it. Courtly office was found for
him in 1580 as secretary to Lord Grey de Wilton
in Ireland. There he wrote the first three books
of *The Faerie Queene*, on whose publication Ralegh,
a neighbour of Spenser in Ireland, insisted in 1590.
Meanwhile, he was working out for himself a moral
philosophy of which one element, Platonism as expounded by the Italian humanist Ficino, may be
discerned in his early *Hymns to Love* and *Beauty*;
while the other element, Christian doctrine, may be
seen blended with Platonism in the later *Hymns to
Heavenly Love* and *Heavenly Beauty*; all four were
published together in 1596. But the full harvest of
his genius is garnered in the romantic allegorical
epic, *The Faerie Queene*; of this, books I–III were

published in 1590, books IV–VI in 1596 and the
complete form, including the stanzas on mutability
in the fragmentary book VII, in 1609. The intention
of Spenser was 'to fashion a gentleman or noble
person in vertuous and gentle discipline'; and this
he achieves by the spirit of his work, though not
by his detail. His method was a continued 'dark
conceit' or allegory, and in this he fails; for the
allegory is discontinuous, and the appearances of
prince Arthur (representative of the comprehensive
virtue of magnanimity) have not the binding effect
that Spenser designed. For the most part he modelled the narrative on Ariosto, though deriving his
sixth book from Malory; the religious and crusading
tone owes something to his Italian contemporary
Tasso's *Gerusalemme Liberata*. But the figures in
The Faerie Queene are not the romantic knights
errant of Ariosto, nor the crusaders of Tasso, but
personified virtues, Biblical, Platonic and Aristotelian,
to wit, Holiness, Temperance, Chastity, Friendship,
Justice and Courtesy; upon these shadowy figures
he confers titles such as The Red Cross Knight,
Sir Guyon and the like. He projected twenty-four
books treating the twelve private and the twelve
political virtues in this manner; only the first six
books have come down to us. The conflicts, perils
and adventures are very much like those of the
romances, and they go on before a scenic background of the poet's own elaboration. The scheme
was ambitious like most Elizabethan schemes, but
Spenser had little constructive skill; he lets the
story drift, interrupts it with delightful but inconsequent episodes, and, worse still, he confuses the

allegorical plan. Sometimes, he is portraying the
conflict between truth and falsehood, sometimes,
between Mary and Elizabeth, sometimes, between
protestantism and Rome, sometimes, between England and Spain. Then, again, the knightly mask
and armour and titles may be stripped from the
abstract virtues and disconcertingly fitted to real
persons; thus, Duessa may be theological error,
or Mary queen of Scots; and prince Arthur may
be Sidney, or Leicester, or Grey de Wilton;
or one person may figure in several guises, as
queen Elizabeth who is the fairy queen, as well
as Belphoebe and Britomart. We watch an un-
ending series of metamorphoses. To go to Spenser
as we might to Bunyan for clear narrative and
easily translatable allegory is to go in vain; his
strength, as we shall see, lies elsewhere, in his lofty
spiritual inspiration and in his art. In any scene
drawn from the real world it would be impossible
to persuade us of the co-existence of beings brought
from the diverse realms of romance, protestant theology, neo-Platonism, contemporary history, legendary
lore and classical mythology. The poet does not
attempt it; he folds their hard outlines about with
the softening veil of allegory and presents them in
pageants and processions, in a dream atmosphere
and enchanted landscape, in golden noon, or star-
lit night, or in magical forests, often near the sound
of waters, which, with the perfumed air, lulls all in-
credulity; or he may establish them in the more firm
and solid caves, like those of Mammon and Despair,
or pleasaunces like the Bower of Acrasia, where
a wonderful dreamy activity pervades the scene.

This art, which weaves words and rhythms into pictures, is one great quality of Spenser's genius.

Though Spenser usually took refuge in allegory and disguise, he was not incapable of dealing with life at first hand, as we may see in book v of *The Faerie Queene*, treating of affairs in the Netherlands, and the drastic proposals for the harrying of Ireland in his prose *View of the present State of Ireland*. His *Complaints* 1591, again, contain, besides the delightful *Muiopotmos* and some elegiac poems like *The Ruins of Time*, *Prosopopoia* or *Mother Hubberd's Tale*, a sarcastic delineation of the intrigues of court and church. He often laments the low estate and mean rewards of poetry now that politicians of the type of Burleigh have succeeded Sidney. His picture of the ignominy of the suppliant at court, in *Colin Clout's Come Home Again* 1591, is based on observation and bitter experience. By virtue of these realistic things, he takes a high place among Elizabethan satirists. Yet love and beauty drew from him his richest music; when he sings most exquisitely, as in his perfect marriage songs *Epithalamium* and *Prothalamium*, no tone of cynicism or harsh note of any kind mars their wonderful melody.

Besides his skill in word-painting, and his unwavering fidelity to the poet's creed of beauty, we should note how his spirit is stirred by the nobler aspects of all the activities of his day; his verse refines them all, heroic adventure, patriotic fervour, queen-worship, puritan exaltation of truth, each yields a finer essence to him to blend with the chivalric temper of which his friend Sidney was

the supreme exemplar. Finally, we may note his
command of his medium of music, rhythm and stanza
form; in the technical skill which distils the utmost
subtlety, grace and strength of expression from
sound, he is one of the great masters; the Spenserian
stanza (a nine-lined stanza, of which the chief features
are the riming bridge at the fourth and fifth lines,
and the closing alexandrine) is only the most
triumphant among many experiments; its later history has been honourable, for it served as a channel
of romance to the arid tracts of eighteenth century
poetry. Keats, Byron and Shelley and many more
poured their music into it; it is our greatest stanzaic
measure.

The poetry of the age is 'thick inlaid' with
mythological allusion, and there are many poems
retelling mythological tales. The first
of real mark is Marlowe's *Hero and
Leander*, in which the gracious, passionate story is
told with a purity of imagination to which neither
Chapman's continuation of the poem nor Shakespeare's two ventures in classic legend, *Venus and
Adonis* and *Lucrece* 1593-4, ever quite attain;
Lodge's *Glaucus and Scylla* 1589, and the anonymous
Britain's Ida, are surpassed by Drayton's *Endymion and Phoebe* 1594, a piece of splendid pastoral
pageantry on the legend of the moon-goddess.
Beaumont's *Salmacis and Hermaphroditus* comes
late in the same school. With these, we may name
the translators of classical and Italian
verse. Stanyhurst's ridiculous hexa-
metric *Vergil* 1582 could not displace Phaer's version
1560, in 'fourteeners,' the measure employed by

Mythological poems — *Translations* (marginal labels)

Arthur Golding in his popular and much-used *Metamorphoses* of Ovid 1567, and in the vastly greater work of George Chapman, the *Iliad* 1598–1611. Chapman's *Odyssey* 1616 was written, for some reason, in heroic couplets, which do not so well recover the pace and energy of the original; both the translations are Elizabethan in their elaborate and frequently ingenious phrasing, and in their expansions of the original. A comparison of Chapman, Pope, Cowper and Lang and Leaf in their treatment of Homer would throw much light on the changing current of literary taste. George Sandys the traveller did the *Metamorphoses* again into couplets 1621. These are by no means all the classical translators, and the industry was so widespread that it sought its raw material in France, Spain and Italy as well. Sir John Harrington made a courtly version of Ariosto's *Orlando Furioso* 1591; Edward Fairfax admirably translated Tasso's *Gerusalemme Liberata* in 1600; Joshua Sylvester's feebly fluent *Divine Weeks and Works* 1590–2, from Du Bartas, had wide influence down to Milton's age.

The group of philosophical and religious poets sounds a note which becomes more insistent in the

Religious and philosophical poems

sequel; Drummond of Hawthornden's religious sonnets, *Flowers of Sion* 1623, illustrate the transition in temper. Before them come Sir John Davies's *Orchestra* 1596, in which the movements of the planets, the sea and human affairs are poetically symbolised in a harmonious dance; and the quatrains of his *Nosce Teipsum* 1598, which, with Dryden-like clearness of verse-argument, discusses the immortality of the soul and the intimate union of soul and body. Fulke Greville's rigidly intellectual poems *Of Humane Knowledge*, *Of Monarchy*, not published till 1633, are too formidable; something of the same quality marks Chapman's *Tears of Peace*; the praise of learning in it is noble, but it is 'craggy' and rather apt to 'break' than refresh the mind. Robert Southwell, the poet of the Roman catholic religion in Elizabeth's days, gives fire by his devotion to the curious conceits and fancies in his *Saint Peter's Complaint* 1615.

The figure of the most profound originality in this group and this age is John Donne, most of whose writings were posthumously **John Donne** published in 1633. *Elegies*, *Satires* (described below), verse *Letters* and *Songs* are all distinguished by the spirit of rebellion, the intensest thrill of emotion, subtlety of intellect and lightning flashes of brilliant phrasing. He rebelled against the long imitative tradition of the Petrarchans; he could no more speak simply of love, like Burns, than they; but he replaced their fine-spun sentiment, worn thin through age-long use, by feeling which retains the furnace heat of experience, animal passion, or an over-intellectualised contempt for women. In general, he is the poet of the metaphysics of sex, moving more rarely on normal levels as in his most exquisite song 'Sweetest love, I do not go.' For the ritualised diction of the Petrarchans, with its circulating catalogue of simile and mythological allusion, he substituted a speech in the main strong and rugged rather than poetical (though often achieving splendid rhythm and colour), and metaphors and parallels drawn from mathematics, alchemy, law, scholasticism and from the most prosaic and unpromising affairs of every day. Carew crystallised the judgment of his time about Donne in his lines 'A king that ruled...the universal monarchy of wit.' Wit, the fiery rapidity of thought and the swift summoning of some image, bizarre but fitting, from his richly-stored erudition, might well be the possession of one who passed from the Roman to the Anglican church, a master of both their theologies. This mental gymnastic contributed to the characteristic 'metaphysical' blend of passion and intellectual ingenuity whether of forensic argument or far-sought conceit which may be seen in the haunting fragment *The Progress of the Soul* and the extravagantly eulogistic elegies, with outbursts of magnificent poetry, entitled *An Anatomy of the World*. Neither his intense individuality, nor the imagination which peers into the backward and abysm of things and is shadowed by the thought of death, could be passed on to his followers; but some habits natural to him became, in them, mere conceits and fantastic ingenuities which were duly castigated in Johnson's *Life of Cowley*. These habits are characteristic of both the secular and the religious 'metaphysicals,' the latter taking their origin from Donne's *Divine Poems,* written when the insolent libertinism of youth had given way to the ascetic devotion of the dean of St Paul's, Donne having by this time been rewarded with belated office in the church.

Another group includes patriotic chroniclers in verse, for prose, verse and drama all take heavy toll of this material. After Spenser, the first of

them is William Warner, whose *Albion's England*
1586–1602 is a history of the usual uncritical kind
from the Flood to his own day. Its rugged fourteen-
syllabled lines are not often poetic nor is its narrative skill very remarkable; it is saved by its
patriotism. Peele has his famous *Farewell to Norris
and Drake* 1589, and Fitzgeffrey his classically
adorned elegy on Drake 1596.   Romance and
Patriotism   chronicle meet in 'well-languaged'
Daniel   Daniel's *Complaint of Rosamond* 1592–
1623; chronicle and reflection are the substance of
his *Civil Wars* 1595–1623, fluent, distinguished but
unexciting. *Tethys' Festival* is the finest of the
masques he wrote for the queen between 1604 and
1610. His patriotic enthusiasm is stirred to its most
powerful expression in *Musophilus* 1599, in praise of
learning, with an inspired prophecy of the triumphs
of English speech; his vein of high-minded morality
runs through *Ulysses and the Siren*, and the gravely
dignified *Epistle to the Lady Margaret*. Musical
grace, a noble austerity of temper, a fine taste in
diction and a slight want of robustness characterise
Drayton   Samuel Daniel; his contemporary, and,
            in some things, pupil, Michael Drayton,
enriched and polished his talent through a lifetime's
assiduous exercise, passing from an earlier heaviness
of matter and style to the levity, suppleness and
metrical ease of *Nimphidia* 1627, a source book of
fairy lore to Herrick. His *Barons' Wars* 1603, and
Poly-Olbion 1613–22, are pious tributes to England,
immense in scale, especially the *Poly-Olbion*; its
thirty songs in twelve-syllabled riming lines survey
the counties, hills, streams, sports, legends and historic

moments of England; the learned notes which accompany them are by the scholar and antiquary John Selden. Like Daniel, Drayton blends together romance and chronicle in *England's Heroical Epistles* 1597-1605 (based on Ovid's *Heroides*), letters of lovers of exalted rank, suggestive of their time and circumstance, expressing real passion, and using the heroic couplet with ease and vigour. His sonnet-sequence *Idea* has been named; his concern with the stage was unprofitable, and his satires are almost negligible; but his *Odes*, pastorals in *The Muses' Elizium* 1630, and *Dowsabel* snatch a grace beyond the reach of his own art. His *Odes* have metrical range and a sure felicity; his mock gallantry anticipates Suckling; his *Ballad of Agincourt* sets a standard, only attained by *Henry V*, of patriotic exaltation. The incessant industry, the varied accomplishment and the Roman massiveness of Drayton make him the most typical of Elizabethan poets.

The pastoral writers are numerous; besides those named as lyrists, George Wither wrote his *Shepherd's* **The** *Hunting* 1615, and *Philarete* 1622, and **Spenserians** William Browne of Tavistock *Britannia's Pastorals* 1613-5, describing, in graceful limpid couplets, country scenes, sometimes simple, sometimes ornate, but less literary than those of his master Spenser; he is a pale anticipatory shadow of Keats. Spenser's mantle of allegory fell upon the shoulders of the Fletchers, cousins of John Fletcher, the dramatist. The elder brother, Phineas, wrote *Piscatory Eclogues*, a novel and agreeable form of pastoral; but more famous is *The Purple*

Island (not published till 1633). In this poem, Phineas (like Giles in *Christ's Victory*) tampered with the Spenserian stanza. *The Purple Island* is an over-elaborate allegory of the human body as an island; the faculties of the mind are treated as inhabitants; and the whole is rounded off with a warfare of vices and virtues, not unlike Bunyan's Mansoul; except in its pedantic plan, the work is poetical, being rich in melody and imagery, though often defaced by an excess of conceit. Giles Fletcher's *Christ's Victory and Triumph* 1610, an epic of the redemption, links Spenser and Milton; the description of the Bower of Vain Delight is not unworthy of Spenser's Bower of Acrasia, while Milton's *Paradise Regained*, of about the same length as Fletcher's poem, owes much to some of the temptations described in it, besides the picture of Satan as an 'aged sire.' Henry More's *Philosophical Poems* 1647, and Joseph Beaumont's *Psyche* 1648, carry on the Spenserian tradition in thought and verse, with an ever-growing tendency to abstraction and neoplatonism; they belong to the influential school of Cambridge Platonists.

Post-renascence satire begins tentatively with Wyatt; Spenser's *Mother Hubberd's Tale* and *Colin Clout's Come Home Again* are born of genuine indignation, as are the satires of Ben Jonson. Much Elizabethan satire is of the nature of the 'character' in verse; Joseph Hall claimed priority for his *Virgidemiarum* 1597; Lodge's *A Fig for Momus* 1589, Marston's *Satires* 1598, Guilpin's *Skialethia* and Donne's *Satires*, published 1633, are all written in heroic couplets with a rough

Satire

unmusical cadence of which the general explanation
is that poets were taught by Persius to regard it as
the inevitable medium for satire; Juvenal is also a
much followed model.   Donne alone has the genius
to make his characters memorable; the acid of contempt bites the lines of his portraits deep into the
plate.   But, speaking generally, besides their obvious
immaturity, these satires suffer through the lack of
large inspiring interests, such as Dryden's politics,
and Pope's solicitude for the dignity of letters.

3.   Prose to the death of James I

We may classify the prose of the time under the
following headings.

Sir Thomas More, in his *Utopia* 1516 (in English
1551), shows the rare constructive dissatisfaction
which figures forth ideal common-
wealths, combined with the still rarer
grip of facts which makes his book a
social prophecy, still awaiting reasonable fulfilment,
of communal possession, universal labour, religious
toleration, even-handed justice and healthful contentment.   Roger Ascham, queen Elizabeth's tutor,
published in 1545 his *Toxophilus*, a eulogy of archery,
with many asides; and, in 1570, the *Schoolmaster*,
discussing classical learning—Italian he hated—
sport, the means to make education palatable and
the making of character.   He sets down his very
sane conclusions in a plain prose which purposely
avoids the ink-horn terms rife in fifteenth century
verse and prose.   Richard Hooker's *Laws of Ecclesiastical Polity* (books I–IV, 1594) is a defence of the

1. Education
and govern-
ment

Anglican position against the Roman catholic and the puritan; its stately rhetoric and rhythmic periods assert with wide philosophical grasp the universal prevalence of law. Hooker rescued theology from the menace of narrowness by his liberal interpretation of the relations between natural law and the divine law of the scriptures.

The contradictions in the character of Francis Bacon 1561–1626 come to light, on the one hand, in his impeachment for corruption, and, on the other, in the vast conquests he projected for science. In *The Advancement of Learning* 1605, afterwards expanded in the Latin *De Augmentiis Scientiarum* 1623, he surveys all knowledge, mapping out three provinces, memory, imagination and reason; in the Latin *Novum Organum*, he tracks down the idols (or phantoms) of the tribe, the den, the market-place and the theatre; next he proposes to interrogate nature by the method of systematic induction, as opposed to the scholastic way of formal deduction. *Novum Organum* is the part brought nearest to perfection of *Instauratio Magna*, Bacon's vast dream of the development of science, through the stages of experiment, ascertainment of causes and prophetic theory, to the final record of all attainable knowledge. It is true that Bacon himself was not a very accurate observer, that he lagged behind the scientific knowledge of his time and that his method of enquiry has been superseded; yet it was he who definitely turned the tide of investigation from medieval to modern methods. The *Essays*, ten in 1597, thirty-eight in 1612, fifty-eight in 1625, are,

2. Philosophy

Bacon

however, Bacon's securest title to literary fame.
They owe something to Montaigne, but, in place
of a leisured abundance, they have, in the typical
instances, a terse compact brevity, the result of a
long process of sifting. They may be divided into
those in which he speaks as politician and statesman
(here he is indebted to Plutarch and Machiavelli);
as moralist and adviser; and as thinker and imaginative writer. His prudence and sagacity, though of
the earth earthy, are almost unassailable. His devotion to the cause of knowledge is that of a supreme
idealist: 'he moved the intellects which moved the
world.' Nevertheless, in more human relationships
his mental force and subtlety are mated curiously
with emotional poverty. His prose has great
pliancy; some essays are in the periodic sentence
of complex structure, some in his 'folded enigma-
tical way,' balanced clauses accumulating sometimes
three deep. His pages are studded with salient
anecdote, quotation and misquotation, especially
from the Roman world, Bacon's model in antiquity.
At their best, they have a magisterial fulness of
thought, a splendour of rhythmic art, an economy
of wording and an arresting quality of figurative
statement far outweighing their lack of orderliness
and coherence; not many things with so many im-
perfections upon them are so freely admitted to be
classic. *The New Atlantis* is Bacon's version of
Utopia.   Burton's *Anatomy of Melancholy* 1621
groups its encyclopaedic learning about the symp-
toms of melancholy; it is a mine of bookish wit,
of modern and antique instances, of scholarlike
irony and humour, and its sentences are stiff with

Latin quotations; it could only have been produced in an age before experimental science had won its footing. Feltham's *Resolves* 1620 are like diluted *Essays* of Bacon.

More's *History of Richard III* and Bacon's *Henry VII* are both weighty historical studies of
3. History, Chronicle and Travel
the newer trustworthy kind which may be contrasted with the older chronicle type in Ralegh's *History of the World*, only memorable now for some passages of a sonorous gloomy eloquence. Holinshed and Speed are less truthful than Camden, whose more critical *Britannia* is in Latin. Stow was the careful chronicler of London, as Harrison, in Holinshed's *Chronicles*, was of English life in town and country. Hakluyt, in his *Principal Navigations* 1589–1600, was the enthusiastic editor of travellers' tales of voyagers and buccaneers, and, in some subtle way, his direct unadorned prose conveys perfectly the sense of action, adventure and colonisation on the Spanish Main and in the north-west passage. His work was continued by Samuel Purchas in his *Pilgrimage* 1613. Coryat's *Crudities* 1611 are European travel-notes, unpretentious and amusing.

Criticism is afoot, as may be seen in Webbe's *Discourse of English Poetry* 1586, and Puttenham's
4. Criticism
Art of English Poesie 1589. Gosson's *School of Abuse* 1579 provoked Sidney, in the next year, to write his *Apology*, which was published posthumously in 1595. Sidney enthrones poetry high above philosophy and history, repelling the puritan assault on the worth and delight of poetry and drama, and, through all the controversy,

keeping an alert ear for the true ring of poetry in
Chevy Chase, Troilus and Criseyde and the 'new
poet's' *Shepherd's Calendar*. But Sidney holds fast
to his learning, upholds the unities and the Senecan
drama and condemns by forecast the romantic
school; in 1580, we must remember, there was
nothing to show that it had any capacity for
grandeur. His prose has the clear eloquence and
felicity of phrasing of his poetry. Daniel for, and
Campion against (though he was an exquisite rimer
himself), debated the question of rime. Bacon philo-
sophised about poetry in *De Augmentiis*, and Ben
Jonson, in the brief paragraphs of his *Discoveries*
1641, uttered pregnant criticism of Bacon and
Shakespeare, and added to the vocabulary of criticism a terminology derived from Roman rhetori-
cians.

The novel, already past its zenith in Italy, makes
an abortive beginning in England with Lyly's
Euphues 1579 and *Euphues and his
England*, didactic tales through which
5. The Novel
move the shadows of renascence youth, discussing
at length and often shrewdly the point of honour,
the purpose of education, the durability of passion,
friendship and atheism, in a tone addressed to the
ladies of Elizabeth's court. Here, Euphuism—a
style already embryonic in Berners's and North's
translations of Guevara's *Dial of Princes*, and in
Pettie's *Petite Palace of Pleasure* 1576, a compilation
of tales—develops to maturity, to be quickly followed by senility and ridicule. Euphuism gets its
artificial emphasis by repetition, antithesis, alliteration, rhetorical questioning, thickly strewn

mythological anecdote and analogies drawn from a
fantastic natural history. It served Falstaff as stuff
for parody, Drayton attacked it and Sidney rejected
some of its extravagances in his more human and
graceful pastoral romance *Arcadia*; still, its mannered disciplined style played a part in providing a
technique of prose. Before the fashion was spent,
Greene wrote *Pandosto* in the same medium and
Lodge *Rosalynde*. Greene then turned to his series
of 'coney-catching' exposures, in the wake of Harman's *Caveat for Vagabonds*, and Dekker followed
suit with his *Gull's Horn Book* 1609. Nashe, the
typical Elizabethan journalist, broke in with his
vivid, picaresque tale *Jack Wilton*. Deloney wrote
novels of craftsmen and apprentices. These romantic and realistic stories correspond in a rough way
to the romances and *fabliaux* of the Middle Ages.
Here must be named the species of writing known
as *Characters*, derived ultimately from Theophrastus.
Sir Thomas Overbury's *Characters* are surpassed in
their witty observation and analytic delineation of
types by Earle's *Microcosmographie* 1628; the vein is
exhausted in the prose characters of Butler, author
of *Hudibras*. It may faintly have influenced the
course of the novel.

Pamphleteering became an enormous industry.
The *Martin Marprelate* controversy stands out by
6. Pamphle-   reason of the vigour of the assailants,
teering   the romantic history of its perambu-
lating press, the fact that bishops were obliged
to call in professional aid and that puritanism here
gave its solitary evidence of a capacity for humour :
the prelates undoubtedly had the worst of it.

Sidney always carried abroad with him Hoby's translation 1561 of Castiglione's *Courtier*, the first
7. Trans-   of many 'courtier books'; the scho-
lators   larly and industrious Philemon Holland translated, about 1600, among other things, Livy and Plutarch's *Morals*. In four notable cases, translators proved themselves competent to distil into English, taking no thought for slavish accuracy, the full flavour of great originals; these are North's Plutarch's *Lives* 1579, from the French of Amyot, Florio's *Montaigne* 1603, Shelton's *Don Quixote* 1612 and, much later, Urquhart's *Rabelais* 1653.

Of all this multifarious prose, rhetorical, ceremonious, exotic, compact, colloquial, over-Latinised or eccentric, we may remark three things. First, that no one has yet appeared to serve as a model in syntax and diction, though Ben Jonson came near to it. Secondly, that it brought much grist to Shakespeare's mill: Holinshed, North's *Plutarch*, the collections of novels, Greene's *Pandosto* (the source of *The Winter's Tale*), Lodge's *Rosalynde* (the source of *As You Like It*) and Montaigne are all contributors to him in different measures. Thirdly, of this type of mannered prose, when encumbrances have been brushed away, thought clarified and imagination infused, Shakespeare himself is the real master in the dialogue of his plays between 1594 and 1604.

4. THE DRAMA

The origins of Elizabethan drama lie far back in the liturgy of the church; there are hardly any traces of classical drama in the Middle Ages, though there are spectacular and faintly dramatic elements in popular carnivals, sword-dances and may-dances. But the church, by converting the services for Easter and Christmas into visual representations with, at first, antiphonal song, and, later, vernacular dialogue, gave birth to the drama destined to maturity in Shakespeare's plays. These liturgical plays date from the eleventh century; they centred about the sepulchre and the manger, and were acted by priests in the church or with its walls for a background. By steps which we cannot precisely date, (i) the subjects were extended till they came to include all the Bible story (strictly called mystery plays) and saints' legends (strictly miracle plays, though this word is applied to both kinds in England). (ii) They passed out of the hands of the church into those of the corporations, who were in the habit of presenting them by the aid of the craft-guilds long before 1378; occasionally, though not regularly, a guild took an incident appropriate to its trade, as Cana, in the case of the Vintners. (iii) These plays, on many incidents of scripture story, legend and even devotional literature, were gathered into cycles and played on Corpus Christi day, and often on succeeding days, replacing, or

Origins

Miracle plays

going on concurrently with, the processions which
celebrated the feast. Most towns had cycles, and
they were often represented on a number of two-
storied wheeled stages or 'pagonds' which passed
in succession round the town to different groups
of spectators. Many details of cost and policing
remain in municipal records, but only five main
cycles are preserved in MSS, generally of the
fifteenth century. Those of York number 48, of
Wakefield (the Towneley mysteries) 32, of Chester
25; there are, besides, the Cornish cycle in dialect,
and a less dramatic group, wrongly called of
Coventry. They are in all kinds of measures, chiefly
lyrical stanzas: all are anonymous, but very. memorable are those written by one of the Towneley
authors, who uses a singular stanza and who, in
the episodes of Cain, of Noah and of Mak the
sheep-stealer, has telling realism and rich humour;
these show the secularising and popularising of
religious drama proceeding apace. There are, in
addition, single plays and fragmentary evidences
of non-clerical material, such as plays on Robin
Hood.

On the heels of the miracle cycles follow, in the
fifteenth century, the moral, or, using the French
word, morality, plays, manifesting the
taste of the time for allegory. The
Castle of Perseverance, the first of them extant,
dates about 1430, and they continue their course for
a century and a half alongside the miracle play,
being enacted, however, on a stationary stage.
Later examples are Skelton's *Magnificence* 1516 ?
and the impressive *Everyman*, in which man,

Morality
plays

summoned by Death to judgment, is deserted by
Fellowship, Jollity, Strength, Pleasure and Beauty,
and accompanied only by the meagre phantom of
his Good Deeds. Moralities are all variations of
a common theme, the struggle for man's soul by
personified vices and virtues. Whereas the miracle
play told the long history from creation to judgment
in prescribed scriptural sequence, the moral play introduced the idea of conflict, invented its stories and
designed emblematic characters, counterbalancing
these advances by falling back for a while upon
lifeless personifications. Some show of comedy was
made out of the vice, said to be the progenitor of the
Shakespearean fool.

Next came the stage of the interlude, a dialogue between characters, in which the morality is
shortened for entertainments in ban-
queting halls, another instance of the
influence of the audience in shaping drama; these
were played by professional players. Several types
of interlude exist; the moral and didactic, such as
Hickscorner c. 1509; the humanist, such as Rastell's
Four Elements c. 1515, and the later *Wit and Science*;
the controversial, such as those of the 'bilious' protestant John Bale, whose *King John* shows the
morality being transformed, very slowly, into the
history play; and, fourthly, the farces, much nearer
akin to the French *soties*, of John Heywood. His
interludes, *The Weather, Love, Johan Johan* and the
Four PP c. 1544, are witty *fabliau*-like tales, portraying genuine social types and carrying comedy
to within reach of classical example.

Classical influence fastens upon comedy and

tragedy about the middle of the sixteenth century.
Classical
influence In comedy, Terence and Plautus are
studied and pillaged; first come school-
master dramas (the renascence schools were much
given to dramatic production) Udall's *Ralph Roister
Doister* 1553 ?, and Stevenson's *Gammer Gurton's
Needle* c. 1550, in which native stuff with some
classical character types is roughly divided into
acts and scenes. Next follow experimenters such as
Gascoigne, Whetstone and Edwards, whose *Damon
and Pythias* 1564 fuses comedy and tragedy and
some degree of characterisation. The kinds welter
together; those in popular tradition acted in the
open or in inn-yards, and those in classical tradition
acted in the inns of court and in the universities;
these lead us to the university wits.

In tragedy, humanist influence set the Senecan
form as model, as may be seen in Sackville and
Norton's *Gorboduc* 1562, and in Hughes's *Misfortunes of Arthur* 1587, both presenting matter of
British history in classical shape with Senecan
accompaniments, ghost, chorus, sententious maxims
and messenger reporting sensational bloodshed; the
dumb-shows in *Gorboduc* are not Senecan but
Italian.

The plays of the university wits cover the years
1580–92; the first of the wits is John Lyly the
The
university
wits Euphuist, among whose eight plays are
Alexander and Campaspe, in which
Alexander the great gives up Cam-
paspe to the painter Apelles; *Mother Bombie*, in
which native stuff is set in a Terentian frame;
Endymion, probably a court-allegory of Leicester,

as *Midas* is of Philip of Spain; *Gallathea* and some
other pastoral masques. His comedies are mostly
of persons of quality, whose artificial codes are the
material of high comedy; at times, he mixes there-
with provincial buffooneries. His witty style and
pleasing talk studded with puns and quips often
sparkle with sprightly polished repartee. The influence of these things extends demonstrably to
A Midsummer Night's Dream, and, by inference,
beyond. It is now thought doubtful whether the
lyrics, which do not appear before 1632, can be by
Lyly's own hand. His success established prose as
the medium for comedy and ensured its discarding
the boisterous humour of English tradition in favour
of lighter, more graceful and more intellectual
substance. George Peele's *Arraignment of Paris*
amends the legend of the three goddesses, and
Diana presents the ball of gold to queen Elizabeth.
His scriptural drama of *David and Bethsabe* has
much graceful blank verse and a shapely plot; this
praise cannot be given to *The Old Wives' Tale*, a
farrago of folklore and literary satire, which gave
Milton hints and figures for his masque of *Comus*.
Robert Greene had more original gift; his *Alphonsus*
is an imitation of *Tamburlaine*; *James IV*, in spite
of its title, is from a novel of Cinthio; *Friar Bacon
and Friar Bungay* compounds the love affairs of
Edward I (as prince of Wales) and the magic skill
of Roger Bacon. Greene has some real passion in
the love stories which he exalts to a high place in
the dramas, and some simple human feeling, especially in his portrayals of long-suffering women, for
whom his own wife may well have sat as a model.

Thomas Lodge's Roman play *The Wounds of Civil War* is very tedious; and the brilliant and varied talent of Nashe did not give anything of importance to the stage. Thomas Kyd was not a university man, but, in his *Spanish Tragedy*, a very popular play, he derived material from Seneca; it is an orgy of revenge and bloodshed; but its deeper interest is its resemblance to the plot of *Hamlet*. On the basis of this, and some references of Nashe, has been built the theory that Kyd was the author of the original *Hamlet* which Shakespeare worked over in the quarto of 1603. Kyd may also be credited with some advance in the involution of character and plot. Christopher Marlowe was the only member of the group whose accomplishment passed beyond the tentative; he is the aggressor against 'jigging veins,' 'mother-wits,' rime in tragedy and the 'conceits' of 'clownage.' His brief dramatic career, if it did not found, at any rate confirmed, the obligation to seek the subjects of high tragedy among people of high rank, and amid the 'stately tents of war.' The ambitious imagination of his irregular genius at first over-reached itself; his first play *Tamburlaine* 1587, and his *Jew of Malta* (Lamb says of Barabas, in this play, 'He kills in sport, poisons whole nunneries, invents infernal machines'), are beyond the confines of likelihood; they portray illimitable lusts, in the one case for conquest, in the other for wealth. The vast outlines of these characters are amazing, but unconvincing: bloodshed and violence usurp the place of natural motive and action. But, in *Edward II*, which, by its realistic historical basis,

Marlowe

compels the poet to concentrate instead of dis-
persing his forces, and in *Dr Faustus*, where the
overwhelming desire to rifle the hidden treasures of
knowledge is a more credible motive, tragedy becomes human; in the case of Faustus, the tragedy
is intensified (if we accept the system of belief), by
the final forfeiture of his immortal soul.   If we
regard Marlowe's accepted triumphs, we may see
that his intrinsic worth is chiefly associated with
two things; first, his mastery of tragic terror, whether
'the reluctant pangs of abdicating royalty' in
Edward II or the agony of the 'exactment of his
(Faustus's) dire compact'; second, his poetical
splendour, those 'brave translunary things' which
Drayton celebrated; he ranks with Chaucer and
Spenser among the great metrical innovators.
Through the instrument of blank verse, he uttered
strains latent but, as yet, undetected in it by any
ear; its various music, its supple submission to all
the demands of thought and beauty, provided the
means to attempt and accomplish the severest tasks,
to chant the loveliness of Helen, to echo the terror
of Faustus's last hour, or to ring exultantly with
stately names, Usumcasane, Theridamas, Persepolis.
This skill made Milton his pupil in verse, as Shakespeare was for the lessons of his early tragedy in
Henry VI, in *Titus Andronicus* (it is to be feared
that Shakespeare wrote it), in *Richard III*, in
Richard II and in the character of Shylock.   In
the light of these things, we may set down at their
justly insignificant value the charges of 'lack of
humour' and propensity to rant.

William Shakespeare was born in 1564 and

educated at the Grammar School of his native town
Shakespeare Stratford-on-Avon. He escaped the
universities. Probably, the waning
fortunes and diminished status of his family rankled
in his mind; his later dealings in Stratford after his
fortune was made, his litigation and purchases of
property and of a coat-of-arms, indicate a resolution
to enforce his rights and to clear a stigma from his
name. After a youth spirited enough to involve
him in a poaching affray and an early marriage, he
turned to London, possibly just before the year of
the Armada, and patched old plays; he soon awoke
the lightly sleeping jealousies of the Bohemian playwrights, especially of Robert Greene. But he won
his standing in London, in a quarrelsome age and
set, by his genius, his engaging temper and his
fertility; he wrote on the average two plays a year
for nearly twenty years, besides narrative poems and
sonnets at the beginning of his career. For all this
Ben Jonson is an unimpeachable witness. So far as
we know, his life was uneventful, though the sonnets
may reflect some desperate passion; we have no
clue to the causes of the changed temper which we
detect in some of his plays between 1601 and 1605.
The cause may have been the fates of Essex, South-
ampton and Pembroke, or it may have been some
compelling importunity within his own mind. After
1608, it is as though he had passed through this
tempestuous ocean strewn with noble wreckage into
a serene sun-bathed haven. He returned to Stratford
about 1611 and died there on 23 April 1616.

The Plays

A rough chronological division of the plays may be made as follows:

I. *Period of Apprenticeship.* 1590–6.

HISTORY	COMEDY	TRAGEDY
Henry VI, parts i, ii and iii	Love's Labour's Lost	Titus Andronicus
King John	The Comedy of Errors	Romeo and Juliet
	The Two Gentlemen of Verona	
Richard II	The Merchant of Venice	
Richard III	A Midsummer Night's Dream	

II. *Middle History and Comedy.* 1596–1601.

	The Taming of the Shrew	
	The Merry Wives of Windsor	
Henry IV, parts i and ii	Much Ado about Nothing	
Henry V	As You Like It	
	Twelfth Night	

III. 1601–8. i. *Plays of disillusion.*

	All's Well that Ends Well (? revision of Love's Labour's Won)	Troilus and Cressida
		Measure for Measure
		Timon of Athens (in part)

Y.   6

ii. *Tragedy.*

HISTORY	COMEDY	TRAGEDY
		Julius Caesar
		Hamlet
		Othello
		King Lear
		Macbeth
		Antony and
		Cleopatra
		Coriolanus

IV. *Period of Romances.* 1608–12.

Henry VIII (in	Pericles (in part)
part)	
	Cymbeline
	The Winter's Tale
	The Tempest

We may consider Shakespeare's work under the headings of comedy, history and tragedy, this being the division adopted in the first folio of 1623.

Comedy is integral and organic in Shakespeare's histories and tragedies as well as a separate species.
Comedy
With this warning, we may outline the varying forms of his comic writing broadly in three sections. In the first, he works through absurdity and creates farce; in the second, he works through grace and youth and creates romance; in the third, through thought and offers ' criticism of life.'

The farce may be that of situation as in *The Taming of the Shrew* and *The Merry Wives of Windsor*, in which we are pledged to laugh though the central situations will not bear thinking on; or of mistaken identity as in *The Comedy of Errors* and

A Midsummer Night's Dream, which depend on ingenuity of construction. It may be absurdities
and oddities of character that he presents; these
make up a lengthy and heterogeneous procession;
figures of ungainly animal vigour, busy with intoxi-
cation, lying, thieving, jesting and singing like
Falstaff and Sir Toby, the consummate spokesman
for the creed of cakes and ale; or Bottom, who, by
sheer reiteration of himself, has become a person of
importance. Next follow the cloudy-witted, like
the artisans of Athens and Dogberry and Verges,
whose brains are fuddled as soon as they are called
upon to act; next, the echoes and parrots, anaemic
and subnormal, Sir Andrew Aguecheek, Slender
and Shallow, born to be spoiled like the Egyptians;
next, those with a large endowment of high spirits
and mother-wit, Maria, Gobbo and Autolycus; and
here, too, we may put the disconcerted boasters
and self-deceivers Parolles, Bardolph and Pistol.
A curious sympathy is extended to them all singly,
whether stupid or alert, which Shakespeare could
never feel for the collective mob.

His romantic comedy goes on under brilliant
skies in palaces and bowers, or in forests or by the
sea-shore, not in Eastcheap taverns or by Gadshill.
In the world of feudal observances, the primitive
impulses of men must be masked. Rank, culture,
leisure, convention, courtesy, disguisings and, above
all, the dominance of the radiantly triumphant creations Portia, Beatrice, Rosalind and Viola; all these
things together weave a web of artificiality in which
men and women are for ever becoming entangled in
comically false positions. Malvolio, who is hopelessly

inflexible and intolerant, suffers most, attempting to enter two worlds, of romance and comedy, which he does not understand. He is an older figure, but, in general, youth is on the prow and Shakespeare culti-vates the belief that youth cannot make irreparable mistakes. Critics like Malvolio and the moody libertine Jaques are outfaced by the impulsive optimists, whose laughter is clear, musical and free. The intrusions of a not very deeply laid villainy in *Much Ado* and *As You Like It* only cloud for a moment the sunshine of love and gaiety. In the last plays, often called specifically 'romances,' the menace of tragedy is not so easily shaken off; they turn chiefly on the theme of sundered families; age has its place and its serener outlook is the result of digested experience, rather than, as in the middle comedies, of heedless fortunate impulse.

Lastly, we may find comedy allied with thought; along this line, Shakespeare developed the fool, from the feudal jester and juggler with words to the observant commentator with a dramatic purpose to serve; Touchstone and his tragic counterpart the fool in *King Lear* are instances. Both reason logically and have the instinct for facts, though they deliver themselves in motley; and they exemplify a generous fidelity contrasted with monstrous impiety. Much the same office is filled by the grave-diggers in *Hamlet*, and the porter in *Macbeth*, auxiliary figures who intensify emotional crises in tragedy. There is wider import in the *macabre* expression of the disillusions of Hamlet, the only humorist among the tragic characters; thought takes a gayer hue in Falstaff, greatest of all comic creations. He is a

rake, spendthrift, glutton, liar and coward for pure
fun; but these things are not the essence of him,
for he is of gentlemanly rank and is a master mind.
He is a rebel against strait-laced authority and the
unthinking man's standards; he will not admit for
himself any moral standards; he ignores uncomfortable facts and evades their consequences by a wit as
nimble and ubiquitous as his body is corpulent and
stationary. With colossal impudence, he betakes
himself to an imaginary world (though it is not
devoid of logic) in which such conceptions as honour
and truth appear the veriest delusions. Just when
he seems to have fortified himself against facts and
laws and to have absolved himself from all punish-
ment, a twinge of the great toe finds him out and his
world breaks down; its foundations were insecure,
for wit cannot defy the gout, and, moreover, the
callous Henry V, who was counted upon as a buttress
against justice, was no true Falstaffian. It appears
from this comedy that truth will out and deride the
perverters of it; but never was sound moralising so
engagingly embroidered.

The chronicle-plays on some of the kings from
John to Henry VIII show a large historical grasp
of this section of the feudal period and
History   a gift of imagining the background of
battlefield, council-chamber, embarkation, the pomp
and retinue of rank as well as the taverns and haunts
of the common soldier. The plays are, in the main,
as historically accurate as their source, which is
Holinshed's *Chronicles*, though there are dramatic
perversions such as making Hotspur of the same
age as prince Hal. *Henry VI, Richard III* and

Richard II are indebted in various ways to Marlowe. The earlier plays on the later period, the
wars of the Roses, are more uniformly tragic, while
the later ones, *Henry IV* parts i and ii and *Henry V*,
are lightened by comedy, the witty insolence of
Falstaff and his satellites. This was Shakespeare's
school of training in portraiture, for characters and
events interest him more than constitutions and
creeds; *King John* does not mention Magna Carta,
Richard II ignores the peasant revolt and *Henry
VIII* the reformation. Yet creed, as an element of
character, is not neglected, as may be seen in the
prayers of Henry V. These regal people are all
brought face to face with harassing circumstance,
'malice domestic, foreign levy'; not many of them
emerge triumphantly. We are never allowed to
forget the toilsomeness of kingly duties; the tinge
of Shakespearean melancholy colours what both
Richard II and Henry V have to say about cere-
mony. The variety and actuality of character is
astonishing; fighting types, statesmen, churchmen,
courtiers, archers, men-at-arms, traitors, parasites,
dreamers, men with deep-grained national traits, all
speak with the accent of life. Women are naturally
less prominent than in the comedies, yet there are
the distinctive figures of Richard II's queen, the
Lady Anne, Lady Percy and Mistress Quickly.
Moreover, these plays are the poet's utterance on the
test question of patriotism. He is a little singular
here, for he adds but few notes to the chorus in
praise of Elizabeth; he drew his inspiration from his
profound affection for the soil and heroes of England
when he wrote the speeches of Faulconbridge,

Talbot, Richard II, John of Gaunt and Henry V. He is for the Tudor settlement, and is a firm believer in the security afforded to the state by rank, though the democratic affability of Henry V was one of the traits which attracted him; the thought of the mob roused his bitterest animosity. Finally, we should note the gift of royal eloquence with which Shakespeare endows all the company of kings.

Shakespeare had already written tragedy before 1601 in the history plays and in *Romeo and Juliet*.

Tragedy
But his later conception of tragedy was not like his romantic idyll, suffused with the warmth and passion and mirth of an Italian summer-night, turned to fatality. These lovers are ' star-crossed '; fate casts a mortal shadow upon their perfect lyrical passion. The tragedies from *Julius Caesar* 1601, to *Coriolanus* 1608, apart from their wider speculative range (perhaps due to Montaigne) present characters at war not so much with fate as with themselves. They are flawed by some frailty or consumed by some overmastering passion, and, by a malign conjunction, upon this weakness the whole weight of adverse circumstance bears too hard for faults to be retrieved, as they might in comedy. It is not the tragedy of weakness, but of weakness betraying strength; character, action and suffering are in a necessary concatenation. We cannot, however, isolate the tragic character; there are nerves and fibres and arteries connecting him with the surrounding world. The poison gathers in these outer places, in Hamlet's uncle-stepfather, in Goneril and Regan, in Iago, in (on one interpretation of them at least) the witches in *Macbeth*, in

the demagogues of *Coriolanus*. The toxin works its
way disastrously to the heart of these heroic figures
and convulses the whole system, noble and ignoble
alike; as in *Hamlet*, where the king and queen,
Polonius, Laertes and Ophelia, Rosencrantz and
Guildenstern are all destroyed before the system is
purged—the rotten thing in the state of Denmark
cleansed.   The plays compel us to take a wider
perspective, else the ransom that evil extorts is too
great a price. The dignity of the protagonists is
sustained by that of the setting; empires, kingdoms,
armies are at stake as well as immortal souls. The
interplay of statecraft, warfare and these passions
that 'o'erleap' themselves, multiplies the imaginative interest, though it is never allowed to force the
tragic character out of focus. Again, there are types
of womanhood—Lady Macbeth and Volumnia, who,
in splendour and power, rival even Macbeth and
Coriolanus; whilst Cleopatra—one of the summits
of Shakespeare's creative genius—altogether over-
shadows Antony. As a foil to these we have the
fated yielding gracefulness of Ophelia and the impulsive self-effacing surrender of Desdemona. It is
to be noted how the diction of the comedies and
histories, clear in meaning and music, and yet finely
adorned, becomes tormented and often violent in the
tragedies, suggesting troublous over-wrought thinking and emotion, which words cannot adequately
convey; there are parallel variations in the blank
verse which can only be hinted at here, but are
fascinating literary studies.

   The significant thing about the sources of Shakespeare is what he made of them; here, as everywhere,

he had the art of distilling the finer essence from every herb. From the thin stock of Italian novels and translations he drew the entrancing perfume of romance; from Holinshed, the strong savour of patriotism; from Plutarch's *Lives*, the sharp flavour of stoic morals.

It is needless to deny that there are blemishes, spots on the sun of Shakespeare, though there are foolish worshippers who seek to deny it; his greatness is firmly enough established by a fourfold test. First, by his creation of character; no other writer has peopled the earth with so large and diverse a company, who haunt the memory and appeal to the affections. Secondly, by the loftiness and delicacy of his morality, stoic, in the main, but inspired by sympathy, widely tolerant of frailty and exuberance, never of calculated evil, calling in very little of transcendental support or 'metaphysical aid' at any great crisis. Thirdly, by his dramatic power in situation and emotion, whether comedy or tragedy. Fourthly, by his poetic gift, his command of rhythm, of imagery and the sense of the inner charm of words. Many dithyrambs have been written on Shakespeare; these four things are set down simply; the student can for himself try them, vary them, expand them with increasing knowledge of the text.

For a hundred years, Ben Jonson 1573–1637 challenged Shakespeare in public favour; Ben Jonson in almost all respects, save intellectual vigour, they were opposites. Jonson's learning was prodigious, as may be seen in the pedantic accuracy of his noble Roman tragedies *Sejanus* 1603 and *Catiline* 1611, and in the erudite notes to his masques. His temperament was harsh, dogmatic and assertive, as revealed in his conversations with Drummond, and in his stage war (in *The Poetaster* and other plays) with Dekker and Marston; yet he was capable of sincere admirations. Again, though there are evidences of romanticism in him, he suppressed them and pronounced himself for rigidly classical formulae in comedy. He introduced definitely to the Elizabethan stage the comedy of manners; realistic social types, at first, as in *Every Man in his Humour* 1598 (not unlike *The Merry Wives of Windsor*), but tending rapidly to become the comedy of 'humours' or of single idiosyncrasies as of Morose in *The Silent Woman* 1609. In Jonson, these 'humours' are neither artificial (as they become in Shadwell, for instance) nor merely photographic, for he penetrates deep into the natures of his creations, as Face, the brilliant scoundrel of *The Alchemist* 1610; there is still more psychological insight in *Volpone* 1605, which also illustrates Jonson's didactic and moral view of his art; comedy, in this play, barely survives in the poisonous atmosphere of loathsome vice. In all these plays, his intellect shapes and fits its material with a fine structural sense. His untiring curiosity is evident in his knowledge of the rogues' dialects of London, and of such lying and blackmailing industries as are pictured in *The Staple of News*, and in the showman's pandemonium, *Bartholomew Fair* 1614, in which appears another colossal Elizabethan conception, Rabbi Zeal-of-the-Land-Busy, to stand beside Sir Epicure Mammon and Volpone. There is a vein of fanciful imaginativeness and lyric beauty in Jonson. His pastoral play, *The Sad Shepherd*, is comparable with Fletcher's *Faithful Shepherdess* in music, grace and pathos; and the verses in *Underwoods* and *The Forest* 1616, putting aside some unpleasant epigrams, form one of the richest hoards of song and witty compliment the age provides. His writing, however censorious, is strong, vivid, the fruit of mental labour and drastic self-criticism; of all the Elizabethans, he held the most exalted opinion of poesy, and fought and hated for its maintenance. He wins sympathy a little slowly, but he compels admiration.

The masque originated in English pageantry and procession, in the forms of disguisings and mummings, in which disguisers went through a significant silent performance. But the name, and some elements which Henry VIII's patronage caused to be incorporated, came from Italy; in its later developments, it was a *salade russe* of scenery, music, poetry, allegory, emblem and dancing. The dancing, at first, was confined to people of rank and quality; Jonson provided for the professional dancers the grotesque anti-masque or antic-masque. Many poets tried their hands at the form, Shakespeare as in *The Tempest*, Chapman, Daniel, Campion and Shirley, but the perfecter of it was Jonson; probably his best is *The Masque of Queens* 1609. The masque became a costly affair, subject to the stage engineer Inigo Jones, whose carpentering was sometimes at enmity with poetry. Nevertheless, some of Jonson's most exquisite lines and concerted music are in these little read poems. The masque had a sunset blazing with glory in Milton's *Comus* 1634.

The remaining Elizabethan drama must be enumerated summarily. Chapman's best comedy Other Eliza- is *All Fools* 1605, and he wrote sensa-
bethan Drama tional tragedies such as *Bussy d'Ambois* 1607, in which there are, nevertheless, many flights of fine reflective poetry. A group of writers deal with domestic subjects and London life; among them is Dekker, best known by Lamb's sentence, 'he has poetry enough for anything.' He reveals a deep vein of humanity, skill in the portrayal of women and poetic fantasy, for instance, in *Old Fortunatus* 1600, and *The Honest Whore* 1604. Other members of the group are Munday, Chettle, Drayton, Rowley, Day and Heywood, whose enormous output includes one masterpiece, *A Woman killed with kindness* 1603. Middleton has bustling and realistic comedies of a low world, *A Trick to catch the old one* 1608, *The Roaring Girl* 1611; and one great scene in his tragedy *The Changeling*; here, as elsewhere, Rowley appears to have braced Middleton to his nobler efforts; *The Witch* has affinities with *Macbeth*. In prose and in verse Middleton has rapidity and ease. Tourneur has poetry in the midst of the gloomy horrors of *The Revenger's Tragedy* and *The Atheist's Tragedy* 1611. Marston hovers between the bombastic and the caustic in his tragic *Antonio and Mellida* 1602. He had a share in the excellent citizen comedy *Eastward Ho!* Beaumont and Fletcher (the latter collaborated with Shakespeare in *Henry VIII* and in *The Two Noble Kinsmen*) are generally thought to have come

nearest to Shakespeare. The fifty-two plays published under their names in 1647 are many men's
work, but chiefly Fletcher's. They wrote together
the tragicomedy *Philaster* 1610, and *The Maid's
Tragedy* 1611, where may be seen creeping in not
only excessively romantic event (common enough in
Shakespeare), but unreality of motive and unaccount-
able transitions of character. *The Knight of the
Burning Pestle* 1609 is a lively bourgeois farce
and parody. Beaumont is generally credited with
balance and judgment, Fletcher with invention,
grace, gaiety, deft construction, a liberal infusion of
licence and a talent for lyrical verse only inferior
to that of Shakespeare. The blank verse of Fletcher
plays fast and loose with even the bare minimum of
restriction retained by Shakespeare in his later
plays: Fletcher has redundant syllables in all
parts of the line; henceforth, until Milton, blank
verse degenerates. Webster, in *The Duchess of
Malfi* 1614, paints a consummate picture of nobility
in woman; no accumulation of horror or suffering
can break her heroic spirit; in this play and in *The
White Devil* he employs sinister Italian themes and
characters with immense tragic effect. Webster has
imaginative genius, pictorial power and Shakespearean penetration into passionate emotion, but
he exercised his gifts too uniformly among images
of mortality and scenes of intolerable cruelty.

Massinger was one of the busiest of collabora-
tors; he is remembered best by *The Roman Actor*
1626, skilfully involving political motive, and *The
Virgin Martyr*, tragedies, and by his comedies *The
City Madam* and *A New Way to pay old Debts*

1626 ?.   He has some command of tragic terror
and writes fluent verse attaining often to dignity
and rhetoric; he constructs with remarkable craftsmanship and economy and these gifts win for him
high rank.   John Ford never deviates from the
events and emotions which drive on to the tragic
outcome; this incisive relentless force leads up to
the scene of Calantha's dancing in *The Broken
Heart* 1629, one of the most powerful, though not
the most natural, out of Shakespeare.   The charge
against Ford—that he signalises the decay of Elizabethan drama—rests less on the unsoundness of his
subjects than on his apparent sympathy with moral
anarchy.   Shirley's tragedies, such as *The Traitor*
1631 and *The Cardinal* 1641, his comedies, such as
Hyde Park 1632, and *The Lady of Pleasure* 1635,
prove him to be last but not least of the great
dramatists.   His famous song, 'The glories of our
blood and state,' is in the short drama (not a
masque) *Ajax and Ulysses*.   Other dramatists are
Randolph, Field and Brome, whose *Merry Beggars*
was the last play staged before the closing of the
theatres from 1642 to 1660, for Davenant's *Siege
of Rhodes* 1656 is more important to opera than
drama.   Shirley and Sir William Davenant seem
to bridge the interval of silence; but, though
Davenant wrote both before and after the restoration, the alterations he made in theatrical conditions,
the introduction of scenery and of women actors,
were soon to be paralleled by a change in the type
of drama; the heroic play of the restoration has
but faint spiritual affinities with the tragedy of the
Jacobeans.

We speak of this vast bulk of drama as romantic; the word has to cover a wide area of meaning. Putting Jonson aside, we may take it to mean that playwrights were careless of the unities, prefering a wider canvas of region and time. They eschewed restraint, for they worked from the model of the complexity of actual life, ignoring the classical method, selection and emphasis of single aspects; they disdained restraint in diction, and, in the later period, in subject—for the age could stomach the strongest stimulants—using inadmissible themes and muffling the shock of moral condemnation. The traditional English admixture of comedy and tragedy is likewise romantic; the same title is used for the many plays in which humanity is transported to some remote or imaginative scene where a lyrical or rhetorical splendour pervades its speech; finally, stress is laid upon passion and feeling. The crowning gift of the English renascence drama, taken as a whole, is its almost infallible power of finding fit and moving utterance for every shade of emotion.

5. Poetry from 1625 to the Restoration

The history of poetry from Donne to Milton presents three main episodes; (i) lyric, which has an almost continuous record from Wyatt to Dryden; (ii) the development of the new heroic couplet and the rise of satire; (iii) endeavours after the heroic poem. Lyric writers were under the influence of Ben Jonson or Donne or both. Jonson banished the Petrarchan tradition, but rarely sings with the 'wood-notes wild' of

Lyric

Shakespeare, and is never tempted to extravagance of imagery; a pupil of Horace, Catullus, Martial, he imported the ideals of elegance, proportion and restraint. For the most part, cavalier lyrists are of the 'tribe of Ben.' Carew often achieves musical perfection and has a graver note in his *Elegy on Donne*; Suckling owes his mockery of gallant usages to the lighter side of Donne's contempt for women, his impetuous gaiety is his own.

Herrick

Herrick's range and accomplishment are the widest, including, in *Hesperides* 1650, Catullan and Anacreontic song, Horatian idyll, the stuff of folklore and country festival, gallant compliment and love tribute to many seductive deities, flowers and their suggestions of transient beauty, verse epistles and some weightier lines on the evil fortunes of his king and country. There is more sincerity of feeling in these than in the distinctly pagan piety of his religious poems *Noble Numbers*. His pure clear feeling and his mastery of metre are the warp and woof of an exquisite fabric, and he has, besides, a flute-like melody and rhythmic subtlety and delicacy which almost conceal the infinite pains he took with his art. Wither, in his early poems, such as 'Shall I wasting in despair?' Waller, in songs like 'Go, Lovely Rose,' and Lovelace, with his fine chivalric note, are much less given to Donne's 'metaphysical' ingenuities than Lord Herbert of Cherbury and Cowley, in Dr Johnson's *Life* of whom is found a destructive criticism of the whole school; neither Milton nor Dryden escaped the contagion, and the religious poets were especially prone to take it. George Herbert's quiet but deeply stirred piety is expressed through images and an order of thought much influenced by Donne, as in poems like *The Pulley* and *Man*. Crashaw has a more passionate note. His *Wishes* and his translation *Music's Duel* are graceful secular poems, but the religious ecstasy and imaginative opulence of *The Flaming Heart* and *The Hymn to St Teresa* are his real claims to remembrance. Vaughan the Silurist, in *Silex Scintillans* 1650, was influenced by Herbert, but he has a deeper vein of mystical thought; he speaks of childhood, nature, light and eternity with subtle insight and with a rare kind of imagery, and he left some impress on Wordsworth. The newly discovered poet Traherne, also a Kelt, has high moments, as in *The Choice* and *The Estate*, but his prose *Centuries of Meditation* show richer emotion and a greater command over style. Habington's *Castara* 1634 contains amorous and religious poems of the metaphysical school; Quarles's *Emblems* are only half literature and that half homespun. We may complete this long chapter in the history of the lyric by the mention of Rochester, Sedley, Dorset, Mrs Aphra Behn and Dryden himself in his plays, each of whom wrote more than one unforgettable song of the cavalier type, often, especially in the case of Rochester, with a note of real passion.

ii. . The heroic couplet, even in the isolated form, is used by Elizabethans such as Spenser, Drayton and Sandys; but it becomes more pointed and antithetical, more epigrammatic and rhetorical and less imaginative in the poems of Edmund Waller about 1623; he introduces

the balanced epithet, places the caesura with more
regularity, has stronger riming words and confines
the sense to the distich. For these things he was
too generously credited by Dryden with 'the reform
of our numbers.' These qualities become more
manifest in Denham's *Cooper's Hill* 1642, and in the
Davideis of Cowley, thought a genius in his day,
whose voluminous output also included so-called
Pindaric odes, imitated later by Dryden, and, with
marked differences, by Gray and by many nineteenth century poets. Marvell, the friend and
assistant of Milton, was, like Cowley, a scholar; his
satires, *Instructions to a Painter* and others, are
inferior to his *Horatian Ode* 1650, and to *The
Bermudas*, and to his amorous and pastoral verse,
such as *The Garden*; these are in octosyllabics of
a 'witty delicacy' in diction and rhythm, and have
fine observation and feeling for the intense hidden
life about him. The drift towards satire, for which
the heroic couplet was the fore-ordained instrument,
is again illustrated in the violent tirades of Oldham,
Satires upon the Jesuits 1679. This carries us well
past the restoration and almost to the revolution.

iii. The heroic poem or epic was the goal of
seventeenth century effort, a perennial ideal of the
Epic renascence. It was discussed by all
critics, and attempted by Cowley in
his *Davideis* 1656 in couplets, by Davenant in his
Gondibert 1651 in quatrains, and, in a more romantic
fashion, by Chamberlayne in *Pharonnida* 1659 in
couplets. It would have been essayed by Dryden
on the subject of king Arthur, had his pension
been paid more regularly. It was finally written

in blank verse by Milton in *Paradise Lost* and *Paradise Regained,* and the mould thereafter was broken.

Milton's early upbringing and the bent of his disposition made him first of all a puritan in spirit, though certainly not in the letter; a cultured puritan and a lover of music. His classical education at St Paul's and at Christ's college, Cambridge 1625-32, developed the instinct for form, beauty and craftmanship which was never to be reconciled with his religious tenets; the Hebraic and the Hellenic in him were both too native and too formidable to yield to any compromise, though his mastery of style may disguise their deep-laid enmity. His models were generally classic, his materials generally scriptural. His residence at Horton in Buckinghamshire touched in him some chords of interest in natural scenes, but not enough to seduce him from books. His journey to France and Italy 1638-9 brought him into relations with scholarship in these countries, and laid the foundations of a continental reputation, which his controversies with Salmasius and Morus and his letters of state, written as Cromwell's Latin secretary, were afterwards to extend. These years of political service 1649-58, undertaken through his keen sense of obligation to the commonwealth, were almost destitute of poetry. At the restoration, his life being surprisingly spared, he resumed the poetical ambitions rudely broken in upon by civil strife; his epic and dramatic poetry appeared between 1660 and 1671.

The Ode on the Nativity 1629 contains some trace

7—2

of metaphysical extravagance, but more remarkable
Early poems are the Miltonic blending of pagan and
scriptural themes, the stately move-
ment, and the imaginative insight, rising to its
height in the flight of the deities of antiquity from
their haunts and oracles. *Il Penseroso* and *L'Allegro*
c. 1632 are richly decorative presentations of two
imagined moods, companion pictures of studious
retreat and festival mirth, wherein is evident the
poet's ear, exact and musical, for all the rhythmic
possibilities of pace and sound inherent in the octosyllabic couplet. *Arcades* is a fragmentary, but
worthy, predecessor of the masque *Comus* 1634; here,
the poet uses a larger canvas; its theme is nearer to
morals and the strict conduct of life; temptation
and chastity are emblematically figured in Comus,
who eloquently presents the snare of vice as an
enrichment of life; and in the Lady, who counters
this with the high and arduous doctrine of restraint.
Platonic, rather than puritanic, idealism underlies
the debate. The art, conscious, varied and perfect,
of the blank verse and the 'Doric delicacy' of the
songs are the highest reach of non-dramatic poetry
to this date. Dr Johnson's criticism that, as a
tale, it moves slowly is much more justifiable than
his strictures on *Lycidas* 1637, which establishes the
model of pastoral elegy drawn from the Sicilians,
and serves as exemplar to Shelley's *Adonais* and
Matthew Arnold's *Thyrsis*. *Lycidas* should be
compared with Milton's earlier *Epitaphium Damonis*.
The death of Edward King is not much more than
a pretext, though the idea of loss allows of the
invocation of nature, English and Sicilian, the

procession of mythical and scriptural mourners and the Christian consolation; 'eloquent distress' is the happy description of the poem by Keats. The passionate note of Milton rings clear for the first time in two digressions; one, on the true nature of fame, condemning poetical triviality; and one, a wrathful puritanic denunciation of hireling clergy. *Lycidas* is in iambic lines of different length and rime arrangement, with some few unrimed lines, slight discords skilfully resolved into the general harmony. Milton's sonnets are the occasional outbursts of smouldering poetic fire kindled during twenty years of politics; some embody sentiments stirred by historical events, as those on the *Piedmontese* and on the *Assault*; some are domestic and personal, as those on his *Wife* and on his *Blindness*; some perpetuate the mood of *L'Allegro*—it never died completely out—as that *To Cyriack Skinner*. Save that he makes free with the *volta* or turn, he adheres to the stricter Italian scheme of the sonnet. He is also a writer of Latin verse, the most accomplished, save perhaps Landor, of all English poets who attempted it.

In 1658 he resumed his intended life-work, which 'posterity should not willingly let die.' The

Paradise Lost

Elizabethan lyric notes are but faintly blown in his great orchestral symphony. It tells, like the miracle-cycles, the story of the fall of man, with the prophecy of his redemption. But the fall of man is preceded by the fall of Lucifer and it is here that the dramatic force of the story is developed; it is not profitable to discuss who is the hero, but it is certain that the attitude

of irreconcilable rebellion against tyranny which
Satan takes up in books I and II is in sympathy
with Milton's temperament and that the official
characterisation of Satan, as the impious rebel and
source of all evil, is crossed and blurred by the
element of Promethean heroism in his nature. We
may get the justest view of Satan if we think of
him as a defeated general, reassembling and inspiring
his forces, by the splendour and irony of his oratory,
and by Machiavellian suggestions, to a renewal of a
forlorn conflict. The latent qualities of pride, envy
and ambition are developed in succeeding books,
where his angelic form loses all its original brightness, and he is degraded. The whole story is
slowly unfolded in the epic manner with large inset
episodes, its scenes placed in the empyrean or in
the circumambient chaos, in paradise or in hell;
only once or twice does it falter in dignity of
conception, never in the solemn grandeur of its
speech. Milton sought 'to justify the ways of
God to man.' Inasmuch as he did this by making
use of a temporary theological system, his poem
is for an age; but it is for all time in its intellectual comprehensiveness, its vast imaginative scale,
its moral sublimity, its descriptive power, whether
shown in clear-cut outlines against vague backgrounds, or in pictures of armies moving 'in perfect
phalanx to the Dorian mood,' or in classic similes.
Whether in its triumphs of oratory, its arguments
on divine things, or its occasional idyllic tenderness,
the sense of dedication is over all. And still there
remain its style, the massive verse paragraphs Milton
designed with 'the sense variously drawn out,' and

its diction of a rich and permanent texture. Words came to him with a long-hoarded wealth of association and with subtle musical values like organ notes with their overtones; and out of these things he wove the true poetic fabric of cadence, imagery and memories.

Paradise is regained, not as a result of the sacrificial offering of the Messiah, but by his resist-

Paradise Re-gained and *Samson Ag-onistes* 1671 ance to Satan—a meaner, more calculating Satan—at the beginning of the ministry in the desert. The poem wants dramatic interest, for we cannot form an anticipation of the fall of Christ. But, as in *Comus*, the offerings of the tempter are set out with no attenuation of their charms; the pictures of the banquet, of the kingdoms and powers of this world, and of Athens, mother of arts, have no superiors in Milton. Here, the prevalent austerity is relieved by imaginative colour; the close, like all Milton's endings, is perfect. His original intention of employing dramatic form for *Paradise Lost* was abandoned, to be revived in *Samson Agonistes*, a subject considered very early, as the famous Trinity manuscript shows. Again, he treats scriptural matter in classic form, choosing the Sophoclean drama. *Samson* is the outcry of a 'gray spirit yearning in desire' for the restoration of the fallen ideals of puritanism; the likeness of the cases of Samson and Milton is evident; the poet contemns the licence and triviality of the court, and expresses his steadfast conviction of the purpose of the Deity, in good time, to crush his foes. The verse, here, is harsher, perhaps more powerful, but with fewer elements of geniality, and the rhythmic norm is, in the choruses, hard to detect.

At heart, Milton was a puritan; to the puritanic spirit he clung more tenaciously than he did even to the humanities. But he was a puritan of a different stamp from Bunyan; the untutored emotion—'enthusiasm' the next century would have called it—of Bunyan has no place in the more disciplined utterance of Milton. He accepted the large outlines of Calvinistic doctrine, though he held the Arian heresy that the Messiah was later born in heaven and not co-eternal with the Father and the Spirit. Satan's right to rebel hangs upon this doctrine, for the exaltation of the Messiah to the right hand of the Almighty—the act of a political tyrant—is Satan's grievance, the *fons et origo*, according to *Paradise Lost*, of all human history. This definitely mapped out scheme of the relations between man and God left little room for mystery, for the feeling of religious awe in face of the unknown; there is no mystery of that kind in *Paradise Lost*.

On the other hand, it is an immense conception, whether we accept it or not, and whether we think it too doctrinaire for epic poetry or not; sublime in its outline and imposing the loftiest standards of action. This moral austerity, and the sense of the duty of holiness, obedience and service, were the elements of Milton's character which appealed to Wordsworth, when he sought in some of his sonnets to intensify the spiritual factors in national life at a later crisis.

6. Prose from 1625 to 1660

The prose of the middle of the seventeenth century reflects the disintegration of national interests. Eliza-

Prose of controversy   beth's religious compromise and the monarchical security of the Tudors collapse; Anglican and dissenter, royalist and com-monwealthsman are at wordy warfare, a struggle soon to become a strife of arms. Religious con-troversy centres about the question of toleration, and the outlines of the argument can be studied in Hales, Chillingworth (*The Religion of Protes-tants*), Lord Falkland, Taylor (*The Liberty of Prophesying* 1646), all tending to find the essentials of agreement in the apostles' creed; the discussion grows wider and more fantastic in Cudworth's *Intellectual System of the Universe* 1678, and closes in Locke's letters *On Toleration* 1689, establishing the validity of the appeal to reason. The hottest

Milton   of the anti-prelatists was Milton; among his pamphlets on this topic is *The Reason of Church Government urged against Prelacy* 1641, which tells us much about himself. He became an independent on perceiving that 'New Presbyter is but old Priest writ large.' He was deep, also, in political controversy (it cost him his eyesight), as in *Eikonoklastes* 1649, a defence of the execution of Charles I, and in his *Second Defence of the English People*, in Latin and autobiographical: but his greatest piece of polemics is his *Areopagitica* 1644, a speech on behalf of unlicensed printing. It failed to persuade the presbyterians to remove the censorship, but it is an imperishable vindication of the rights of thought against tyranny and prescription. Round the central tenet of liberty Milton grouped, though by an afterthought, all his prose, on divorce, on church and on state, except his idealised picture of Miltonic schooling, *The Tractate on Education* 1644. More philosophic minds than Milton's set themselves to solve these urgent problems; Thomas Hobbes, in his *Leviathan* 1651, traces the history of society from its aboriginal state of internecine war through the 'social contract' to its logical outcome in absolute monarchy, which is established on grounds of universal self-interest, not, as heretofore, by divine right. The prose of Hobbes has a grim tenacious power which irritated into activity a widespread opposition. Harrington's *Oceana* 1656, and Filmer's *Patriarcha* 1680, and Algernon Sidney's *Discourses* treat of these topics, while Locke's *Civil Government* 1690 reflects the whig settlement of the revolution. His *Essay concerning the Human Understanding* 1690 lays a broad foundation for the metaphysical theory of the eighteenth century. Another great writer fashioned by these troublous times was Clarendon, whose *History of the Great Rebellion*, begun in 1641, published 1702–4, proves him a maker of history and a great statesman in a time of intrigue and cabals. It is not impartial or critical history, for the dice are heavily weighted against the parliamentarians, nor does it pierce to the currents and movements of which events are merely the surface ripples; but it has high literary power, its record is unfolded with sustained dignity of speech; in description of warfare and political narrative it is masterly and it is unmatched in its gallery of historical portraits.

Other recorders are May in his *History of the Long Parliament* 1647, and Fuller in his series beginning with *Good Thoughts in Bad Times* and closing with *The Worthies of England* 1662. Nearer still to the type of memoir are the diaries of Evelyn and Pepys 1660–9, the latter a historical document of importance and a piquant example of self-revelation. Of letter-writers must be mentioned Howell for his witty and entertaining *Familiar Letters, Domestic and Foreign* 1655, and Dorothy Osborne, for the letters to her fiancé, Sir William Temple.

There are other minds who appear detached from current strife; a group of divines and a group akin to the essayists. The eloquence of the pulpit begins in Elizabeth's reign with Lancelot Andrewes and with Donne, splendid in strange harmonies of prose, expressing spiritual intimacy and wonder; it continues parallel with the great French preachers Bourdaloue and Bossuet, through Fuller the incessant humorist and Jeremy Taylor, South of cogent wit, and Barrow, a man of science and pulpiteer. Taylor is among the three or four great Anglican orators; his sermons are deeply versed in the classics and the fathers, full of human sympathy, multi-divisional in method, rich in imaginative decoration and simile, and complete in knowledge of oratorical art. On the puritan side, there is much less learning and much less elaboration, with a correspondingly intense concentration on the affairs of the individual soul. Richard Baxter wrote many volumes—' a cartload '

Non-contro-versial prose.
i. The Divines

the infamous Jeffreys said—besides *The Saints'
Everlasting Rest* 1650. But the greatest of puritan
preachers was John Bunyan, who,
better than Byron, deserves the title
'the Pilgrim of Eternity.' The central experience
of Bunyan's life is recorded in *Grace Abounding to
the Chief of Sinners* 1666. During his imprisonment
he discovered his power of giving concrete expression
to inner experience. *The Pilgrim's Progress* 1678–
84 took shape as a dream-allegory; its materials
were drawn from his own spiritual history; from
the scriptures and commentaries upon them; from
chap-books, emblem-books and popular romances;
from the actual persecutions of dissenters; and from
the roadside life of his day. His power lies, first,
in his intimate portrayal of a widespread order of
religious experience; next, in narrative skill and in
a sense of character so vivid that we forget he is
writing an allegory; thirdly, in the vital zest and
energy of his style, familiar, racy, shrewd, a perfect
dialect for the unlearned. The abstractions do not
live so concretely in *The Holy War* 1682 as in this
'similitude of a dream'; *The Life and Death of
Mr Badman* 1680 is often praised, but the realistic
narrative of tradesmen's thievery is too thickly
strewn with Biblical phrase and discussion. The
fine spirit of Sir Thomas Browne,
almost our first egoist, is compounded
of curiosity, mysticism, charity and strange learning.
His purpose in *Religio Medici* 1643 is to define his
faith; in reality he draws the cloak of Christianity
over an engaging collection of heresies. 'There is
all Africa and her prodigies in us,' he says; he

Bunyan [side note]

*ii. Essayists.
Browne* [side note]

compels his religion to be reconciled with these marvels; the result is the revelation of a kingdom of the mind whose new beauty and wonder stir him to an ecstasy of thought and language. His *Pseudodoxia* or *Vulgar Errors* 1646 is a storehouse of older credulous knowledge veined with scepticism, and of learned divagation. *The Garden of Cyrus* ransacks nature in pursuit of the ubiquitous quincunx, while *Christian Morals* and *A Letter to a Friend* give some sense of his high stoical ethics. His noblest gifts are exercised in the fifth chapter of his *Hydriotaphia* or *Urn Burial* 1658, a gorgeous prose elegy on fame, antiquity and death, viewing man as he stands in the perspective of the present, the past and eternity, and moved thereby to the various emotions of melancholy, compassion and exaltation. The prose in which these things are expressed has vast imaginative range, profound reflection, a quite individual and fascinating humour, whimsical and arresting thought, where what the age called 'wit' is blended with sumptuous phrasing and poetic rhythm; and, over all, there is a solemn sublimity in the strangely harmonious periods. There is a great school of prose eloquence concerning mortality, which includes Ralegh's *History*, the essay on *Death* wrongly attributed to Bacon, Drummond's *Cypress Grove* and Jeremy Taylor's *Holy Dying*.

Cowley's *Essays* 1667 on such subjects as *Liberty, Solitude, The Garden*, have the intimacy of personal revelation, picturing, in the main, a man disillusioned but not discontented, seeking retirement and its grave pleasures. He perceived the right function of the essay form, and hit happily

upon the ideal essay style. He may well illustrate
the transition from the older to the newer school
of prose. Izaak Walton says in his preface to
The Compleat Angler 1653, 'I have made myself
a recreation of a recreation' and mixed thereto
'some innocent mirth.' The book has for its literary
ancestry pastoral and piscatorial eclogues 'old-
fashioned poetry but choicely good'; and it records
with a like felicitous simplicity the complacent joys
and callousness, the varied fishing-lore and some of
the rather irrelevant classical learning of Piscator.
The opening is a triumph of prose descriptive of
sport and nature; and the final benediction 'upon
all that are lovers of virtue; and dare trust in
His providence; and be quiet; and go a Angling,'
harmonises with Walton's undisturbed remoteness
from the restless age. His *Lives* of five notable
divines are masterpieces of biography, redolent of
the personalities of his subjects, as old gardens are
of perfumes.

As to the matter of all this prose we note the
widespread polemical activity, the louder bayings
of puritanism, the gentler accents of toleration,
a general anxiety of thought, becoming, at times,
a deep-toned melancholy, and a new tendency towards realism. As to style, there is a welter of
forms; some few writers, Hobbes, Walton and
Bunyan among them, cultivate a direct, incisive
manner; but men of learning are in the main
over-Latinised in diction, or over-decorative for the
plain man's affairs; Milton, Taylor and Browne
are instances. Some again are parenthetical and
structurally helpless; Milton and Clarendon both

suffer in this way, though both are masters of the grand style. Some writers are excessively oratorical and periodic; this charge lies against Milton—as great a sinner as he is a master—and Taylor. Milton, Taylor, Browne and Clarendon are monuments, not models; the making of modern prose style was the business of the next generation.

BOOK IV

THE LITERATURE OF THE MIDDLE CLASSES 1660–1800

1. PROSE FROM DRYDEN TO SWIFT 1660–1720

THE renascence as it comes to us from Italy blazes into a splendid consummation in Milton. Henceforth, so far as writing is touched by literary influences, these come to us from the renascence as coloured by its passage through France. The exiled court returned from its long vacation with the habits, manners, ideas and literary interests of France. But these affect mainly the literature of the court. There is a competing influence, that of the citizen class, the humanised descendants of the triumphant but intolerant commonwealthsmen; this and other developments, such as the liberation of the press, the party cleavage into whig and tory, the patronage of literature by the politicians, are reflected in the writings of Dryden, Congreve, Addison, Steele, Pope, Swift and Defoe.

Prose undergoes a disciplinary process; it was exercised in the pulpit, by Tillotson, to whose 'clear, plain and short sentences' Dryden overstated his debt; in the essay, by the learned

amateur Sir William Temple; in political debate,
by Halifax, whose defensive *Character
of a Trimmer* and *Advice to a Dissenter*
1687 give him a rank only below
Dryden; in pamphleteering; in journalism, by
L'Estrange; and by writers on science. Bishop Sprat,
secretary of the Royal Society (in which Dryden,
Pepys and Charles II were enrolled), told in a famous
sentence how they exacted from their members 'a
close, naked, natural way of speaking,' the reverse
of the imaginative splendour of the school of Browne.
The final outcome was modern prose, fit for 'the
average purpose'; its diction and metaphors no
longer at the mercy of the Latinising rhetorician;
its short harmonious sentences not modelled on
the wheeling periods of Cicero, but having their
emphasis, pause and rhythm determined by the
sentence of conversation. The conversational ideal
also prescribed for modern prose its tone of equality
with the reader, and its vivid happy pictorial
manner in the quick suggestive way of the good
talker; wit, elegance, clearness, point, animation,
these are the qualities of Congreve's comedies and
Dryden's criticism.

The making of modern prose

John Dryden 1631–1700 was the literary dictator
of his day, eminent in prose, verse and drama.
His main concern in prose was with
criticism, which judges confusedly at
first, having for its accepted models French interpretations of Horace and Aristotle and finding no
consonance between these and the work of the
Elizabethan giants before the flood. Dryden with
his genuine love of the best in letters came nearest

Dryden

to reconciling the two interests; all his prefaces
and essays turn on these matters; *An Essay of
Dramatic Poesy* 1668 is rather academic, though
splendid in praise; the *Preface* to the *Fables* 1700
is more independent, for here he sees Chaucer clear
through many mists. Keen perception, generosity,
freshness and zest distinguish him throughout.
Dennis and Rymer, rather pedantic critics, and
the Frenchman Saint-Évremond, long resident in
England, can only be named.

Jonathan Swift 1667–1745, dean of St Patrick's,
Dublin, the supreme genius of unpoetic prose, produced in 1704 *The Battle of the Books*
and *A Tale of a Tub*, treatises dealing
in trenchant satirical fashion with literary squabbles
concerning ancients and moderns, and with the
dissensions of Christian sects. He had a period of
almost regal power as a tory politician 1710–3, won
by such brilliant political pamphlets as *The Conduct
of the Allies* 1711; the intimate side of this part of
his life is recorded in the delightful *Journal to Stella*
with its 'little language' and its traces of genial
humour, only paralleled in his chaffing of the as-
trologer Partridge. Afterwards, he suffered the
bitterness of a proud and masterful mind possessing
immense nervous energy yet condemned to engage
in the pettiest occupations; physically, he was a
sufferer; his mysterious love-affairs fell into con-
fusion; furious emotions fermented within him,
generating a morbid misanthropy, which coloured
too darkly his passion for reason and justice.
Irony is his distinguishing mark, as may be seen
in *The Argument against abolishing Christianity*

Swift

1708, and in the hideously tragical mirth of *A Modest Proposal* 1722, which suggested that the superfluous children of the Irish poor should be disposed of by being served up as food. Irony is accompanied by invective and some malice in his *Drapier's Letters* 1724, against the monopoly of Wood's half-pence in Ireland. All his resources are brought into play in *Gulliver's Travels* 1726. Its narrative skill, whimsical invention and meticulous detail have made it, by a strange destiny, a child's classic; the concurrent irony becomes more searching and more repulsive in successive degradations of humanity, till, in the fourth book, man is stripped of every shred of honour, decency, morality and reasonableness, and becomes a cowering and nauseous Yahoo. The method of his irony is either to conduct some assumption of unreason with all gravity to its disconcerting conclusions, or to set truth blazing in the very lines of the pictures which the complacent and the hypocritical draw of themselves. Swift's is the model of all plain unadorned styles; in lucidity, directness, force and in the perfect conveyance of thought into the fewest and most effective words he has no equal. No genius at once so universal in range and so penetrating in criticism of society appeared again till Burke.

With Swift should be named his friend Dr John Arbuthnot, a man of fine character, whose gifts were like the more genial half of Swift's. He was the inspiring spirit of the Scriblerus club in which Pope, Gay and Congreve were also concerned, and was the author of the tory *History of John Bull* 1712.

8—2

Addison and Steele were the first to find articulate and polite utterance for the prevailing part
The Spectator
of the new nation, the puritan middle classes. The extravagance, insolence and licence of the restoration era had provoked a reaction in the direction of morality and order; and the increase in wealth and the very influential institution of the coffee-house brought something of amenity into the outlook of the middle classes. Addison and Steele made their fellow citizens—sound in heart and understanding but without established traditions—conscious of themselves; it was an office of national importance, and it is difficult to imagine a more propitious conjunction of the hour and the men. With extraordinary tact, they varied preaching with ridicule, pictorial example with appeals to sentiment, all with an engaging air of enjoyment. They gave a decisive turn to the national mind, becoming its accepted censors in morals, manners, dress, literary taste and conversation. In nothing was their influence more necessary or more powerful than in restoring the status and dignity of women by awakening their self-respect and enlarging their horizons; in this, Steele's chivalry is more attractive than Addison's condescension. In fact, we may say generally that, while Addison has a more urbane culture, a more retired observation, a quicker eye for eccentricity, a defter irony, Steele, who is less aloof, has a greater warmth of feeling and more generous impulses. It was Steele who initiated the whole enterprise by means of *The Tatler* (appearing three days a week 1709–11), a miscellaneous sheet containing news, stories, domestic

sketches, admonition, poetry and learning. Addison
was drawn into the undertaking, and, when *The
Spectator* began on the cessation of *The Tatler*, he
wrote more than half of its 555 issues between
March 1711 and December 1712. *The Spectator*
appeared daily and, discarding news, confined itself
to a single essay. Mr Spectator is Addison's creation, the Spectator club is Steele's; both have an
honourable part in the characterisation of the
perennially charming feudal aristocrat Sir Roger
de Coverly. Besides these papers, there were lay
sermons, tales, allegories, correspondence, accounts
of functions, of visits to the theatre and criticism
such as Addison's papers on ballads and on *Paradise
Lost*. The two banished political rancour from
their journal (though Steele's pronounced whiggism
found an outlet in some later ventures), and avoided
personal scandal; they endeavoured, in Addison's
words, to 'enliven morality with wit and temper
wit with morality'; so that, while the restoration
poured ridicule upon virtue, these writers poured
ridicule upon vice, and they found the whole nation
with them. Addison achieved a perfect style for
these essays, easy, effortless, colloquial, but correct
and never without dignity; Steele is more negligent
in choice of word and in syntax, but in pathetic and
domestic scenes he strikes a chord beyond Addison's
range.

Daniel Defoe or Foe 1660?–1731 belonged to the
obscurer side of the journalism which sprang up
when the censorship was withdrawn
in 1695. Numerous ephemeral sheets
preceded him, but his *Review*, written in Newgate

Defoe

prison, afforded some hints for the first numbers of
The Tatler. He was a busy and effective pamphleteer
for twenty years before turning to fiction. He had
an amazingly ready pen, a prosaic but racy and
copious style, a journalist's eye for those details which
take the public taste, an extraordinary knowledge
of what everybody was doing and what they were
paid for it, and an unmatched faculty for colouring
fiction with the hue of truth; the gift is at its height
in his *Journal of the Plague Year* 1722. All this
realistic writing and describing served him in the
best stead when he wrote at the age of sixty his
first novel, *Robinson Crusoe*, the epic of the plain
devout man overcoming adverse nature. His narrative power was exhibited also in other fiction,
such as *Captain Singleton* 1720, *Moll Flanders* 1721
and other stories generally nearer to the manner of
Nashe than to the modern novel.

2. POETRY FROM DRYDEN TO POPE

The emergence of the heroic couplet as the main
vehicle of poetry has been traced. Dryden is the
first master of the measure in which
satire, elegy, panegyric, debate, epistolary matter, criticism and miscellaneous learning
were to find expression for a century. After some
early metaphysical attempts, Dryden produced his
Annus Mirabilis 1666, in quatrains, on the fire,
plague and war of that year. For fourteen years,
his attention was given to drama in heroic couplets,
and, with this practice behind him, he produced
Absalom and Achitophel 1681, a sketch of the

Dryden

political situation in which Charles II, Shaftesbury
and Monmouth were the principal figures. The
poem has supreme skill in political argumenta-
tion and presents a gallery of portraits including
Zimri, Achitophel and Shimei, masterpieces which
show forth the individual and the type in one
figure; their clear outlines and ingenious choice of
detail make them unanswerable, because the statements are either next door to the truth, or cannot
be refuted without uncomfortable disclosures. In
the warfare of satires which followed, Dryden was
irritated into attacking Shadwell and Settle, in the
second part of *Absalom* and in *Macflecknoe* 1682;
he gives decisive proof, apparently, of their claim
to all the titles of infamy; then, after an interlude
on their poetical incapacity, he sends them hurtling
into the realms of dullness. There is no other
personal invective so explicit yet so tempered by
artistic execution. His later exercises in the couplet
include *Religio Laici* 1682, a rational Anglican's
case, while *The Hind and the Panther* 1687 is his
apologia on the occasion of his conversion to the
Roman church; *The Fables* 1700 are adaptations
in the same measure chiefly from Boccaccio and
Chaucer. The most notable of many translations
was his *Vergil*; and he wrote, besides, lyric verse
in his plays, and pindarics such as *Alexander's
Feast* and *An Ode to Mistress Anne Killigrew*.
He left the couplet varied in accent and pause,
a vehicle for prosaic thought and diction, effectively
rimed, with the sense contained, for the most part,
within the limits of the riming lines. There are
other couplet writers between Dryden and Pope,

such as Granville and the earl of Dorset, Garth
(*The Dispensary* 1699) and Blackmore. Of more
Hudibras importance is Samuel Butler's *Hudi-
bras 1663–8, a parody in octosyllabic
couplets of *Don Quixote*, victimising the presbyterians in the figure of the knight Hudibras, and the
independents in that of his squire Ralpho. It is
hard and bitter in sentiment, and weak in construction but amazingly clever in idea, compression,
imagery and rime; the mind becomes restive under
its incessant explosions of wit. In some other writings,
Butler shares with Swift a hatred of the new science.
This octosyllabic form began early to challenge the
sway of the decasyllabic; most of Swift's verse (*On
the Death of Dr Swift, Cadenus and Vanessa*), Prior's
Alma, Gay's *Fables*, Dyer's *Grongar Hill*, Parnell's
Night-Piece, Matthew Green's *The Spleen*, show for
what various moods it could be used.

Alexander Pope 1688–1744 is the typical poet of
the generation after Dryden; a town-dweller, suspi-
Pope cious of enthusiasm, a satirist, a critic,
devoid of lyric gift, accepting authority
from France, a skilled and conscientious artist in
form, much beholden to a shibboleth called 'nature,'
compounded of scraps from Boileau, Horace and
Aristotle with a strong infusion of eighteenth century
common sense—a thing as remote as possible from
'nature' as Wordsworth thought of it. Pope's poetry,
practically all in the heroic couplet, included
criticism, satire, translation and ethics; in his
Essay on Criticism 1711, he had attained perfect
ease and polish. His satires are of three classes;
(i) the brilliant mock-heroic *Rape of the Lock* 1712–4,

a gay satire of the cavalier world; (ii) *The Dunciad* 1728, of which the part attacking dullness is excellent and necessary, but the personal abuse of Grub street hacks and of Theobald (who exposed the textual failings in Pope's edition of Shakespeare 1725), does Pope himself a disservice; (iii) his most mature and most accomplished *Epistles* (including the masterly one to Arbuthnot 1735) and the *Imitations of Horace* 1733–9. These are a mingled yarn of the best and worst in Pope; there is sane judgment, fine irony, concern for letters, loyal friendship to Swift, Arbuthnot, Gay and the rest of Scriblerus circle; but accompanying these things are personalities such as the malicious and plausible distortion of Addison and the venomous portrait of Hervey. His translations of the *Iliad* 1715–20, and *Odyssey* (with coadjutors) are masterly, though far from literal, re-interpretations, in pointed antithetical couplets, after the taste of the time; but they undoubtedly retain something of the Homeric lightness and energy. *An Essay on Man* 1733 elaborates a philosophy based on the inconsequent optimism of the brilliant but superficial Bolingbroke. It is worth notice that, in his early pastorals and in his emotional poems *Eloisa to Abelard* and his *Elegy on an Unfortunate Lady*, he gives evidence of a vein of romantic feeling afterwards unworked. Pope is a master of the secondary rhetorical kinds of poetry, or, to put the matter in other words, the inner urgency which drove him to composition does not appear to have been delight in beauty or imaginative vision. He is a craftsman of infinite patience, aiming at polished perfection of speech.

To achieve this he employs the arts of elegance, lucidity, antithesis and 'wit,' which by Pope's time had come to mean the incisive and memorable expression of familiar ideas. His tendency to compress his meaning into single lines or, at most, into the distich, together with his extraordinary power of crystallising thought into words, produces the effect of a shower of metrical epigrams; it reveals, too, the lack of such wide-sweeping imaginative conception as would require the space of the paragraph for its statement. Within the line the break comes generally after the second or third foot; at first, the effect is apt to be monotonous; after a time we realise with what delicate and subtle skill the variations of stress are proportioned to their purpose, whether of oracular statement, pathos, satire or eulogy. These effects are what Pope offers in compensation for his abandonment of the bolder freedoms of Dryden, whose couplet had a constant tendency to *enjambement*, that is to overflow, to triple riming lines and to alexandrines. Criticism, since Wordsworth, has been prone to belittle Pope; and it cannot be denied that there were uncomfortable traits in his character. Nevertheless the last word on him ought rather to be an acknowledgment of his conscientious and unceasing devotion to his craft of letters.

3. PROSE OF THE LATER EIGHTEENTH CENTURY 1720 TO 1800

The prose of theology centred about the deistic or rationalist controversy; the opponents of revealed religion were writers such as Bolingbroke, Shaftes-

Prose of doctrine bury, author of *Characteristics* 1711, Tindal, Conyers Middleton and Toland, while on the orthodox side were Butler, author of *The Analogy* 1736, close-knit and exhaustive in its argument, and William Law, famous for his mystical and evangelical *Serious Call* 1728. In philosophy, Locke's empiricism was varied by Berkeley's idealist doctrine that matter only exists for mind, and by Hume's development of it, that the mind itself is but a succession of ideas. Hume wrote with great literary charm, but Berkeley, as in his *Dialogues between Hylas and Philonous* 1713, developed a style of grace, lucidity and power hardly to be paralleled in any other philosophical writing. With these should be associated Mandeville's *Fable of the Bees*, which opens in verse, a vigorous, penetrating and misanthropical survey of society, to which the mystic, William Law, made an effective reply.

Steele's *Guardian*, one of many ventures which flourished for a little time when *The Spectator* came

The Essay to an end, was without a really notable successor until Johnson in the *Rambler* 1750, and in his later *Idler* and *Rasselas* 1759 (which is not much more than a bound volume of *Ramblers*), proved that a man might have many gifts of heart and brain, learning, shrewdness, sympathy, humour, religion, wisdom and yet not be able to dissipate melancholy or to achieve the lightness of the perfect essay style. Sir Joshua Reynolds's *Discourses* brought art criticism within the range of the essay; Ruskin and Pater are the chief of many later disciples. Goldsmith, in *The Citizen of the*

World, adopts the pretence of being a Chinaman surveying naïvely the follies and oddities of Englishmen. But the Addisonian tradition of the essay was worked out, and, when the essay was revived by Lamb and Hazlitt, it was fundamentally changed in manner and matter. Meanwhile must be noted the foundation of the modern newspaper press (for instance, *The Times* and *The Morning Post*), the relations of which to literature at large are not yet fully determined.

Of memoirs and letters this is our golden age, almost challenging the supremacy of France. Swift's
Memoirs and Letters *Journal to Stella* 1710–3 portrays intimately the foremost figures in society, literature and politics, at the end of Anne's reign. Swift moves in these circles on a footing of perfect equality. Pope's polished letters were put forth and advertised in characteristic subterranean fashion; Lady Mary Wortley Montagu's show her a bluestocking possessed of a keen sardonic wit; Gray's are the *locus classicus* for the change of attitude towards what had hitherto been thought forbidding and monstrous in natural scenes; Chesterfield's are brilliant, courtly and wise, intending 'to fashion a gentleman in noble discipline' after French and English models; the other aspect of them is commented on by Wesley in his *Journal* thus: 'He was a man of much wit, middling sense and some learning; but as absolutely void of virtue, as any Jew, Turk, or Heathen, that ever lived.' Walpole's vivid epistolary style records the gossip, personal tastes, antipathies, reflections of a busy leisure and wide-ranging mind, with an air of

intimacy, a quick sense of the comic and some measure of malice, a mixture which makes his letters an incessant source of amusement. But none of these letter-writers has a sense of style so inborn, so delicate as Cowper's; his material is simply that which passes before our own observation, but he charms attention by subtle grace and simplicity of description; the elements are mixed in infallible proportions. Madame D'Arblay's *Journal*, beginning 1786, gives a vivid and personal account of her uncomfortable office at the court of queen Charlotte. The *Letters of Junius* 1769–72, which contain virulent invective against the duke of Bedford and others of the king's party, have the fortune to embody a mystery of authorship; opinion leans, though hesitatingly, towards Sir Philip Francis as the writer.

In biography, the age has such masterpieces as Gibbon's *Autobiography*, Boswell's *Life of Johnson* 1791, and Johnson's *Lives of the Poets* Biography 1779–81. There was, no doubt, a large vein of folly in Boswell, but he had uncommon skill in providing opportunities for the play of Johnson's personality, an artist's sense for the salient aspects of an incident, a rare measure of hero-worship, a retentive memory and an engaging narrative style, with the result that of no other man have we a presentation so intimate, so detailed and so unforgettable as to manner, habits, garb and speech. It is from Boswell's *Life* more than from his own writings Dr Johnson that we derive our picture of Johnson, marked by disease, awkward in gait, emphatic in assertion, a lover of talk and of clubs, as well as our impression of his courage, independence,

British intellect, with its largeness of grasp in
some things and insular speculative narrowness
in others, his readiness to argue all causes, his
melancholy, his piety, his benevolence, his immovable prejudices against the whig dogs and the
Scots. Except for the three months' tour in the
Hebrides, Boswell cannot have met Johnson on an
average more than ten days a year in the twenty
years of their acquaintance. In view of all this,
it is clear that Macaulay's first sketch of Boswell
(Macaulay made some amends in a later essay)
as the fortunate fool of literature is an injustice.
Johnson's other writings are numerous, including the
great *Dictionary* 1755, the edition of Shakespeare
1765 with its splendid preface, and his *Journey to
the Western Isles* 1775; but the crown of his writing
is the *Lives of the Poets* 1779-81, combining biography and criticism. Literary anecdote keeps its
savour in these pages, but the *Lives* also afford
a body of criticism in which the canons of the
pseudo-classical school reveal both their strength and
their weakness. His understanding and sagacity
make such lives as those of Dryden and Pope
almost final pronouncements, but his lack of sensitiveness for imaginative expression and for a freer
music than Pope could charm from the heroic
couplet, to say nothing of his church and state
prejudices, render the account of Gray nugatory
and that of Milton only partially valid. His earlier
involved sentence structure and polysyllabic diction
are tempered by this time to a finer strength and
a mature ease. The *Letter to Lord Chesterfield* gave
a death-blow to the system of patronage under

which writers had successively profited and starved since the restoration; henceforth, the author was to appeal direct to the public.

History in the modern sense, like the essay, letter-writing and the novel, is a creation of the age of prose and reason. Hume's

History

History of England 1762 is a different thing from the garrulous though generally accurate contemporary records of Burnet's *History of my own Times* 1723. Hume's writing is clear and spirited, he has narrative skill, sense of character and philosophic reflection; Smollett's continuation is simply vigorous hack-work. Robertson's *Histories of Scotland* and of *Charles V* are in the rotund Latinised style which took a new lease of life in Dr Johnson's time. He examined with some care such material as the age provided, and is accurate in the main. No such qualification need be put upon *The Decline and Fall of the Roman Empire* 1776–88

Gibbon

of Gibbon, one of the masterpieces of historical writing. First, he brought together by tireless and minute research an unimaginable mass of detail which his historical sagacity interpreted with rare judgment; next, he chose his vantage ground so as to present in panoramic succession the major events of thirteen hundred years—the spread of Christianity, the barbarian irruptions, the rise of Mohammadanism, the record of the Persian empire, Arabic civilisation, the crusades, closing his survey with the brilliant relation of the fall of Constantinople. How masterly is his control of his multifarious material may be seen in the fact that, for the years 476–1453, he changes the scale of the work and yet maintains unfalteringly his sense of proportion. Gibbon's attitude, to which his *Autobiography* gives consummate expression, is in the main that of impartial detachment, except towards religion and zeal; these things (he was much influenced by Voltaire) provoked his ironic scepticism, as in his famous account of the spread of Christianity. His style has a long resounding march and energy in sentence, paragraph and chapter; its system of balanced rhetorical clauses is well suited to express the pros and cons of his well-considered statements. The monumental quality of his achievement may be judged from the fact that modern scholars, though they revise details, make no proposals to supersede his work as a whole.

Edmund Burke is the greatest of all political orators by virtue of his minute knowledge of events, piercing insight, imaginative grasp and magnificent rhetorical endowment. In his earlier speeches on English affairs, such as *Thoughts on the Present Discontents* 1770, and on colonial politics, such as his *American Speeches* 1774–5, he investigates problems as they are illuminated by past experience, is generous towards progressive hopes, condemns meticulous legality and aims at 'reason, justice and humanity' by means of a practical and high-minded expediency. Yet all his eloquence failed to avert the war of independence. The French revolution set him face to face with a more profound social upheaval and forced him back to a conservative upholding of inherited institutions, for which he has been accused of inconsistency. In *The French Revolution* 1790, and

Burke

Letters on a Regicide Peace 1795-7, he formulated
his creed of the state as an organism of slow bene-
ficent growth enshrining the 'permanent reason' of
the race as against popular illusions—which he ab-
horred as much as he did abstract politics—while,
at the same time, embodying the conception of moral
duty and forbidding revolution. He lifted political
discussion out of the sphere of mere argument by
his analogy between the state and the world; and
he called in imagination, sentiment, the whole nature
of man in fact, to assist the reason in the exercise
of judgment; in this respect, he may be counted
something of a romantic. His oratory shares in
the revival of the long swelling sentence, though,
within it, he manages admirably his antithetical
clauses and enlightening illustration; he has an
unequalled gift for the accumulative method and
for interfusing poetic phrase and imagery of oriental
richness so that it seems one with his thought. All
subsequent political speculation is deeply in debt
to Burke.

4. THE NOVEL

The backward record of the novel might stretch
to the Greek romances; but its more significant
features were not compounded till the eighteenth
century. Long and detailed realistic narrative is
seen in Bunyan, Defoe and Swift; character sketch-
ing in Addison, and, on the domestic side, in Steele;
the association of naturally related characters in
real circumstances, plot and situation are found
in Fielding; while sentiment, erotic emotion and

Y.   9

the sense of tragedy are added by Richardson.

Richardson Richardson's *Pamela or Virtue Re-warded* 1740 and *Sir Charles Grandison* (portraying an insufferable masculine ideal) are inferior to his *Clarissa Harlowe* 1748. When fairly entered upon, this novel enchains the reader; it has a Ford-like tenacity in respect of its tragic theme, the undoing of Clarissa by Lovelace, fecklessly seconded by her rigid and unimaginative family. Its insistence on feeling to the exclusion of almost all else, and its stuffy conception of virtue may seem unhealthy; its interminable length, its epistolary form, its diffuse and endlessly analytic style make a great dead weight to lift; but the book rises to the rank of a classic; it was accepted as such in France and Germany, where its influence was enormous. Henry Fielding, after dabbling in the

Fielding drama, turned novelist to ridicule *Pamela* in *Joseph Andrews* 1742; this revealed to him his vocation and in *Tom Jones* 1749 he proved himself the possessor of the strongest and most comprehensive understanding among the English novelists. The tale is plotted on epic scale, the conventions of which are wittily utilised in the initial chapters of each book. Its range of incident is wide, the events set in country houses, inns and by the roadside; the London part of the tale is the least attractive. The book is full of living men and women, of broad humorous comedy of situation and character and of a widely tolerant spirit exacting a standard remorseless in its castigation of hypocrisy, treachery and calculating propriety. Fielding is not invaded by the hot-house

sensibility, the conscious glow of feeling of Richardson and Sterne; his whole world is manlier in its
acceptance of things as they come. Neither the
Swift-like irony on the subject of 'greatness' in
Jonathan Wild 1743, nor his later novel *Amelia* 1751,
attains the proportions of *Tom Jones*. *A Journey
from this World to the Next* has brilliant satire in
the chapters describing Elysium. Fielding writes
the masculine flexible English of the scholar and
the man of the world, the best of all middle styles.

Sterne   Laurence Sterne's *Tristram Shandy*
1760–7 defies all the canons of order
and development; it is an eccentric fantasy having
for its ancestry Rabelais, Cervantes, Burton and
Arbuthnot. No thread of story runs through the
work, no possible world is reflected therein, but
rare turns of humour and pathos, and, above all,
character appear; Uncle Toby, and Corporal Trim
especially, are figures constantly being elaborated
by subtle touches delineating gesture, speech, the
absorbing pursuit of their wayward hobbies, and
their generous human feeling. The style is shot
with iridescent colour, full of Rabelaisian pedantry
and allusive innuendo, yet answering, on occasion,
to every call of emotion or description. Sterne's
Sentimental Journey 1768 is a document showing
forth the 'sensibility' of the time, the high-wrought
feeling perpetually threatening tears, which actually
flood the page in Mackenzie's *Man of Feeling* 1771.

Goldsmith   Goldsmith's charming idyll *The Vicar
of Wakefield* 1766 is feeble in struc-
ture, being but a series of incidents in a chequered
family history loosely bound together; but its

9—2

humanity and sympathy, its delicate touch on humour, pathos, satire and tragedy, and its limpid musical prose ensure for it a place among the great prose writings of the eighteenth century.

Smollett   Smollett's picaresque novels *Roderick Random* 1748, *Peregrine Pickle* 1751 and *Humphry Clinker* (in letter form) 1771 often reflect his rather harsh and irritable temper, but they have extraordinary wealth of comic adventure drifting easily to blows, variety of character, including national types, doctors and sailors—the shadier and more insolent predominating—and a coarse racy speech, all of which were doubtless enriched in his own travels by land and sea.

We may briefly indicate several lines of development which the novel followed; first, that of romance,

Minor novelists   of such varying shades as we see in Walpole's *Castle of Otranto* 1764, Beckford's *Vathek* (in English) 1786, Mrs Radcliffe's *Mysteries of Udolpho* 1794 and the novels of other terror-mongers such as 'Monk' Lewis, who were parodied in Jane Austen's *Northanger Abbey*. Next, novels of edification such as Godwin's *Caleb Williams* 1794, turning on the pathology of crime; and the Rousseau-like educational story *Sandford and Merton*, and those of Hannah More and Miss Edgeworth. Thirdly, we may note the beginnings of the novel of local colour, Irish in Miss Edgeworth's *Castle Rackrent* 1800, Scottish in Galt's *Annals of the Parish* 1821 and Miss Ferrier's *Inheritance* 1824, these last two in the wake of Sir Walter. Lastly, most important in its immediate results, the novel of manners or domestic satire; in this, Fanny

Burney's *Evelina* 1778, rich in character sketches, precedes the masterpieces of Jane Austen.

Jane Austen 1775–1817, in her *Sense and Sensibility* 1811, *Pride and Prejudice, Mansfield Park, Emma, Northanger Abbey* and *Persuasion* 1816, adapts the comedy of manners to the novel. Her circle is small, and no doubt she was confirmed in her tendency to realism by a reaction from the novels of mystery, which she ridiculed in *Northanger Abbey*. She delineates the upper middle class family of the southern counties, its relatives, its emigrations to Bath, and, more rarely, to town, and its absorbing interest in marriages and dowries; these constitute the two inches of ivory on which, as she herself said, she worked with a fine brush. Grant this miniature circle and the absence, for the most part, of tragic and vehement matter, and she must be allowed to attain perfection in her art; not only by reason of her remarkable restraint, her sure instinct for proportion and for selection of salient detail, her unfaltering consistency in character-drawing, but, also, by her style; for, whether in the dialogue, or in the finely ironic phrasing of her comment, she never fails in aptness and a kind of fastidiously used force. She lives and moves in the company of her characters, like Dickens, but, whilst he is in a continual state of exuberant excitement about them, Jane Austen is always alert, sane, unsentimental, witty, rather like Meredith's comic spirit abroad. She imparts to the atmosphere in which we view her characters some quality of sharpness and clearness, so that they make an ineffaceable

impression upon us and we know them through
and through.

5. The eighteenth century tradition and the rise of romance in poetry

The tradition of Pope continues in writings in
couplet which stretch in a thinning line down
The successors to Byron. Addison's *Campaign* 1704,
of Pope Tickell's fine *Elegy on Addison*, Parnell's *Hermit*, Young's satires, *The Universal Passion*
1725–8, Johnson's *London* 1738 and *The Vanity of
Human Wishes* 1749, Churchill's lampoons *The
Rosciad* 1761 and others, Goldsmith's *Traveller*
1764, Darwin's *Loves of the Plants* 1789 (richly
burlesqued in *The Anti-Jacobin*), Rogers's *Pleasures
of Memory* 1792, Campbell's *Pleasures of Hope* 1799,
Crabbe's narratives, from *The Library* 1781 to *Tales
of the Hall* 1819, Byron's *English Bards and Scotch
Reviewers* 1809; these make up a catalogue, which
could be easily extended, of poems of which the
themes are satire, panegyric, elegy (death and the
churchyard were much in the mind of the eighteenth
century), learning and didacticism; much more
rarely do we find poets treating of passion, nature
or large historic event. Some of the titles indicate
what proved to be the besetting sin of this age of
intellectual analysis, namely abstraction and personification. Some poets use the typical measure,
the couplet, but are less didactic, as Gay in
Trivia, or the Art of Walking the Streets of London
1716, and Prior, though his light and sparkling
'society verses' such as *The Female Phaeton, To*

a Child of Quality and *Jinny the Just* are far
superior. Other writers are of the didactic tradition
in subject but not in form, using, for instance, blank
verse, as Akenside's *Pleasures of Imagination* 1744,
and Young's *Night Thoughts* 1742–4; they and
many others followed Milton, but, not having access
to his springs of inspiration, were prone to write
a diction 'glossy and unfeeling' or large, circum-
locutory and ineffective; much more understanding
of blank verse was shown in the Miltonic burlesque
(not in the least malicious), *The Splendid Shilling*
by John Philips. Other poets of the age are partly
in the pseudo-classic tradition; but the fortunes of
Pope's school are falling and we seek out more
curiously the forerunners of the rising dynasty.
The heralds of   They are heard even in the moment of
romance   Pope's supremacy; they besiege the
classical citadel on many sides. First, we see men
turning from the town to the fields in Thomson's
Seasons 1726–30, accurate and sensitive descriptions
of quiet aspects of nature, though, in diction, too
imitative of Milton; in Parnell's *Night-Piece,* in
Dyer's *Grongar Hill* 1727, in Allan Ramsay's
Gentle Shepherd 1725, in Gray's *Elegy* 1751 and
in his *Letters,* in Collins's exquisite *Ode to Evening*
1747, in Goldsmith's *Deserted Village* 1770, in
Cowper's *Task* 1785 and in the *Songs* and *Poems* of
Burns. Next, we may note the use of the Spenserian
stanza in Shenstone's *Schoolmistress* 1742 and in
Thomson's *Castle of Indolence* 1748, in some part
a real re-animation of the spirit of Spenser; Milton's
early poems count for something, too, with Gray
and Collins. When we remember that the earliest

name in Johnson's *Lives* is that of Cowley 1618–
67, it becomes significant that Spenser was edited
by Thomas Warton 1754, Chaucer by Tyrwhitt 1775,
and Shakespeare by Pope 1725, by Theobald 1734,
by Warburton 1749 and by Johnson 1765. A number
of works which, earlier, would have been called
contemptuously 'Gothic' came to light in the second
half of the century. Thomas Warton's learned
History of Poetry 1774–81 reopened the closed book
of medieval romance; ballads were brought fully
to light in Percy's *Reliques of Ancient English
Poetry* 1765. Gray's *Triumphs of Owen* and *Fatal
Sisters* are from the Welsh and Norse. The High-
lands are the scene of the cloudy and gloomy
heroics of Macpherson's pseudo-Gaelic *Ossian* 1762.
Chatterton's *Rowley Poems*, purporting to be of the
fifteenth century, show an interest in the past which
takes a scholarly turn in Gray's more erudite odes,
The Bard and the nobly conceived *Progress of
Poesy*. Something must be set down also to the
religious revival led by John Wesley; it does much
more than produce the hymns of Cowper and the
rich, vigorous and triumphant *Song to David* 1763,
of Christopher Smart.

Of the great mass of writing thus summarily
dismissed we may dwell for a moment on one or two
outstanding things. It is evident that the splendid
rhetoric tinged with melancholy of Johnson's *Vanity
of Human Wishes*, and the happy delineations of
characters in the circle of Dr Johnson's club in
Goldsmith's *Retaliation* 1774, are of an earlier date
Gray's *Elegy*   in spirit than Gray's *Elegy* 1751. There
is a magic appeal in the solitary figure

of the *Elegy*, even though we cannot form any human picture of him, reflecting in a mood of resignation in the hushed twilight landscape upon the lot of the rustic poor, who are foiled of fame, yet doomed, like all their fellows, to the inevitable grave. The appeal partly lies in the finely phrased truisms, about feelings the occasions of which are common to all; partly in the implicit human cry for sympathy. The polished diction and the rhythm have a rare quality which transcends the formal balanced epithets and the excessive use of inversion, things which, in themselves, would stamp Gray's genius as of his age. He is far from being clear from the vices of his school—witness his personification and abstraction and want of the free lyrical note in the *Eton College* ode; yet, by his feeling for the wilder aspects of nature in his *Letters*, and for humbler human beings as in the *Elegy*, and by his sensitiveness to the imaginative worth of other literatures, Welsh, Norse and the poetry of Dante, he is on the side of romance. He was the widest read man of his day, a critic of fine insight and historical sense, and he was not ignorant of science. William Collins, like Gray, wrote in the form of the elaborate academic ode; it would be an instructive exercise to trace the form of the ode, whether pindaric, pseudo-pindaric, or of regular successive stanzas, through Wordsworth, Coleridge, Shelley, Keats down to Swinburne, who pronounced the ode the supreme form of lyric poetry. The *Ode to Evening* is the masterpiece of Collins; there is fastidious art and classic self-possession in his *Ode to Simplicity*; and, in the *Dirge in Cymbeline* and

'How sleep the brave,' he proved himself the most exquisite lyrist between the Elizabethans and Blake. Chatterton's fine *Ballad of Charity* ought also to be singled out both for its intrinsic quality and for its later influence on Coleridge, Keats and the pre-Raphaelites.

All this means a wider range of poetic subject; it points to a liberating of emotion and to a revival

Signs of transition

of imaginative faculties, which had been gradually but finally dulled during the puritan ascendency, the cavalier reaction, and the age of prose and reason. Again, when Pope counselled poets to follow 'nature,' his meaning was that they should portray man as he appears in his social environment; as this conception of the function of poetry loses sway, the embittered partisan attitude of the urban poets yields to more frank and unsuspicious feeling and to enthusiasm; the rigid rationalistic temper gives way before the invasions of mystical and religious thought in Blake and Cowper; abuse, debate, preaching and generalities are replaced by solitary introspection and reverie, or by communings with nature, or with things of sensuous beauty; individualism, tentative in Cowper, pronounced in Blake and Burns, takes the place of an attempt to write to an artificial pattern in the school of Pope; feelings which give colour to unexciting but intimate events are expressed poetically in Cowper, and the child-mind finds its first understanding spokesman in Blake. These changes are accompanied by a less frequent use of the long-established couplet, the flat blank verse line or the octosyllabic couplet, which

was to have, however, a new lease of life in the
Christabel form established by Coleridge; and this
was only one example of a fresh metrical inventiveness which set in with the revival of lyric, and of
which the latest master was Swinburne. As a result
of all this we get, at the end of the century, writers
of the classical tradition side by side with romantic
innovators. George Crabbe 1754–1832, in his verse
Crabbe   form and in his satirical temper, is old-
fashioned; the realism of his description
of country folk in a way anticipates Wordsworth,
but is without Wordsworth's sympathy; he began
describing the villages he knew in a fit of revulsion
from Goldsmith's sentimentalism. His pictures of
nature and the sea are most intimately observed,
and though he is apt to see the harsher aspects, he
paints what he sees vividly and arrestingly. *The
Borough* 1810, *Tales in Verse* 1812, and *Tales of the
Hall* 1819 make up a series of narratives, including
character sketches and tragic biographies, for the
most part of people of higher rank than those in
The Village 1783. His tales are not altogether
sombre; some are touched with humorous observation, and there are unexpected flashes of romantic
feeling; most of the tales have unmistakable force
and grip and strong satirical power.

William Cowper 1731–1800 is another figure of
the transition. His *Table Talk*, *Expostulation* and
Cowper   the like are in the tradition of Pope;
but he came to protest against its
artifice; he sought to translate Homer more
simply than Pope and he deserted the couplet for
blank verse. Above all, he revolted against the

town. 'Chartered boroughs,' he says, 'are public plagues.' The *Winter Evening* in *The Task* argues that man has an innate love of natural objects, which not all the seductions and vices of cities can obliterate. *The Task* 1785, which heralds the return of poetic style, has a curious diversity of theme; the most persistent interest in it is the recounting of all the simple delights and observations of country life, the coming of spring, the sound of distant bells, the light occupations of the gardener, the gambollings of pets and animals, much in the manner of Vergil's *Georgics*. With this, there is a large admixture of exhortation, of evangelical doctrine, of challenges to deists and of the opinions of a scholarly recluse possessing a religious temper. He has many sallies of humour, boisterous, as in *John Gilpin*, Prior-like in other verses, quite individual, as in *The Colubriad*. His music has a larger volume in the unfinished *Yardley Oak* 1791; and there is intense feeling in the pathetic poems to *Mary Unwin* and the lines *On the Receipt of my Mother's Picture*; the terror of his own mental experience gives the power of profound gloom to *The Castaway*. The lines *On the Loss of the Royal George* may take a place among patriotic lyrics such as Thomson's *Rule Britannia*, Garrick's *Hearts of Oak* and the war lyrics of Campbell, in which rhythmic effects are generally much surer than the diction and imagery.

William Blake 1757–1827, mystic, poet and engraver, is an isolated, not to say miraculous,

Blake

phenomenon in his day. He is not inspired in any way by his age; he remained almost unknown during his life and he did not found any school. His *Prophetic Books* are not yet fully elucidated, though it is clear enough that they anticipate the liberal doctrines of the next generation; as in Shelley, reason and custom are accused of fettering imagination and goodness, priestcraft and kingcraft are condemned, and 'great things are done when men and mountains meet.' The last books *Jerusalem* and *Milton* are overcharged with the vast spectral images and symbols which haunted him habitually. His genius is more unmistakably at play in his shorter poems in *Poetical Sketches*, as early as 1783, and *Songs of Innocence* 1789. In some of these he recaptures perfectly the lyric note of the Elizabethans; in others, the very spirit of childhood speaks out its impulses and delights in its own voice of simple magic; in this identification of himself with the child-mind, Blake has no peer. *Songs of Experience* 1794 have some sinister discords breaking in upon the melody of innocence. Something of the range of Blake's lyrical genius—its strength and its sensitiveness—may be realised from a comparison of 'the fervent beauty and vigour of music' of *The Tiger*, with 'the fierce floral life and radiant riot of childish power and pleasure' in *Songs of Innocence*.

We must think of Robert Burns 1759-96 as coming late in a line of great tradition rather than as a conscious herald of romantic revolt; he was, in fact, an admirer of English eighteenth century literature. He continues the tradition of Scots poetry, which in a diminished way had been upheld by Allan Ramsay (*Poems* 1721) and Fergusson (*Poems* 1773) and by

Burns

many unknown local poets of the type of Davie
Sillar, Lapraik and Simson, recipients of some of
the most human verses of Burns. It is true that
some elements in the tradition and in Burns
coincided with the movement towards romance in
England—the love of the soil and animals; the
feeling for natural scenes; the revival of the lyric
note; the democratic doctrine, which hit well with
his pugnacious independence; the assertion of the
worth of humble folk; the piety of the hearth-side;
the unashamed utterance of strong instinctive
passions; the return to past heroism and history,
sometimes with a Jacobite tinge; the sensitiveness
to the imaginative and supernatural in folklore. On
the other hand, his unsparing and irreverent satire
of religious hypocrisy, as in *Holy Willie's Prayer*,
and of all hereditary pretensions; his love of strong
rustic liquors and gaieties, as in *The Jolly Beggars*,
and the mirthful narratives, such as *The Twa Dogs*
and *Tam o'Shanter*, which swing along with reckless
speed yet have full and exact detail, and incisive
vividness of expression; these things are like enough
to some aspects of Dunbar, but they are not much
in consonance with the aims of Wordsworth or of
Keats. Burns's *Songs*, perhaps even more than his
Poems, are rooted fast in a rich native soil; the
Songs are, for the most part, words invented or
elaborated from some suggestive or musical existing
phrase, to fit the melodies of old Scots folk-songs.
In these, perhaps his highest genius is shown, in
their exquisite sensitiveness, their absolute fidelity
to experience (compare them, for instance, with the
generalised emotions of his verses in English), the

beauty and simplicity and power of his diction and rhythm, especially when he utters passionate feelings of tragic or pathetic intensity.

6. THE DRAMA FROM 1660

The story of the drama from the re-opening of the theatres at the restoration to modern days is a tale of mediocrity relieved by occasional flashes of comic splendour. The first episode is that of the heroic play, a grotesque form of tragedy, drawn, as Dryden says in his preface to the most famous of them *The Conquest of Granada* 1670, 'far above the ordinary proportion of the stage'; heroic romance and French tragedy share the responsibility for the matter and form of these plays, which were generally in heroic couplets. Next came the series of Shakespearean imitations and revisions; there was much incompetent botching, but Dryden's *All for Love* 1677, a remaking of *Antony and Cleopatra*, is worthy of its theme. Nathaniel Lee's *Rival Queens* 1677 is fitfully poetical; and Otway in *Venice Preserved* 1682 evolves a most moving tragic conclusion out of a conflict between loyalty and passion, in spite of the comparative bareness of his diction. Garrick took some liberties with the text of Shakespeare, but at least he restored dignity to his profession. Shelley's *Cenci* is the only other tragedy in the Elizabethan tradition that our drama can boast. A succession of rhetorical tragedies may be traced in the eighteenth century, Addison's *Cato* 1713, Young's *Revenge* 1721, Thomson's *Sophonisba* 1730, Dr Johnson's *Irene* 1749;

but a brilliant series of burlesques, *The Rehearsal* 1671, Fielding's *Tom Thumb* 1730 and Sheridan's *Critic* 1779 hounded the type to death. Citizen tragedy made a momentary appearance in Lillo's *George Barnwell* 1731. Gay's *Beggar's Opera* 1722, a travesty of fashionable Italian opera, took the town by storm, but is not in itself any great thing. Comedy has much more to show. The realistic comedies of Shadwell, a fruitful creator of Jonsonian humours, picture the Alsatian aspects of London life; Dryden's comedies, such as *Sir Martin Mar-All* and *The Spanish Friar* 1681, are mostly *tours de force*; he joined in the foray which pillaged Molière for characters and situations and cheapened them on their way across the channel. A finer product is the comedy of manners, such as Etherege's *The Man of Mode* 1676, the comedy of Wycherley (*The* Restoration *Plain Dealer* 1677) and of the brilliant comedy trio, Congreve (*The Way of the World* 1700), Vanbrugh (*The Relapse* 1697) and Farquhar (*The Beaux' Stratagem* 1707). It is the wittiest comedy of an actual society that we have; it portrays a world of heartless infidelity, of reckless adventure in pursuit of lawless pleasure, of the droll *contretemps* which arise out of plentiful intrigue; but the infinite grace of speech of the culprits redeems them for literature. Into this orgy of licence Jeremy Collier, a non-juring divine, hurled his *View of the Immorality of the Stage* 1698; but its immediate result was a decline in art; comedy was brought back to a clean way of writing only to become the tearful sentimental thing it is in Steele's *Conscious Lovers* 1722, and in the figure of Faulkland

in Sheridan's *The Rivals* 1775. In the reaction from
this school, the last writers of comedy till our own
day, the Irishmen Goldsmith and Sheridan, produced their masterpieces. Goldsmith in *The Good-
Natured Man* and in *She Stoops to Conquer* 1773

Goldsmith and Sheridan has a real sense of character, especially
of the pleasantly grotesque (for which
he might have taken himself as, in some measure,
a model), comic invention, natural sentiment and
amusing dialogue. Sheridan chooses his material
for plot and character in *The School for Scandal*
1777 from earlier plays, from Vanbrugh and Molière;
it is a richer, more urbane world than Goldsmith's,
with entangling social conventions, concerns with
legacies, marriages of convenience, idle coquetry
and scandal-mongering; the usual world of high
artificial comedy. But the dialogue, though also in
that tradition, is his own, the quintessence of verbal
wit. The earlier *Rivals* is, for the most part, farce
enriched by the figures of Bob Acres and Mrs
Malaprop. *The Critic*, with its play inset, is unsur-
passed in the brilliance of its literary parody.
Though his comedy is still artificial, and though
most of his characters are old types, yet the
effectiveness of his situations and surprises, his
pointed criticisms of manners and, above all, his wit
of idea and speech, compel laughter, and his style
makes him enduringly readable. From this time
forward there is a long intermission; no plays which
are at once literature and suited for the stage are to
be found until we come to two Irishmen of our own
day, Wilde and Synge.

BOOK V

THE REVIVAL OF ROMANCE 1798–1832

1. NEW CONDITIONS AND INTERESTS IN LITERATURE

WE have seen that many new forces are stirring by the end of the century; the twin processes of evolution and revolution are at work. But the conscious revolution, the sense that old fetters must be snapped and a new way of life entered upon, waits for the declaration of Wordsworth and Coleridge in *Lyrical Ballads* 1798. For what they accomplished and what they adumbrated in the nineteenth century, many names have been proposed; 'the return to nature,' 'the romantic revival,' 'the renascence of wonder,' 'the awakening of imaginative sensibility,' 'the convalescence of the feeling for beauty.' But no single name can define the diverse gifts exemplified, let us say, in *Michael, Kubla Khan, Marmion, The Eve of St Agnes* and *Prometheus Unbound*, though it is easy to see that all of them differ from *The Rape of the Lock* and *The Vanity of Human Wishes*. The enquiry into causes and evidences might take us far afield; we may concentrate attention upon two or three points.

i.   Economic and political changes lie behind.
The most powerful influence is that of Rousseau

Rousseau
(himself indebted to Thomson's *Seasons*)
working through the French revolu-
tion.   Rousseau's comprehensive return to nature
involved, in the main, three things, all of which were
to germinate in English literature; first, a return to
the country, next, the unchecked expression of the
emotions, thirdly the levelling of all social distinc-
tions; these things all contribute to the ideal of
the primitive unsophisticated man wandering in the
forests, the natural habitat of virtuous unrestrained
simplicity.   The fundamental doctrine of liberty was
worked out in prison reform, or slave liberation, in
the benevolent idealism of Shelley or the individualism of Byron; in Germany, in defiance of oppression,
it gave birth to a nation.   Wordsworth, Coleridge
and Southey all proclaimed an ardent youthful
sympathy with the French revolution; all of them
recoiled from its implications and methods, and
younger generations, represented by Shelley and
Browning, looked on them askance, as 'lost leaders'
in the great cause of freedom.

ii.   The same insurgent spirit is at work, also, in
criticism.   To this chapter belong Wordsworth's

Changes in
critical method
theorising contentions (afterwards tempered by Coleridge) as to the material
best suited for poetic treatment, as to an appropriate
diction, and as to the function of metre.   The same
rebellion against rule, reason and uniformity underlies changes in the type of the critical magazine;
the earlier *Edinburgh* 1802, *Quarterly* 1809 and
Blackwood 1817 adhered substantially to the older

10—2

canons. They were powerful enough to delay the acceptance of Wordsworth, Shelley and Keats, though Jeffrey of *The Edinburgh* in the end softened some of his strictures upon Wordsworth, and spoke generously of Keats. But, meanwhile, the truer critical method of imaginative insight and sympathy had been born in the writings of Lamb, Coleridge, Hazlitt and De Quincey.

iii. We have already noted the evolution of a deep-felt sympathy between man and nature, and Subjects of the a recognition of beauty in the simple new poetry emotions, in eighteenth century poetry; these were to be the texts of all Wordsworth's prophesyings. But, in other ways also, the new poetic genius is irresistible. Wherever at any earlier time poets had seen the vision of beauty or caught the strains of a true music the romantic genius claimed the inheritance. The art and mythology of Greece, the historic scenes of Italy and the Mediterranean shores, the exotic customs of the east, the chivalry, superstition and faith of the Middle Ages, the life of the Border with its insatiable feuds and its singular heroism; the new poets essayed all these themes; sometimes attempting to gild refined gold, as in Keats's *Endymion*, but more often loading every rift with richer ore as in *La Belle Dame sans Merci* and in *The Eve of St Agnes*. Subjects were found, moreover, beyond the horizon of these remote and historic matters. A crude and unimpressive treatment of the supernatural had pervaded the novels of the school of Walpole; Keats and his contemporaries strike chords that ordinarily lie silent far within the threshold of rational consciousness, yielding echoes only when unknown terrors, longings, dreams and ecstasies are stirred, such as find utterance, for instance, in *Tintern Abbey*, *The Ancient Mariner* and *Suspiria*; furthermore, they may be seen learning to divine between what is merely neurotic and disordered and the finer issues of mystery and terror, in the successive versions of *The Ancient Mariner* and in Keats's omissions from the *Ode on Melancholy*.

We may remark, also, a tendency towards picture and tale in place of analysis and disquisition (though there is didactic and reforming poetry of supreme quality in Wordsworth and Shelley). In Coleridge and Keats, colour and imagery are so vibrant and profuse that they appear like enchantments seen through the magic casements of the *Ode to the Nightingale*. Some of the writers of this school cause that thrill of the perfectly chosen word which gratifies at once the expectation of ear, imagination and understanding more often than has anyone since Shakespeare. The disciples of Keats, the pre-Raphaelites, cultivated a studied exactness of imagery, and the method degenerates, no doubt, into the modern vice of word-painting. Indeed, the pathology of romanticism is a revelation of the manner in which good customs corrupt the world.

There are resemblances between the earlier nineteenth century and the earlier creative period, the Elizabethan. Here, again, we find widened horizons, the flood-tide of poetic energy and the worship of beauty; but, while the earlier group dealt mainly with the world of action and affairs, the later, with exceptions, as in Byron and Scott, has a less adventurous, more introspective cast. Except Scott, there are few creators of characters, and no very notable contribution to comedy; and the later age has no drama.

A moment may be given here to a distinction which is constantly confronting us in the nineteenth century; that between romantic and classic. It is not necessarily a distinction of subject, for some of the triumphs of romance are, in Shelley, Keats and Swinburne, on classic themes; nor is it a case of the presence or absence of imagination, though this might serve to differentiate broadly the pseudo-classic eighteenth century. There is imagination in both the true romantic and the true classic; but the latter, with firm self-possession, restrains it in obedience to an instinct for perfect form, while the romantic, in a mood of excitement, gives it free rein; the instinct for form is by no means conspicuous in *The Excursion*, or *Prometheus Unbound*. The classic designs with clarity of outline; the romantic is purposefully vague, and is prone to run riot in decoration and colour; the classic presents emotion pure and intense, the romantic seeks out shades of feeling and powers in nature which can only be half distilled into words; the classic tends, on the whole, towards a statuesque type, the romantic prefers to suggest veiled immensities and indefinable ecstasies. These are general statements, but, if there is any truth in them, the early nineteenth century, though it is called romantic, produces masterpieces in both kinds; the 'bare sheer penetrating power' which Matthew

Romantic and classic

Arnold emphasises in Wordsworth is, for instance,
classic; but, in the main, the works we are to discuss
would fall under the other category.

2. POETRY FROM 1798 TO 1832

William Wordsworth 1770–1850, in *Descriptive
Sketches*, and Coleridge, in *Religious Musings*, had
both written verse not distinguishable
Wordsworth from some of that of the eighteenth
century before their intimacy at Stowey led to the
staking out of the complementary claims of the
natural and the imaginative in poetry. The significant portions of Wordsworth's development are told
in his *Prelude* 1805 (not published till 1850), a confessional monologue, which proves him, like Milton,
an egoist with an unshakable conviction of his
mission to teach, and shows, too, how much of his
poetry was of the stuff of his own emotions and
reflections. His mind—deep, slow-moving but not
speculatively comprehensive—took profound impres-
sions in his youth; after the moral crisis at about
the age of thirty, he was not often open to fresh
imaginative stimulus. The consequences are, first,
that much of his voluminous later work is repetition
in a muffled voice of what had already been fault-
lessly uttered, and, secondly, that many large tracts
of experience were closed to him; for instance,
comedy, the tumultuous side of sex, individual
enmities and many aspects of beauty outside nature.
The Prelude modifies the usual picture of Wordsworth
as a staid, austere, ruminative person; his youth
at least was adventurous and impetuous, while his

first experiences of nature were of its formidable
conscience-haunting aspects. An impulsive idealism
led him to take his third Cambridge vacation in
France, where he participated in the high hopes of
the Girondists. The turn given to these hopes by
Robespierre left him without faith, and the rational
doctrines of Godwin's *Political Justice* availed
nothing against his spiritual unrest
and despair. His sister, Dorothy,
diagnosed the malady and prescribed a life amid
the temperate stillness and calm power of nature.
The intensity of the crisis imprinted the cause of
recovery deeply in his mind, and he became the
high priest of a new gospel. Moreover, in the simple
folk who dwelt closest to the soil he realised the
value of the feeling and charity condemned by
Godwin, and the poignancy of the primeval events
which 'having been must ever be.' At this propitious
moment, he made the acquaintance of Coleridge, who
helped to kindle his imaginative and expressive
power; together, they projected *Lyrical Ballads*
1798; between this date and 1807, most of Wordsworth's enduring work was written, though he lived,
winning slow but sure recognition, till 1850. Like
all nature poets, he had great descriptive skill,
whether of minute or larger aspects; but nature was,
for him, much more than a gallery of magnificent
landscapes, or a background for action, or even a
scene whose physical elements might seem to sort
with varying human moods; for him, man and nature
have spiritual identity, and his endeavour was to
pierce to the spirit that 'impels all thinking things,
all objects of all thought and rolls through all

Poetry of nature

things.' The heart of his creed, as affirmed in
Tintern Abbey 1798, is that the refreshing of worn
spirits, the inspiration to kindliness and goodwill,
the perception of truth, the power to see into the
life of things, come through continued intercourse
with nature and the contemplative rapture which it
induces in those who are properly attuned and wisely
passive. In the noble *Fragment from the Recluse*,
however, this passivity is replaced, in part, by a
vital creative effort of imagination working upon the
world, an idea akin to Coleridge's ' In our life alone
does nature live.' There are many corollaries to
such a doctrine, and they form the basis of many
of Wordsworth's lyrics—that the beauty of nature
could be transmuted into human frame and feature,
as in ' Three years she grew '; that the woods, the
starry sky and the lonely hills could inform the soul
with the noblest learning, as in *Brougham Castle*,
The Tables Turned, and *Expostulation and Reply* ;
that memories are ineffaceable and bring in their
train a wealth of consolation and delight, as in
Daffodils, and *Stepping Westward*; and that
obedience to duty is the condition of stability,
repose and joy, as in the *Ode to Duty*. The sum
of his beliefs on much of this matter may be found
in the discussions of the Wanderer and the Solitary
in books I and II of *The Excursion* 1814, while, in
later books, the Pastor illustrates them in the lives
of his parishioners.

Much of Wordsworth's poetry of man is involved,
therefore, in his poetry of nature; in the *Fragment
from the Recluse* he announced the
novelty of his theme, the exquisite

Poetry of man

mutual fitness of the mind of man and the external world. We may regard this aspect of his work under three main headings, of childhood, of rustic life and of liberty and patriotism.

i. His poetry of childhood is tinged by the remembrance of his own infancy, when the world

Childhood had been lighted by some bright gleam which he interpreted to be the result of a spiritual vision freshly come from a celestial home. He thinks of his mature imaginings as efforts to recapture the truths which infancy possesses without effort; this is the meaning of the line 'The child is father to the man,' which prefaces the great *Ode on the Intimations of Immortality* 1803-6. The ode records the passing of this vision with the years; yet the bonds of the two worlds are not altogether severed; sometimes, still, a sound, a recollection, is wafted from those mightier waters to this smaller earth; and, in compensation for the loss, there is gained the deep human experience which modulates its grief into sympathy; on this part of the ode, the best comment is contained in *Tintern Abbey* and in the *Peele Castle* lines. His other poems of childhood have some touches of insight, but, in the main, childhood remained an abstraction to him.

ii. The poems of rustic life are based on his belief that there 'the essential passions of the heart speak a plainer and more emphatic language'; if with this we link his principle that 'the feeling de-

Rustic life veloped gives importance to the action and situation, and not the action and situation to the feeling,' we fathom his intention in *The Affliction of Margaret, Michael, Ruth, The*

Brothers, Resolution and Independence, the Matthew poems, and those of the Lucy who dwelt near his Cumberland home. The narratives are bare, almost trivial, but they have the suffusion of intense pure feeling, pathetic or tragic, and need no other appeal. These poems of children, peasants and half-witted creatures at first stirred repugnance; they are now thought by some to be among the most characteristic of his writings. He is not quite a realist, his rustics are not always real rustics, but the feelings are real feelings, the deepest, simplest and most widespread that we know.

iii. Liberty, the first high aim of the French revolution, was a rallying cry for all these **Liberty and patriotism** romantic poets, but the interpretations of it varied widely. For Wordsworth, liberty had always a close relation with discipline in the individual. In another sense, as in the sonnet 'The world is too much with us,' it meant freedom from material fetters. Again, in sonnets such as *The Venetian Republic,* and 'It is not to be thought of,' it lifted him to a larger historic utterance than did any other subject. His patriotism was a call to England to wake from moral slumber, as in the sonnets which invoke Milton's name. Although his ideal of *The Happy Warrior* is pacific—a stoic self-control, a calm contempt of circumstance, an immovable faith in good and honour, yet he had a spark of pugnacity in him which is fanned to a flame in his martial summons *To the Men of Kent.*

Other influences touched him from time to time; Milton was his model in his numerous sonnets—he was a great practiser and experimenter of metrical forms; the reading of Vergil suggested to him his *Laodamia* 1814; Scott, his faintly romantic *Brougham Castle,* and *The White Doe* 1807. Finally, one should note in him much of that kind of poetry whose main appeals are through vague suggestion, subtle rhythm and magical halo, such, for instance, as *Yew-Trees,* the sonnet on *King's College Chapel* and *The Solitary Reaper.*

Samuel Taylor Coleridge 1772–1834, philosopher, psychologist, critic, talker and journalist, as well as poet, took for his sphere, when he and Wordsworth projected *Lyrical Ballads,* 'persons and characters supernatural, or at least romantic; yet so as to transfer from our inward nature a human interest and a semblance of truth sufficient to procure for these shadows of imagination that willing suspension of disbelief for the moment which constitutes poetic faith.'

Coleridge

His output was large and varied, as we shall see, but his genius was supremely exercised by the kind of theme thus defined; *The Ancient Mariner, Christabel* and *Kubla Khan* all belong to his *annus memorabilis* 1797–8. An opium dream gave birth to *Kubla Khan,* with its voluptuous pictorial splendour, its sounds echoing from wild mysterious haunts, its workings of occult powers and its weird and fascinating harmonies of rhythm. *The Ancient Mariner* is a model in little of the whole of one aspect of romanticism. Its appeal is to the imagination, it is impregnated with the supernatural; in remote, untrodden regions, the poet describes scenes of arctic cold or sultry tropical heat, the dwelling-places of the uncanny omens and superstitions of sailors; to

each scene he gives a vigour of outline, a brilliance
of colour, and curiously real sounds, that bewitch us
into granting the 'willing suspension of disbelief
which constitutes poetic faith.' With the same
audacity, he enchains our interest in a series of
outlandish events and figures breaking abruptly
upon the vision, the Ancient Mariner, the albatross,
the phantom ship, the dead men rising, the crimson
lights and the angels' songs; there are, too, homely
things such as the harbour, the wedding feast and
the praying hermit; enough to remind us faintly
that we are in a dream. Nature plays a significant
part in the whole effect; the vaster elements, the
sun, the sea, the stars and, above all, the moon are
drawn with a few bold impressive strokes; in contrast, there is the fresh murmuring beauty of the
month of June; there are, too, the albatross and
the watersnakes, the imaginative counterparts of the
animals in Cowper and Burns; nature, moreover, has
a strange sympathy with the events of the story, for
some upheaval or portent precedes each supernatural
happening; the most impressive imagery is from the
same source, 'At one stride came the dark,' 'I pass
like night from land to land.' The simplicity of
wording throughout is matched by the choice of
metre, the simple ballad form, rich in traditions to
which Coleridge and Keats above all were most
delicately sensitive. All this abundant stuff of
romance is steadied by a sure art, ennobled by
seriousness and beauty, and its unity is secured in
the action and suffering of the Mariner, in his moods
of remorse, loneliness, gloom, fear, penitence and
calm, portrayed with a psychology as true as it is

subtle. *Christabel* chooses a medieval background and makes brilliant use of its chivalric trappings; its second part, indeed, is Scott-like and definite, though the famous lines on severed friendship are beyond the scope of Scott. But the first part is Coleridge's masterpiece; it pictures a world full of foreboding, every movement and sound is a whisper of doom, and the simple words seem to tremble with a secret menace; inexplicable overmastering terror pervades the scene, 'A thing to dream of not to tell,' which spreads its maleficent tyranny out through the air, 'The night-birds all that hour were still.' The invisible deformity of Geraldine, like the more gracious influences which Wordsworth knew, is 'felt in the blood, and felt along the heart.' The four-beat measure of the poem, though not as original as Coleridge thought it, gave potent aid to the music of poetry, and Scott, though with a less fine ear, tried it in the *Lay*, and Byron in *The Siege of Corinth*.

The promise of this sudden fertile spring in 1798 was unfulfilled: the rest of his life was given to philosophy, eloquence and criticism, and everywhere he was dogged by his malady of irresolution and his besetting sin of drug-taking. Most of what is memorable, therefore, in his voluminous production, is to be sought among the writings of his youth; there are poems of the romantic kind, *Alice du Clos*, *The Dark Ladye*, *Lewti* and *Love*; Wordsworthian poems such as *The Nightingale* and *Fears in Solitude* and other descriptive pieces; poems inspired by childhood, especially by his own son, Hartley, such as *Frost at Midnight*: poems, also, which give us

the inward experience from which he wove his
spectral dreams, such as *The Pains of Sleep*, and
Dejection, which records the loss of his shaping
power of imagination and the failure for him of
the doctrine of the healing of nature. Still, there
remain his vigorous translation of Schiller's *Wallenstein*, and his political odes, *To the Departing Year*
1796, and *France* 1798, which last utters a revulsion,
parallel to that of Wordsworth, from the hopes
earlier inspired by the revolution.

Robert Southey 1774–1843 was a relative by
marriage of Coleridge and the friend of Wordsworth,
the 'Lepidus of the triumvirate' once
called the Lake school. He formed a
colossal project of writing epics on the mythologies
with which his omnivorous reading had made him
acquainted; the fruits of this project were his narratives *Thalaba* 1801 (a favourite of Shelley), *Madoc*
1805, *The Curse of Kehama* 1810 and *Roderick, the
last of the Goths* 1814, perhaps the best of these
epics, because, from early years, Southey had had a
keen affection for the poetry of Spain and Portugal.
The romantic instinct for adventurous story, un-
familiar scenery and pageantry is evident; but
neither in Wordsworth's nor in Coleridge's way
could he produce the illusion of reality; the poems
have a bookish inflexibility of imagination for all
their purity of diction and careful versification.
Some of his ballads and lyrics, tragic and humorous,
have won more favour than is accorded to his
ambitious epic narratives.

To Sir Walter Scott 1771–1832 fell the task of
commending romance to the public taste, and

this he did by the verse-tales written between the
Scott years of Trafalgar and Waterloo, among
them *The Lay of the Last Minstrel*
1805, *Marmion* 1808, *The Lady of the Lake* 1810
and *The Lord of the Isles* 1815. He was nearer to
the still widespread tradition of the past century,
that part of it, at least, which derives from Fielding,
than the other romantic poets, and so gained a hearing
more quickly. After a hundred years of sedentary
poetry, of argument, satire and melancholy, he
restored one of the Homeric functions, the representation of physical action; the tale came to its
own again in the wake of the ballad. Scott, like
some other poets, began writing ballads in emulation
of the German poet Bürger's *Lenore*; he published
The Minstrelsy of the Scottish Border 1802–3, but
he soon turned to the tale, enhancing its appeal by
his directness and simplicity, by his unerring instinct
for the salient features of scenery and place, and by
his pictures of border life, with its feuds and chival-
ries; he was nourished on its history and ballads
and folk-memories. He makes, in addition, a high
appeal to national consciousness, as may be seen in
his tributes to Nelson, Fox and Pitt. His rhythm,
like a moss-trooping gallop, is not always free from
commonplace (though he has a keen sense of the
music of names); he draws character in broad outline; but whatever he lacks in subtlety he makes
up in a singularly healthy manliness of temper.
Yet his finest art is not in his tales, but in his
lyrics; in *The Pibroch, Coronach, Brignall Banks,
County Guy, Proud Maisie* and in a dozen others, he
is perfect.

The personality of George Gordon, Lord Byron 1788-1824 has, for later ages, unduly obscured his poetic work; the tempestuous egoism, volume of passion, irrepressible confessions of the poet and the romantic variety of his adventures attract and repel. Like Shelley, he was a votary of freedom; though, at first, it meant for him the freedom of the individual will, the conception becomes loftier in *The Prisoner of Chillon*, and, in the glorious end of his career, he became the advocate of the awakening nationality of Greece. *Hours of Idleness* 1807 did not foretell the real lyrical talent which he afterwards developed, whether of the resounding martial type of *Sennacherib*, or the curiously explanatory passion of 'When we two parted' and 'There's not a joy the world can give' or the pure magic of 'There be none of Beauty's daughters'; personal passions and recollections seem to inspire the longer-breathed *Dream* and *Darkness*. *English Bards and Scotch Reviewers* 1809 is a piece of youthful bluster, but with the promise of power. It indicates his satirical temper and his sympathy with the school of Pope. Fame came to him with his descriptive itinerary *Childe Harold* i and ii 1812, where partly the imagined character, and partly the historic and heroic memories of southern Europe won the instant ear of the public. Before parts iii and iv 1816-7 were written, Byron had become an exile in Italy and an intimate of Shelley. The infinitely wider power of these later cantos is due to these causes, as is likewise the stronger feeling for mountain and ocean which recurs in *Manfred* and *Don Juan*, where,

Byron

as in Shelley, it is interwoven with passion. Italy, at the same time, inspired his poems to *Venice, Tasso* and *Dante* 1819. By his series of verse tales from *The Giaour* 1813 to *The Island* 1823, he drove Scott from Scott's own field; in the earlier half-dozen tales, with their pictures of oriental and southern crime, headlong passion, exotic scenery and savage realism, he delineates 'the Byronic hero.' Conrad, Lara and the rest of them pass through the stages of unnatural crime, guilt-stricken conscience, fevered energy and cynical contempt, to a final angry isolation; the type is pictured for the last time in Byron's greatest non-satirical work, *Manfred.* Another drama, *Cain,* depicts a different kind of guilty rebel. His dramas of political intrigue, *Marino Faliero* 1820 and *The Two Foscari,* are *tours de force*; they have now no advocates. But, whilst writing them, Byron was discovering that the heroic and romantic were not his spheres; satire, realism, the normal levels of life, these are the materials of his abiding work in *Don Juan* 1818–22, the fully accomplished successor to his experimental *Beppo.* The loosely strung episodes of *Don Juan,* the rapid changes of emotional key, the swift revulsions from sentiment to mockery, the uncensored report of everything seen or experienced, the total disregard of decorum, exactly fitted Byron's matured genius, as did the *ottava rima* measure, to which, at his best, he gave a new perfection. His expression here attains the rightness and precision of his *Letters*; the torrent of vivid diction, colloquial and unsought, sweeps rhythm, rime, wit, dialogue and rhetoric along with it in its abounding power. *The Vision of Judgment*

1822, a parody of Southey's poem to George III of the same title, is the most sustained piece of satirical invective in English. When Byron has passed the stage of Titanic posing, power is his supreme quality, and his power is not only a mental tonic, but it carries us past his careless craftsmanship and all the faults which are set in high relief by his nearness to Shelley and Keats.

The poetry of Percy Bysshe Shelley 1792–1822 reflects the complexity of his character. Some of

Shelley

his actions, his ill-starred marriage, his visions and propaganda leave the impression not so much of a child as of a spirit from another sphere, not moving in the orbit of common men—thinking this life but the interlude of a nightmare. Yet there were many ways in which he stood in quite normal relations with his fellows; a fascinating and companionable figure is revealed, for instance, in his *Letter to Maria Gisborne* and in *Julian and Maddalo*. But there were in him almost irreconcilable traits of dejection and of idealism; his *Euganean Hills* embodies both moods. His pessimism becomes morbid in some of his self-portrayals in *Adonais* and in *Stanzas written in Dejection near Naples*. It takes the form, at other times, of an acute sense of isolation, as in *Alastor*, though this mood gives rise to some of his supreme work, expressing the desire for ideal companionship in *The Sensitive Plant*, and the fulfilment of this desire in the fervid passion and symbolic backgrounds of *Epipsychidion*, the poem which best illustrates his debt to Plato's *Symposium*. Perhaps, also, out of the same root of dejection sprang the complete

11—2

abandonment of himself to the immense elemental forces of nature, which is illustrated in the *Ode to the West Wind* and in the close of *Adonais*.

His all-pervading idealism inspires, first of all, his lifelong battle with oppression. In his generation, the watchword of liberty won back some of the glamour it had had for Wordsworth; tyrannies and monarchies had been restored in Greece, Italy, France and Spain. The early *Revolt of Islam* 1818, the *Ode to Liberty*, ennobled by historic imagination, the *Ode to Naples* and *Hellas* 1822 invoke freedom and, at the same time, arraign priest and king and tyrant, as, with an intenser hate, do his political satires, chief among them *The Masque of Anarchy* 1819. In *Prometheus Unbound* 1820 the object of his scorn is the traditional and dogmatic conception of God. Prometheus stands for the saviours of mankind, Jupiter for the tyrant God, created by custom and ruling by fear, who is dethroned by the rising of Demogorgon, the spirit of justice, dwelling in eternity. There follows in act iv the lyric rapture, a great chorus of spirit voices, which celebrates the rejuvenation of the earth. None of the poets prophesies larger hopes for man than Shelley, who owes something in this respect to the better part of Godwin. The poet pictures an earth overflowing with love and joy, its inhabitants sceptreless, equal, just, gentle, wise. But, with his generous vehement mind, he effects the transition to the golden age at one prodigious stroke. He had little faculty for enquiry, for the slow accumulation of experience, for the testing of hypothesis, for the dreary journey between the intractable real and the visionary ideal.

This failing has laid him open to the charge that he lacks humanity, that, in Matthew Arnold's words, he is no more than 'a beautiful ineffectual angel.' Nevertheless, he is intensely in earnest in his religion of universal love and freedom. The assertion of the supremacy of love and freedom would no doubt have been the solution of his last enigmatic fragment, *The Triumph of Life*. His theory of the One, the encircling creative mind, is not clearly elaborated, but is partially expressed in the triumphant close of *Adonais* (his splendid elegy on Keats), in *Mont Blanc*, and in his prose *Defence of Poetry*. Shelley is one of the poets' poets; everything that passes through his mind becomes saturated in poetry; but the singularity of his gift is that he obliterates the defining line between matter and spirit, between the solid earth and man's thought, between the real and the imagined; the two are involved together in his 'translucent' pictures of nature, especially regarding the more lawless things, wind, sea and light; but all his imagery, perpetually recurring yet always fresh, has this quality of mingling the spiritual and the material. He has the Turneresque vision which sees and retains the splendid moments, the ethereal hues, the spiritual beauty and power of a scene; any of his numerous voyages by rivers, caverns, oceans and mountain sides, in *Alastor*, *The Witch of Atlas* and other poems, will serve as illustration. He is no great creator of characters; his analytic mind reduced them, in *Adonais*, for instance, to abstractions, which move in the middle region between earth and spirit. There is, however, one striking and masterly exception, *The Cenci* 1819, a drama of

Italian lust and revenge, which, in its power and
objectivity, and in its picture of the wronged Beatrice
Cenci, rivals the later Elizabethans; here, the poet
purposely eschewed what he called 'mere poetry.'
But 'mere poetry' was his native element, as one
may see in his wealth of lyric verse.   Shakespeare,
Burns and Shelley are the monarchs of English
lyric; in swift energy of thought, in miraculous
melody, in emotional ecstasy, in profuse imagery,
and, at times, in a rare faculty of myth-making, we
shall search in vain for the peers of songs such as
'Worlds on worlds are rolling ever,' 'My soul is like
a boat,' 'The world's great age begins anew,' *The
Cloud, Arethusa, To a Skylark*, 'I arise from dreams
of thee,' 'Swiftly walk over the western wave,'
'Rarely, rarely, comest thou,' and many others.
Finally, mention must be made of a number of excellent translations, the best of them from Greek.

John Keats 1795–1821 was but faintly touched
by the political revolution, but his early *Sleep and
Poetry* 1817 proves him conscious of
Keats   the revolution in literature.   The first
awakening of his art came through his introduction
by Leigh Hunt to Spenser, Sandys and other
Jacobean poets, from whose influence he never
entirely escaped.   It was from them, as much as
from Lemprière's *Dictionary*, that he gathered his
knowledge of classical story.   Chapman's *Homer* he
celebrated in one of his most perfect sonnets, a form
in which he rivals the greatest masters.   Beauty
was the magnet to his imagination; it drew him to
Grecian art and mythology, to the Middle Ages and
to nature.   *Endymion* 1818 is a mingled yarn of

luscious scenes and veiled allegory, with many faults
(which the poet himself acknowledged in his manly
preface) of diction, verse and feeling. It is 'prentice
work' and yet contains such things as the ode to
Pan, the song to sorrow and the Bacchic chorus.
But his conception of Hellenism was to be clarified
and exalted by his growing imaginative powers and,
perhaps, by the influence of the Elgin marbles. In
expression, he was never quite what Shelley called
him, a Greek; the Elizabethan habit of beautiful
interpolation remained to the end in different degrees
in *Hyperion* and in the odes, *To a Grecian Urn*, *To
Psyche* and *To Maia*. The ode *To a Grecian Urn*
contrasts the disappointing satisfactions of life with
the arrested but expectant joyousness of art, and
closes with a tenet of which all his work is an ex-
pansion, 'Beauty is Truth, Truth Beauty.' *Hyperion*
remains a fragment, though the poet attempted to
complete it, while removing its excessive Miltonic
inversions. The Miltonic theme, the defeat of the
Saturnian gods, and something of Milton's epic scale
and verse structure persist; the poem is Keats's
highest intellectual reach, and, in the words of
Oceanus and Mnemosyne, it embodies his final conception of beauty, as it is enriched by the elements
of memory, power and sorrow.

His imagination pierced just as unerringly into
the poetic aspects of the Middle Ages. In his tales
Isabella, The Eve of St Agnes, The Eve of St Mark,
the scenes pass like the slow unfolding of rich
tapestries; the mind is constantly being engaged by
new beauties of cunning decoration, of surprising
contrast in colour, shape and sound. *Lamia*, the story

of the serpent-woman, is in the kind of heroic couplet
which Keats learned, curiously enough, from Dryden.
The brief unearthly masterpiece *La Belle Dame
sans Merci* is supreme in its class; it is compounded
of bitter personal sorrow, of nature, of chivalry,
faery, enchantment, magic, dream and mortal horror;
it is told in ballad form with a consummate reticence
befitting its ghostly theme, the undoing of men by
evil powers, which use beauty as their lure.

Keats's conception of nature was sensuous: colour,
shape, sound, perfume and touch make their simul-
taneous siege on the senses in, for instance, *Psyche*
and in the flawless *Autumn.* There is the same
concreteness when he pictures the haunt of the
nightingale, the verdurous glooms, moss-carpeted,
flower-scented, thrilled with sound, which entrance
him to wish, like Shelley, for death. The *Nightingale*
ode, however, is a revelation of mood, like the odes
on *Indolence* and *Melancholy,* whose long-hidden
shrine the poet discovers, by a finely imagined
paradox, in the very temple of delight. The magical
perfection of the phrasing in these odes is the gift
which entitles Keats, in Matthew Arnold's words, to
rank 'with Shakespeare.' Of his other poems, the
Mermaid tavern lines, *Fancy, Robin Hood* and
'Bards of Passion' are delightful, as is the song 'In
a drear-nighted December'; the dramas *Otho* and
King Stephen and the comic poem *The Cap and
Bells* are almost negligible.

Of Landor's voluminous poetry, some of the best,
as in the mythic and idyllic *Hellenics* 1846, is marked

Other poets   by definite form, classic purity of lan-
                guage and appropriateness of imagery;

of many exquisite short verses, *Rose Aylmer* is the most famous. With one aspect of Wordsworth we may associate *The Farmer's Boy* 1800 of Robert Bloomfield and the *Descriptive Poems* 1820 of John Clare. The nearest akin to Scott is James Hogg, the Ettrick shepherd, whose *Queen's Wake* 1813 shows an intimate understanding of the ballad, while, in *The Poetic Mirror* 1816, he skilfully parodied Scott, Southey, Wordsworth and himself; his *Kilmeny* is a graceful fairy tale. With Byron, we should most naturally associate his biographer, Thomas Moore, whose largest work, *Lalla Rookh* 1817 is a collection of gorgeous eastern tales, embroidered on a prose ground, brilliant in a kind of facile melody and narrative. He is somewhat stronger in his lyric poetry, which was inspired to patriotism by Emmet, as in *Irish Melodies* 1807–34. He has also a gift of stinging banter in his satirical squibs *The Twopenny Post-Bag* and *The Fudge Family in Paris* 1818, exercising a pungent and ingenious wit upon the regent and Castlereagh. The mantle of Shelley fell, if anywhere, upon Thomas Lovell Beddoes, though Beddoes is equally of the tribe of the Elizabethan dramatists of mortality in his *Death's Jest Book* 1850; perhaps his rarest power is shown in some of his lyrics, such as the enchanting *Dream Pedlary*. Nearer to Keats stand his friends Leigh Hunt (*The Story of Rimini* 1816), Thomas Hood (*The Midsummer Fairies* 1827, and *Eugene Aram*) and John Hamilton Reynolds (*The Garden of Florence* and *The Fancy*). Hood is better remembered for many comic poems, though his constitutional bent was towards tragedy: his humanitarian

verses, such as *The Song of the Shirt*, ring true. A
fiercer writer is Ebenezer Elliott, whose *Corn Law
Rhymes* belong to 1831. Lamb, Hartley Coleridge
in his sonnets, and Wolfe win their places in
anthologies by one or two triumphs. Parody,
whether of poetical or political absurdities, produces
some of its classic triumphs in *The Anti-Jacobin*
1797–8, by Ellis, Hookham Frere and Canning; *The
Needy Knife-Grinder*, for instance, victimises the
sentimental revolutionism and hapless metrical in-
ventions of Southey, and *The Loves of the Triangles*
ridicules the misdirected poetic energies of Erasmus
Darwin. The *Rejected Addresses* 1812 of James and
Horace Smith pink some of the foibles of Crabbe,
Scott, Moore and other poets of the time.

3. PROSE FROM 1800 TO 1832

The prose of the period is almost equally swayed
by the revolutionary and romantic interests, but,
until we come to Carlyle, there is nothing of the
sweep of Burke and Gibbon; the memorable writing
of 1790–1832 is in the novel or in essay and criticism.

We have already traced the history of the novel
down to Jane Austen. As in her case, Scott had
I. The novel.   much of the eighteenth century in
Scott   him; he is in the succession of Fielding
and Smollett. But he vastly extended its province,
inventing the historical novel and adding other
elements of the largest promise. He turned from
the verse tale in 1815 and wrote, in all, thirty-one
novels. He began with Scottish history, dealing
with the events of 1745 in *Waverley*, the covenanters
in *Old Mortality* and Mary queen of Scots in *The*

Abbot. With *Ivanhoe* 1820 began his tales of
English history and the Middle Ages; to this group
belong, also, *The Fortunes of Nigel, Woodstock* and
Kenilworth. Foreign scenes are the background of
The Talisman and *Quentin Durward*; of the more
domestic kind, *Guy Mannering, St Ronan's Well* and
The Heart of Midlothian are all masterpieces. Scott
established the European canons of the historical
novel, in regard to the proportions of history and
invention, the general fidelity of portraiture of known
persons and their exclusion, in the main, from the
central places in the tale, the broadly accurate realisa-
tion of past national life in profuse and picturesque
detail, the credible play of public events upon
private fortunes and the adoption of a slightly
archaic speech. To these things, he added a romantic
care for local scenery, steeped in the atmosphere of
memory and affection. He comes nearest to Shakespeare in the fecundity and diversity of his creations.
Just exception may be taken to some of his inanimate
heroes and heroines and their rhetorical dialogue;
but, in the representation of national types, especially
of all ranks of Scots, from monarch to crofter,
speaking their native dialect, and, in particular,
when pitted against the Sassenach, he has amazing
truth and vitality; in his command of the supernatural, his *Wandering Willie's Tale* is not to be
surpassed. Some of his most effective characterisation is achieved in his prefatory figures, such as
Cleishbotham and Old Mortality. We may always
rely on him for fine chivalry, courageous loyalty,
shrewd humour and true pathos. His large, sane
and vigorous personality, and its struggle with

disaster at the close, afforded material for a classic biography, the *Life*, by his son-in-law Lockhart. Neglecting minor novelists, two others must be mentioned before we come to the great Victorians; J. J. Morier, whose *Hajji Baba* 1824 is an entertaining and veracious chronicle of the east; and Thomas Love Peacock, who satirised, in conversation-novels like *Crotchet Castle* 1831, the manias and singularities of poets and philosophers; whilst, in *Maid Marian* 1822, he gave, with a tonic admixture of satire, an entrancing picture of the times which inspired Scott's *Ivanhoe*. Peacock sprinkles his novels with lyrics like an Elizabethan romancer; his Attic purity of style and fineness of wit have been unduly neglected.

Most of the poets exercised themselves also in criticism ; Wordsworth in his prefaces, Coleridge in

II. Criticism *Biographia Literaria* 1817, Scott in the introductory parts of his novels, Southey in many reviews and biographies (out of which grew his classic lives of Nelson and of Wesley), Shelley in his *Defence of Poetry*, a subtle and eloquent study of the working of creative imagination, Keats and Byron in their brilliant *Letters*: all reflected upon and discussed their individual relations

Coleridge to poetry. Of these, Coleridge ranged farthest; he was probably influenced by Schlegel in his formulation of an aesthetic philosophy based on a distinction between imagination and fancy, to which Wordsworth also gave his assent. There was another equally important mission for criticism, to recover the buried riches of English renascence literature. In this quest, Coleridge,

Lamb, De Quincey, Hazlitt, Leigh Hunt, Scott (as in his lives of Dryden and of Swift), were all engaged. Coleridge, though his work is preserved only in fragments in *Biographia Literaria* and in notes on Elizabethan drama, is the most original; for, with a poet's sensitiveness and a philosopher's analytic insight, he imagines afresh the conditions of creation in another mind and traces the steps in the evolution of a masterpiece; on all estimates of Shakespeare and Wordsworth since his day he has left an abiding impress. Lamb's different way may be seen in the fact that some of his best criticism of Shakespeare is in essays on actors; the human aspect of literature was more to him than the critical. His brief inspired notes to his perfect anthology, *Specimens of the Dramatic Poets* 1808, are the high-water mark of impressionist criticism. His fine insight enables him, in his *Tales from Shakespear* 1807 (the comedies were done by his sister Mary), to retain the 'exact emphasis of the original.'

William Hazlitt 1778–1830, in works written between 1817 and 1820, *The Characters of Shakespeare's Plays*, *The English Poets*, *The English Comic Writers*, has left a body of sane, spirited, human judgment in a manner which infects the reader with the critic's own enjoyment; his standards, like Lamb's, are personal, but he takes a wider range, seeing character not in isolation, but in contact with other men and manners; he has even more of the pure zest, 'gusto' he calls it, of letters than Dryden. De Quincey, also, must have a niche here, both for his share in the elucidation of *Macbeth* and for his essays on rhetoric and style, where he formulates the illuminating distinction between the literature of knowledge and that of power.

The essay cannot be sharply divided from criticism. The magazines, *The Edinburgh*, *The Quarterly*, *Blackwood's*, *The London* and *Fraser's* provided a means of expression and sometimes a means of livelihood to writers such as Gifford, Southey, Hazlitt, Sydney Smith, Leigh Hunt, De Quincey and, later, Carlyle. Hazlitt's forceful, though not always just, review of notabilities in 1825, *The Spirit of the Age*, is only the last of a series in which brain-stuff, wit, sharp challenge, skilful overture, raciness and exactness of writing are extraordinarily abundant. The lively and copious *Noctes Ambrosianae* of John Wilson (Christopher North) appeared in *Blackwood*.

III. The essay

The Magazines

Walter Savage Landor 1775–1864 is best remembered for his *Imaginary Conversations* 1824–9, and for the extensions of them in *Pentameron* and *Pericles and Aspasia*. The speakers are men and women chosen from history, Hannibal, Marius, Godiva, Anne Boleyn, Spenser— there are hundreds of them; their speech is veined with lively human touches and with memories of idyllic scenes, but there is hardly any narrative fibre. His own independent and, in some ways, unadaptable principles are reflected; he is like Swinburne, a republican but no democrat. He is as cunning in another order of prose-writing as De Quincey, in contrast with whom he stands in the classic lucidity, lightness and plastic beauty of his expression. Thomas De

Landor

De Quincey

Quincey 1785–1859 wrote work prodigious in bulk; besides criticism, he produced long essays such as those on the Caesars and the Essenes; confessional prose, like the *Opium-Eater* and the *Autobiographical Sketches*; reviews of the works of his contemporaries, and stories and fantasias.   In these last, he is greatest; his richly wrought prose, poetry in all but regularly recurrent rhythm, is perfect in narratives such as *The English Mail-Coach*, *The Spanish Military Nun* and *The Revolt of the Tartars*, where his harmonious periods suggest, with immense power, the movement of multitudes over vast steppes and deserts, through unspeakable sufferings.   The 'prose of impassioned reverie' is seen in his *Dream Fugue* and in *Suspiria*.   The shifting cloud-matter of dreams is marshalled as logic orders it in the one; the profoundest tortures and despondencies of the mind are symbolised in the other.   He perceived a psychological correspondence between vision and 'rhythmus,' and his ample cumulative periods cohere in ceremonious patterns, falling, at the same time, with infallible music upon the ear.

Charles Lamb 1775–1834 with his delicacy and strong understanding and waywardness, remains
Lamb
unique.   The *Essays* and *Last Essays of Elia* 1820–5 are intimate revelations of his tastes, antipathies and moods.   Three or four subjects engage him chiefly: old-fashioned London scenes, such as the Temple and India house; characters who inhabit them, possessing odd twists of habit and disposition; his near relations, painted with fine penetration and forbearance; matters, too, of comic extravagance, or of imaginative fantasy, or

of pathetic wistful regret. All this is told by one who was rich in humanity, in love with life, who bore disastrous blows with fortitude. His most engaging quality, even more evident in his letters, is his humour; pun, repartee, grave exaggeration, grotesque narrative, whimsical turns of thought, reminiscent anecdote, kindly ridicule, delicate irony —he runs through the whole gamut of humour with the finest taste, and is equally sure in his pathos. His style, though intimately personal, extracts essences from many rare herbs, Jacobean prose writers, seventeenth century lyrists and dramatists; he is a connoisseur in words and prose rhythms; whether simple or elaborate, he makes them delicately flexible and adaptable to his moods. The immensely voluminous democrat William Cobbett is a more pugnacious egoist; his political thought and utterance, in his *Weekly Political Register* 1802–35, were not always strictly under control or strictly consistent, but he is saved for literature by his style, which is strong, simple and direct. In his *Rural Rides* and in his *Advice to Young Men and Young Women* 1830, where, sometimes, the softening light of memory falls upon the page, he is a classic writer, one whose sense of the purport of words is matched by economy in their use.

Cobbett

BOOK VI

THE VICTORIAN AGE

1. CURRENTS OF THOUGHT

In 1832, the energies of the romantic revival were dispersed; thought, political and religious, comes more insistently into literature, and, in spite of the poetry of Tennyson, Browning, the pre-Raphaelites and the Oxford poets, we are in an age of prose. Two main currents—with many tributaries —may be detected, the rationalist, an English tradition from Locke and Hume, confirmed in Benthamism and utilitarianism; and, on the other hand, the religious, culminating once in the catholic reaction of the Oxford movement, and, again, in the broad church party, with Maurice at its head. The rationalists are reinforced, first, by the widespread speculative doubt which Carlyle, Tennyson and Browning sought to dispel in *Sartor Resartus, In Memoriam* and *La Saisiaz*; secondly, by the vast evolutionary hypothesis of science, interpreted very largely in materialistic ways. Religious feeling was fostered by the transcendental philosophy which Coleridge unsystematically poured into the ears of clever young men at Highgate; Carlyle's ironic picture of him in the *Life of Sterling* is well known.

Carlyle, however, was the most potent apostle of the new idealism, which was our largest debt to Germany; though it did not provide him with a working faith. The Oxford movement turned back to medieval tradition by the assertion of authority in the church, by the appeal to feeling and by the use of ritual; in this last, it showed an interesting approach to the pre-Raphaelites; Morris found much of his inspiration in the Middle Ages, and the same aspect in Scott powerfully attracted Newman. In politics, we become aware of the incarnation of some of the ideas of Rousseau in governmental forms when the Reform bill was passed in 1832. In many ways, democracy was foiled of its expression; but its demands and its hopes enter largely into the works of men so diverse in outlook as Dickens, Ruskin and William Morris; the newspaper and the modern novel are the mouthpieces of the democratic state. Democracy and science join hands in trade, invention and communication; for literature, their conjunction is more significant in the fiction of Thackeray, George Eliot, Dickens and Thomas Hardy. Science produced its own masters of writing, the greatest of whom was Huxley.

2. VICTORIAN POETRY 1832–1900

As an artist, Alfred, Lord Tennyson 1809–92 worked most securely in lyric and idyllic material; he was impelled, however, by the spirit of the age, to weave contemporary thought into his art. He sought to cope with his own profound grief at the death of Arthur Hallam

Tennyson

and to bring to terms his crumbling beliefs and the new doctrines of science in *In Memoriam* 1850. He attained, finally, an optimism based on feeling, an instinctive conviction of immortality and a sense of all-pervading Divine law, which were balm to the troubled spirits of his day. This closeness to his time gives his thought a bygone air, though the craftsmanship retains its primal beauty and skill. Under the same impulse, he wrote *Idylls of the King* 1859–85, 'shadowing Sense at war with Soul.' Here are recorded the ideals and prowess of the knights of the Round Table, the organised powers of righteousness, and its disintegration, first by the guilty passion of Lancelot, next by the pursuit of the wandering fires of enthusiasm, as of the Grail, by men unfitted for the quest. The final note is, again, optimistic, as may be seen in the passage at the close on the changing of 'the old order,' and in the later poem *Merlin and the Gleam*. However lofty the ideal unfolded in them, the *Idylls* are now, in a manner, faded. If we bear in mind the art of Tennyson's predecessor Malory, it is easily seen that the fault lies in the treatment of the material; it cannot serve—Keats and Scott never tried to make it—as a vehicle for overt preaching. This judgment is confirmed when we see that the earlier-written idylls, such as *Morte d'Arthur*, with no allegorical interpolation, are of higher poetic worth. Tennyson could never quite command the large metaphysical utterance of Wordsworth and Shelley; we may note, too, that, in long poems, he is generally wanting in structural gift, though *Maud* is an exception. The conclusion is that these more ambitious works are

not likely to be the most prized; and the same
sentence would apply—were it not for the sprinkling
of magical lyrics—to *The Princess* 1847, and to the
historical dramas, with some reservation in the case
of *Becket* 1884.   FitzGerald thought that Tennyson
never advanced upon the two volumes of 1842.
Ulysses represents his classically inspired verse (including his most powerful single poem *Lucretius*) in
which he was uniformly triumphant; *Sir Galahad*
and the *Lady of Shalott* show him gleaning in the
Middle Ages, though he never proved himself a true
medievalist; *Locksley Hall* prophesies later poems of
social concern; *The Gardener's Daughter* is of the
form of village idyll to which *Enoch Arden* 1864
belongs.   *The Dream of Fair Women* is the most
exquisite of his too rare dream-galleries; 'Break,
break, break' illustrates, as does his swan-song
Crossing the Bar the Tennysonian lyric, which
crystallises deep-felt emotion round some fitting
image in nature.   His many volumes, down to the
last, *The Death of Œnone* 1892, comprise, besides
these things, the lyrical monodrama *Maud* 1855,
which, along with overstrained melodramatic and
morbid elements, embodies some of his most
passionate and subtle writing; patriotic poems,
finely tempered and stirring when celebrating heroic
action, as in *The Revenge* and *The Heavy Brigade*,
though, at times, sinking to insularity; and poems
of character, to which belong his humorous dialect
poems, *The Northern Farmer* and others.   He is a
nature poet, of the order, though not with the fulness,
of Keats; he broods expectantly before his object
until vision and reflection generate the inevitable

phrase; either in minute observation or broad atmospheric effect, nature is an element in all his verse, though it has never the overmastering importance that it has in Wordsworth and Keats. He is a great 'inventor of harmonies'; the lines to Vergil, to Milton, the blank verse of *Morte d'Arthur, Ulysses, Tithonus,* the stanzas of *The Palace of Art* and lyrics such as 'Tears, idle tears,' come instantly to mind. His vision of beauty is expressed with mastery of rhythm, phrasing, whether simple or gorgeous, sound-values, alliteration, haunting suggestion, and is adorned with innumerable allusions, the spoils of his wide and scholarly culture; and all is polished and perfected with an art only equalled by that of Pope among English poets.

Robert Browning 1812–89 shares with Tennyson the supremacy of Victorian poetry, though his fame was slower of confirmation. He was

Browning

remote from traditional schools of poetry and he had not Tennyson's flawless technique with which to win the public ear. Browning was a detached spectator, Tennyson a fellow-sufferer with his age; Browning, in a sense, was cosmopolitan; Tennyson, like Dickens, English to the core. Both were addicted to the contemporary habit —Browning more than Tennyson—of thinking religious things out in poetry; it is evident in *Christmas Eve and Easter Day* 1850; and *La Saisiaz* 1878 is Browning's *In Memoriam.* Browning proved himself the subtler intellect, and, by temperament, the more convinced optimist. His poetry reflects politics little enough, and he takes from science chiefly what can be spiritually interpreted, as in

Rabbi Ben Ezra. Of his earlier poems, *Paracelsus*
1835 remains one of his most stimulating achieve-
ments; *Sordello* 1840 completely discouraged his
public. Something was retrieved, however, by the
grace and power of *Pippa Passes* 1841, the first of
the series named *Bells and Pomegranates.* After
many dramatic lyrics and romances in this series,
and after a number of plays, the best of them *A
Blot in the 'Scutcheon* 1843, he came to his pre-
ordained form the dramatic monologue, a comprehensive soliloquy absorbing into itself surrounding
scenery and persons, and bringing all that is perti-
nent to the chosen moment by the channels of
memory, association and reflection. He employed
this form in *Men and Women* 1855, in *Dramatis
Personae* 1864, and in *Dramatic Idyls* 1879–80, in
which last, action divides the interest with analysis.
His agile curiosity, odd garnerings of knowledge,
peculiar vigilant humour and power of synthesising
all into a consistent picture are illustrated in types
of many lands and ages, as, for example, Karshish,
Fra Lippo Lippi, the bishop of St Praxed's, Mr Sludge,
bishop Blougram, Caliban and Cleon. *Cleon* and
Artemis Prologuises remind us of Browning's high
devotion to Greece, the best fruit of which was his
Balaustion's Adventure 1871; but his imagination
moved more freely and surely in the Italy of the
renascence. Though not quite a trustworthy critic,
he was keenly interested in music and art, still more
in the souls of musicians and artists; in the same
way he regarded his lovers, most of whom, signifi-
cantly, fail in their quest. All these poems give
evidence of a subtle sense of character, as indicated

by thoughts and longings before these crystallise
into action; he lays bare the soul by the application
of a sudden test; nothing could be more unlike
the long slow gradient of interest in Wordsworth's
poems. Browning is sharply conscious of detail, of
edges, of salient divisions in nature, humanity and
thought, especially if they border on the grotesque
or evil. In a later series of poems, *The Ring and
the Book* 1868-9, *Fifine at the Fair* 1872, *Red Cotton
Night-Cap Country* 1873 and *The Inn Album* 1875,
he seems to aim specifically at crushing truth out of
pestiferous accumulations of falsehood. Of these,
The Ring and the Book is his masterpiece, in respect
of constructive power, cunning detail, vivid ex-
posure of complex motive, unfaltering appropriateness
of speech and outlook to each character in the
ten-times repeated story, notably when he portrays
the four most prominent characters, Guido, Capon-
sacchi, Pompilia and the pope. His last volume
Asolando 1889 recalls his early freshness and wealth
of lyric, and echoes again his lifelong creed that
failure, evil and misery are but opportunities for
victory afforded by a far-seeing Divine Love to the
immortal soul of man. 'No weakness, no contempt'
is true of Browning as of Milton. This robust energy
and manliness, this grappling with the actual, in
order to wring from it a heightened sense of the
worth of life, this scorn of lethargy, though it may
wear the mask of morality, are likely for long to
make the poet a rare remedial and tonic companion.
As to style, though it would be a grave error to suppose that he entirely eschewed grace, sweetness and
melodic variety to challenge attention by oddities

and novelties, it is clear that his diction and
rhythm have the quality of aggressive pungent
singularity oftener than that of exquisite beauty;
he has a special fondness for the shock of the actual,
in the midst of the imaginative, picture, and for
prosaic rhythms among those of poetry. It is unfortunate that he often lays himself open to a just
charge of obscurity; it comes of over-swiftness of
thought, of excess of detail and of too great compression; but, perhaps, it is, in truth, a more serious
charge that he too often falls back into the mood of
prose.

With him may be named his wife, Elizabeth
Barrett Browning, whose exquisite *Sonnets from the
Portuguese* 1850 are inspired by a rare
passion and devotion. Her touch is
surest in lyric, especially in the lyric of sympathy,
as in *Cowper's Grave* and *The Cry of the Children*;
but she also wrote romance like *The Romaunt of
Margret* and *The Rhyme of the Duchess May*, and
celebrated the Italian struggle for liberty in *Casa
Guidi Windows* 1851, whilst her long verse novel
Aurora Leigh 1857 has passages of insight, exaltation and beauty, strongly phrased, though it exhibits
many defects of style and construction. Most of her
poems expose her extraordinary carelessness in rime.

Matthew Arnold 1822–88 seems, in his *Poems*
1853, and *New Poems* 1867, to retreat from life,
baffled by its outward complexity; a
tone of melancholy and loneliness pervades *Dover Beach*, a wistful consciousness that he
could not attain the faith which he envied in others.
This, with a deep reverence for truth and noble

Mrs Browning

Matthew
Arnold

character, inspires *Rugby Chapel* and some other poems, where a quiet beauty and rare distinction give way, at times, to a more poignant cry; the stoic resolution upon which he falls back is the basis of poems of the type of *The Last Word*. A curious beauty haunts *The Forsaken Merman*; and fine natural descriptive powers are exercised in *The Scholar Gypsy* and in *Stanzas from the Grande Chartreuse*. He shows that he is finely sensitive to the spiritual thought of other poets—Goethe, Wordsworth, Heine, Byron and Shakespeare—in *Memorial Verses*, the Obermann poems, *Heine's Grave* and the sonnet on Shakespeare. *Merope* and his other classical poems are less marked by ' excellent action,' restraint, proportion and keeping than are his admirable narratives *Sohrab and Rustum* and *Balder Dead*, with their limpid unencumbered speech, and his elegiac poems, above all *Thyrsis*.

Clough This last is an elegy on Arnold's friend and fellow-student at Oxford, Arthur Hugh Clough, a mind of the same order, whose ' piping took a troubled sound,' like Arnold's. Clough's *Bothie of Tober-na-Vuolich* 1848 has more elasticity of spirit and more humour than have any of Arnold's poems, and his lyrics, especially the memorable ' Say not the struggle naught availeth,' are inspired by stronger hopefulness of conviction.

The phrase pre-Raphaelite has reference to the colouring, the minute elaboration and the religious **The Pre-Raphaelites** mysticism of the early Italian painters. In poetry, it is a convenient title for anti-classical poets, such as the Rossettis, Morris and, in part, Swinburne. Dante Gabriel Rossetti's

translations, *Dante and his Circle* 1861, remind us
of his Italian blood; his *Poems* 1870
and *Ballads and Sonnets* 1881 give us
The Blessed Damozel, the sonnet-sequence *The House
of Life* and his London street poem *Jenny*. His
ballads—historical, as in *The White Ship* and *The
King's Tragedy*, menacing and unearthly in *Sister
Helen* and others which make use of the essentially
romantic motive 'the evil powers of nature assailing
man through his sense of beauty'—are among his
most notable work. *The House of Life* is a record
of the passion and mystery of love; sensuous as its
imagery often is, its intense emotion sets it spiritually aglow. There is no swift torrent of words,
but the molten passion is moulded into exquisite
pictorial shapes by the painter's regard for form
and composition. All Rossetti's writing has slow
fastidious distinctness, sumptuous phrasing and
close-packed imagery and subtle and varied musical
appeal. His sister, Christina Rossetti,
was much more spontaneous, as we
may see in the delicate lyrical abandon and quick
repetitions of songs such as *A Birthday*; her poems,
mostly lyrical, are unique in their blending of
opposite qualities, the power of miniature wizardry
(in *Goblin Market*), the religious ecstasy of a finely
devout spirit, the keen sense of physical beauty and
colour, and subtle simplicity in rhythm and phrasing;
she divides with Keble (*The Christian Year*) and
Newman (*The Dream of Gerontius*) the title of the
chief religious poet since Vaughan.

William Morris 1834–96 was the most voluminous
of Victorian poets, and by far (though Rossetti was

D. G. Rossetti

Christina
Rossetti

painter as well as poet) the most active in other
William
Morris decorative arts, for which he chose the
general title 'designing.' He imitated
the pictorial aspects of many other poets' work;
Rossetti, Chaucer, Tennyson, Browning and the
sagas all left some impress on him. His prevailing
inclinations were towards medieval forms, even
when he tells the classical tale, *The Life and
Death of Jason* 1867, and the twelve classical stories
which alternate with the twelve medieval and
oriental legends in *The Earthly Paradise* 1868–70.
This collection is after the fashion of *The Canterbury
Tales*, though the tellers meet in a remote imaginary
island. His earlier *Defence of Guenevere* 1858 had
a poignancy, a sense of bitter strife in the conscience,
symbolised in colours and figures of a feverish
brightness and sharpness, which disappeared from
the 'tapestry-work and low music' of *The Earthly
Paradise*. For, here, we have, instead, brilliantly
coloured shadows in a brilliantly coloured shadow
land; a large equable movement, whether in stanza
or couplet, a pervading note of melancholy, and no
humour. Yet these are memorable retellings of
famous tales, without the Tennysonian intrusions of
sermon and counsel. Greater than these, however,
are the poems, of epic rather than of romantic
temper, inspired by the northern sagas, some of
which Morris translated in prose as well as in verse.
Sigurd the Volsung 1876 has some of the berserk
force, the immense passion, the heroic battling, the
relentless spirit of the Scandinavian originals. He
undertook other translations such as the *Odyssey*,
the *Aeneid* and *Beowulf*. Of his prose romances,
some picture medieval utopias, as *The Dream of*

John Ball, others primitive Teutonic life, such as *The House of the Wolfings* 1889; all are in a simple coloured prose which has the effect of poetry.

Other poets must be more briefly named: Dobell, author of the fine ballad *Keith of Ravelston*; Aytoun, now remembered for the *Bon Gaultier Ballads*, which are humorous in intention, like *The Ingoldsby Legends* of R. H. Barham; W. M. Praed whose 'society' verse almost equals Prior's, and C. S. Calverley, a master of parody. Arthur O'Shaughnessy and Lord de Tabley wrote lyrics of fine musical power; P. J. Bailey, in the extraordinarily unequal *Festus* 1839, and R. H. Horne, in *Orion* 1843, are writers of epic verse. Coventry Patmore's *Odes* prove him a master of the theory and practice of rhythm. High thought and feeling, boldness of imagination and mastery of poetic diction win for Francis Thompson his place among the major poets.

Other Poets

Three others remain to be spoken of, one at some length—Edward FitzGerald, George Meredith and Algernon Charles Swinburne. Among the poems of Meredith, the so-called sonnets *Modern Love* give us one of his subtlest tragical studies of temperaments at war with one another. The song entitled *The Lark Ascending* has a pure and marvellously sustained melody, as has also *The Woods of Westermain*, where the music is interwoven with the doctrine set out in *Earth and Man*: that earth, which has patiently fostered many generations, is the surest source of wisdom and health, however austere the discipline. FitzGerald, in *Rubáiyát of Omar Khayyám* 1859, professed to translate the quatrains of

Meredith

FitzGerald

a Persian poet; his version is, in fact, a poem of the
nineteenth century, in an eastern setting, the finest
imaginative expression of the creed of hedonism.
FitzGerald seeks to drown the age-long questionings
as to man's fate in the cup of voluptuous content.
The questions, however, still echo through the verse
and receive sardonic rejoinders. The wistful and
ironic tone of the poem, its opulence of colour, bold
and novel imagery and the haunting music of the
rhythm and stanza give it enduring charm.

With an intensely individual temper, Algernon
Charles Swinburne 1837–1909 unites a keen sus-
ceptibility to the influence of other
Swinburne   poets.   His deepest affinity is with
Shelley, an earlier intellectual revolutionary, though
Swinburne's creed insists more on liberty than on
equality or fraternity; he has Shelley's antagonism
to priests and kings, and Landor's paganism.   The
cause of liberty and the leaders in the cause, Mazzini
and Hugo, inspire the great poems of his middle
period, *A Song of Italy* 1867, and *Songs before Sunrise* 1871.   Like Shelley, he has native kinship with
the Greek poets; it is evident in *Atalanta in Calydon*
1865 with its exquisitely musical choruses, and in
the more austere *Erechtheus* 1876.   Like Shelley's,
too, is his power of penetration into nature; his
landscapes have the same expressiveness of mood.
No English poet is to be compared with him, however, in the sense of the power and beauty and
mystery of the sea, as shown in *A Forsaken Garden*,
By the North Sea, *A Swimmer's Dream*, and many
another poem.   The spirit of rebellion, of insurgent
youth, inspires his *Poems and Ballads* 1866; while
Laus Veneris and *Dolores* show his keen sense of

feminine beauty. Nothing is hidden of the animal stirrings, the languor and revulsions of love, of passion, with its train of exaltation and bitterness, and of death, whose wide empire of quiet promises relief from the ache of intolerable desire. This exotic material, recorded in marvellously musical verse, is less prominent in the *Poems and Ballads* of 1878 and of 1889, and other volumes of lyric verse. Other themes—patriotism; ballads of the sea; a series of memorial poems, including those to Landor, Kossuth, Baudelaire (the beautiful and disturbing *Ave atque Vale*), Marlowe (*In the Bay*); sonnets on Elizabethan dramatists;—mingle with his poems of liberation. Other volumes included splendid medieval romances *Tristram of Lyonesse* 1882, and *The Tale of Balen* 1896; and also his dramatic trilogy *Chastelard* 1865, *Bothwell* 1874 and *Mary Stuart* 1881, each of which shows how lasting upon him was the influence of the Elizabethans. We may sometimes feel that he conjures too readily with the poet's symbols—stars, wind, storm, light, spray, sleep, pain, sorrow, death—and that the facile silver tones and the easy emphasis of alliteration can hardly be consonant with deeply felt passion. Yet he is a pioneer, and remains the sovereign of a new kingdom of rhythm and metrical form. In intricate and dainty forms such as the triolet and ballade, in billowy roller-like measures as in the *Hymn to Proserpine*, in the stanzas of *The Garden of Proserpine*, *Itylus* and other poems, with brief, strong closing lines, and in the transformed couplet of *Tristram* (to name only a few cases), he brought to light inexhaustible springs of new metrical art.

3. THE VICTORIAN NOVEL

Charles Dickens 1812–70 wrote best when his subjects were those of memory and observation;

Dickens

poverty oppressed his childhood and youth, and in those days he acquired intimate knowledge of the lower classes and of London street life; the imprisonment of his father, the original of Micawber, accounts for a number of pictures of debtors' prisons; his experience as a reporter took him to provincial towns, travelling by coach and sojourning in inns, and his descriptions of these mark him a successor of Fielding. His two years' stay in a solicitor's office is the source of his brilliant gallery of lawyer portraits. The everyday life of humble people, their toil, distresses, enmities, volubilities and diet, the background and atmosphere of their dwellings, are set forth with amazing vividness. He suffuses the grey and desolate realism of Crabbe with the warm colours of humour and pathos. He is always prone to force the note; none of his characters deliver themselves quite like men of this world; but whereas characters like Mrs Gamp, Micawber, Pecksniff, Gradgrind, Peggotty, Gargery and the Wellers are over-emphasised in the manner of Ben Jonson's 'humours,' they are at least a sublimation of truth; while figures such as Monk in *Oliver Twist* and Steerforth are drawn from the outside and we have no interest in them; like his plots, with their lost wills, murders and kidnappings, and some of his descriptions of the pathos of unmerited suffering, they are theatrical, a strain in Dickens which played him false in many ways. He was too ready to sacrifice probability to a situation; hence, a too persistent use of coincidence. His casual and hurried method of printing monthly parts no doubt affected the construction of his stories, as it did Thackeray's, for the worse; for, though they are crowded with incident, only rarely do they unfold themselves by an inner necessity; in this matter, his historical novels *Barnaby Rudge* 1841, and *A Tale of Two Cities* 1859, stand a little apart. He sometimes allowed his artistic conscience to be overborne by concurrence with the standards of his audience; and he did not always succeed in raising his splendidly generous hatreds of child drudgery, religious hypocrisy, legal fraud, tyrannical schools and debtors' prisons from the rank of propaganda to that of art. But, whatever his defects, there remain his abounding vitality, human sympathy, irresistible farcical fun, immense widening of the boundaries of fiction and humour, represented in five or six of his best stories, say *The Pickwick Papers* 1837–9, *The Old Curiosity Shop* 1840, *Martin Chuzzlewit* 1843, *David Copperfield* 1849–50, *Great Expectations* 1860–1 and the Christmas books.

In William Makepeace Thackeray 1811–63, the world portrayed, the art of portraying and the

Thackeray temper of the novelist are widely different from those of Dickens. Thackeray's is the world of the upper classes, of clubs, professions, London society with its more sophisticated, less open expression. His sense of character in his greater works *Vanity Fair* 1847–8, *Pendennis* 1849–50, *Henry Esmond* 1852, *The*

Newcomes 1854–5 is marvellously sure; Becky Sharp, Arthur Pendennis, the Major, Harry Foker, Esmond, Beatrix, Lady Castlewood, Colonel Newcome, all are creations original, perfectly sustained and finished; his apprehension of social atmosphere and relations, and his management of episodes are equally unerring. It is a world not of heroes—most of his attractive characters have a strain of pathetic feebleness in them—but of widespread generous qualities. There is, no doubt, an interpolation of unimpressive moralising which obtrudes itself irritatingly upon his art, and a running comment of potent ridicule or sharp irony; but this does not affect the truth of his vision, though it may, for a time, conceal the balance, sanity and true gentleness of the writer's character. The cynical tone of *Vanity Fair* softens in successive books until, in *The Newcomes*, it becomes a tender melancholy which, in the death of the colonel, expresses, with fine imaginative restraint, intense emotion on the most common of human occasions. His stories are not well composed, having rather the uncalculated episodic succession of life, just as they have its curiously fascinating blend of bitter and sweet. Some hold *Esmond* to be his masterpiece; it is an astonishing, sympathetic re-creation of the life of queen Anne's day, taking full advantage of a magnificent opportunity; perhaps the delicacy and strength of Thackeray's disposition are best shown in the solution of the difficult aesthetic and moral problems inherent in the tale. Besides these major works, he wrote much in the nature of journalism, burlesque and extravaganza, *The Yellow-plush Papers*, *Barry Lyndon* with its fine incisive

Y.   13

touch, *Codlingsby* a parody of Disraeli, *The English Humourists* (who are chosen from his favourite eighteenth century), and the delightful *Roundabout Papers*. Throughout, he expresses himself in an easy, limpid, unmannered, accomplished style.

In the case of George Eliot (Mary Ann Evans) 1819–80, as in many others of her time, ancestral faith failed and she fell back upon a 'religion of humanity'; she is almost the only philosophically trained mind among the English novelists. Her philosophy is at once her strength and her weakness; for, on the one hand, it enabled her, along with her sympathy, her fine 'intelligence of the heart,' to pierce through the single action and indicate its universal significance and its attachments for common humanity. On the other hand, the tendency to abstraction grew upon her in her later, drier novels, *Felix Holt* 1866, and *Daniel Deronda* 1876. Her recollections of people closely attached to the farms, inns and towns of the midlands by birth, breeding and religious tradition, with their narrow outlook, shrewd homely humour, domestic pride, views of duty, marriage and the like formed the staple of her surest art, and found their liveliest expression in *Adam Bede* 1859, *The Mill on the Floss* 1860, the classically constructed *Silas Marner* 1861, and *Middlemarch* 1871–2. Her own intense emotional experience made her portray life as, on the whole, a grim affair, especially for her women characters; but these earlier novels have the relief of penetrating humour and observation, as we may see in the cases of the Tulliver aunts and Mrs Poyser. Like Dickens and Thackeray, she also essayed the

George Eliot

historical novel in *Romola* 1863, a tale of Savonarola and Florence.

The novel was also the form of expression chosen by the Brontës, Charlotte and Emily, untamed spirits cribbed and confined on the edge of the Yorkshire moors. *Wuthering Heights* 1848, Emily's single novel (she also wrote some piercing verse), gives a picture of undisciplined characters, of passion sometimes exalted, sometimes ferocious, which are well sorted with 'the shrewd bleak soil' and the wild moods of nature, portrayed often with an eerie suggestion of the supernatural.

Charlotte's stories, *Jane Eyre* 1847, and *Villette* 1852, based on her own history, and *Shirley* 1849, based on her sister Emily's, are less forbidding, though mostly devoid of humour and marred by overstrained elements as in the case of the maniac's wife in *Jane Eyre*. But she had a subtle sense of the working of women's passions; the sufferings and rewards of love in women of commonplace appearance are her central concern; by the light of her own experience and intuitions, she makes an open and outspoken revelation of the heart with what Swinburne calls the 'occult inexplicable force of nature.' She has, too, in *Villette* some powerful strokes of satire. With her may be named Mrs Gaskell, whose biography of Charlotte is a masterpiece, as is also *Cranford* 1853, a finely detailed picture of a quiet rural society whose surface is ruffled by small and charming adventures; like Miss Mitford's *Our Village* 1824–32, *Cranford* has a delicate feminine grace and light humorous observation. The unfinished *Wives and Daughters* is the

13—2

best of Mrs Gaskell's other novels (*Mary Barton,
Sylvia's Lovers*), but, though they have more modern
and more tragic substance, they never recover the
perfect art of *Cranford*.

These are the major names; there remain to be
merely catalogued before we close this record of
Minor the novel with Stevenson and Meredith,
Novelists Disraeli's brilliant political stories *Con-
ingsby* 1844, *Sybil* 1845 and *Tancred* 1847; historical
novels, such as *The Last Days of Pompeii*, of Bulwer-
Lytton; the propaganda stories of Charles Reade,
such as *Hard Cash* 1863, and his one masterpiece, the
full and vivid medieval story *The Cloister and the
Hearth* 1861; fluent and pleasing sketches of
cathedral-city character and humour in Trollope's
Barchester series; the breezy Smollett-like yarns of
Marryat; pictures of the stage Irishman as in Lover's
Handy Andy and Lever's *Charles O'Malley*;
Kingsley's novel of Elizabethan seamen and Spanish
new-world treachery in *Westward Ho!* 1855, and
his delineations of social distress in *Yeast* and *Alton
Locke*; we must also chronicle *Lorna Doone*, Blackmore's great romance of Exmoor; and almost the
chief of travel-books, unless Kinglake's *Eothen* 1844
should challenge the title, Borrow's *Bible in Spain*
1843, together with his novels *Lavengro* 1851 and
The Romany Rye 1857. In these works, autobiography, a vivid sense of open-air life and adventure,
and intimate gypsy lore blend with an arresting
brilliance and tang of style. The open air is the
native habitat, also, of Richard Jefferies, as in his
Wild Life in a Southern County 1879, a successor
to Gilbert White's *Natural History of Selborne* 1789,

and a forerunner of a large and attractive modern literature in which a writer deals with such aspects of bird-, animal-, insect- or plant-life, as may fall within the range of his own close observation.

The kinds of novel are numerous, and the boundaries between them are easily obscured; but the general currents are clear. The eighteenth century novel began, in Fielding and Richardson, in the fashion of realism. The novelists of terror and Sir Walter Scott widened the range of the novel by the introduction of romance and history; in Scott's wake follow all the historical novelists and the romancers of the 'sword and cloak' school; the one genius in this company is R. L. Stevenson. Jane Austen upholds the realistic tradition; but while, in Fielding and Smollett, the typical background is that of travel, Jane Austen keeps within the domestic circle that she knew from her own experience. Dickens and Thackeray also maintain the realistic tradition, though the worlds they portray are widely different, and though both attempted the historical novel as well. To the women novelists, George Eliot and the Brontës, we owe, in all probability, a deeper strain of introspection in character, a closer psychological enquiry and a more open expression of passionate moods. Novels of propaganda have rarely attained the highest rank, though both Dickens and Charles Reade made trial of them. The work of Samuel Butler, Thomas Hardy and George Meredith has two interests; firstly, it illustrates the resolute and exact temper of science at work in fiction; secondly, it puts upon the novelist of our day the obligation to approach life with an implicit 'metaphysic,' that is to say, with a comprehensive judgment of the worth of life. Meredith speaks reassuringly and optimistically on this subject; Hardy sees man in the grip of an ironic destiny. Hardy is also the novelist who has most powerfully used the motive of the hereditary claims of the soil and atmosphere of a man's birthplace.

We may take Robert Louis Stevenson 1850–94 as the representative of the romantic novelists; he is a chronicler of adventure, mystery and surprise; R. L. Steven- sometimes he sets his tale in remote son ages and places, as in *The Black Arrow* 1888; but, for the most part, he is inspired by the memory and spell of Scottish scenes, 'the cold old huddle of grey hills' of his native country; the eighteenth century is the period of the Scottish tales, *Kidnapped, Catriona* and *Weir of Hermiston.* This last unfinished book, a torso in granite, leaves the impression of irresistible power in its chief character, going blindly to work and driving towards inevitable tragedy. Things gruesome and malignant are the themes of some of his short stories, as in his brilliant psychological fantasy *Dr Jekyll and Mr Hyde.* His essays *Virginibus Puerisque, Memories and Portraits* and *Across the Plains* are in the wake of Hazlitt; they have not the earlier writer's pungency and force, but they are wider-travelled and have a more engaging temper and humour; the delightful *Letters* are of the same order. He first won his spurs in *Treasure Island* 1882, which gives amazing definiteness to boyish imaginings of piracy and is the classic of its kind; something of the same

imaginative insight into the child-mind marks his
Child's Garden of Verse. It used to be the fashion
to call Stevenson's style artificial or precious; it
was the fruit of constant and assiduous labour, and
is a little mannered; it has, nevertheless, lucidity,
buoyancy and humour in a remarkable degree.

George Meredith 1828–1909 takes his figures
from the surviving feudalism of England and from
George the world between the commons and
Meredith the peers. He found in the classes of
high rank and deep-rooted tradition, in which the
best of the men are natural rulers, though they may
not be great thinkers, and the best of the women
are leisured, cultured, vital and witty, the scene
and matter of his art. The appendages of such a
world—scholars, tutors, solicitors, yeomen, cricketers,
prize-fighters and the rather luridly portrayed *demi-
monde*—vary and enrich the scene; while the incalculable shifts of those who hover hankeringly
at the boundaries of the set provide the theme of
exquisite high comedy, as in *Evan Harrington* 1861.
The characters are often brought together in spacious
country houses; such a company as the brothers of
Sir Austin Feverel may remind us of Peacock's
assemblies of intellectual humorists; Peacockian, too,
are the lavish praises of wine and scholarship; but
there is nothing in Peacock to compare with the
strong-shouldered, competent, game-winning Red-
worth, in *Diana of the Crossways.* Meredith has an
acute sense of the conventions of caste and his
tragedies are connected, though not always directly,
with defiances of them by characters in the earlier
novels, *The Ordeal of Richard Feverel* 1859, and

Rhoda Fleming 1865. The later books, *One of Our Conquerors* 1891, *Lord Ormont and his Aminta* and *The Amazing Marriage* 1895, are less concerned with caste than with rebellions against the tyranny of the marriage bond. Meredith is more than a mere showman of his world in action; with penetrating and ramifying insight, he tracks the dubious courses of emotion, desire, conflicts of will with reason or convention or authority. He portrays, with Shakespearean delicacy, the quick pulse and unflawed beauty of a first passion in Richard Feverel; love but the ghost of a passion in Dacier in *Diana*; egoism masquerading as love in Sir Willoughby Patterne; and he is equally authoritative on friendship and patriotism. We do not go to him for narrative— though there are sketches of swift and exciting incident, such as that of Carinthia and the mad dog in *The Amazing Marriage*—but for analysis; he is the surgeon of the social body, whose diagnosis, made with sure intuition and consummate craft, commands our acquiescence. Complexity is necessary to the full display of his skill; the minute exhibition of this complexity may account, in part, for the excesses in diction which may be justly charged against him. These are not quite the same as faults of over-compression of thought; the brilliance and sparkle of epigram, the deft counterstrokes of wit, the critical reflections, which make the reading of *Diana* a pleasing mental excitement, become too oracular and descend in too bewildering a shower in the later books. He is more than psychologist and analyst; he is an ironist, choosing his point of view and uttering his comment as the instrument of the

comic spirit. His keenest shafts are reserved not
for humanity at large, for he is an optimist; but
for vanity, egoism, sentimentalism and rigid formu-
larism; his surest aim is taken in *The Egoist* 1879;
but all his prose is shot through with irony, the
method of which, and its great literary prototypes,
are set out in the incomparable *Essay on the Comic
Spirit*. *Beauchamp's Career* 1875 is the only novel
he wrote whose development is determined by
English political ideas. Meredith seems to rise into
an ampler air on broader pinions, to view a larger
panorama, in *Emilia in England* 1864, and *Vittoria*
1866, where the almost epical matter is the strife
between Austria and Italy, and where he creates
his supreme woman figure, the artist and patriot
Emilia. To the novels, there has recently 1912 been
added the rich treasury of counsel, wit and criticism
contained in his *Letters*.

4. HISTORY, CRITICISM AND SCIENCE 1830–1900

Thomas Carlyle 1795–1881 unites the functions
of man of letters, historian and prophet. His earlier
essays are divided between the interests
Carlyle
of German romance and such bio-
graphical subjects as Burns, Samuel Johnson and
Voltaire. With *Sartor Resartus* 1834, a faintly
veiled autobiography centring about the spiritual
new birth which he owed largely to Goethe, come
into play his 'philosophico-poetical' thought and his
teeming psalmodic style. His first large historical
work was *The French Revolution* 1837, the most
brilliant of all, pictorially, whether in characters like

Mirabeau and Danton, or in vivid scenes such as the fall of the Bastille, the flight to Varennes, or the death of Louis XVI. His doctrine that history is the biography of great men (the basis, also, of his lectures *Heroes and Hero-Worship* 1840) is more fully developed in *Cromwell's Letters and Speeches* 1845, which swiftly reversed the national verdict of generations; and in *Frederick the Great* 1858–65, the work which made the largest tax on his mental energies and nervous resources. These compositions precede the modern school in their methods of research, though they exemplify Carlyle's untiring industry. He was no single-minded historian, for he sought to show how the age might best manage its affairs, to be prophet and poet as well as recorder. The prophetic and sometimes dyspeptic strain becomes more rife in *Chartism* 1839, *Past and Present* 1843, *Latter-Day Pamphlets* 1850 and *Shooting Niagara* 1867; this last is his only writing of any length after the death of his brilliant but unhappy wife in 1866. Shorn of their volcanic eloquence and graphic splendours, his precepts are two, a mystic philosophy and hard work. His mysticism, like the Earth Spirit in Goethe's *Faust*, resolves the visible universe into the mere vesture of eternal mind; urged by this thought, Carlyle assails the materialism and luxury of his 'sceptico-epicurean' generation. On the other hand, he conceived of action and toil as the only sources of bodily and spiritual health, the only solvents of doubt and misery; he had nothing but withering scorn for the expedients of ballot-boxes, Reform Bills, the dismal sciences of economics and evolution, and the 'Hebrew old-clothes' of orthodox religious belief (on this, see the *Life of Sterling*). He came to worship force, which he too easily assumed to be identical with righteousness. His prejudices and antagonisms and a certain ferocity of expression render him an untrustworthy critic of his time, and he oftener saw the truth in some lightning flash of intuition, than in the processes of philosophising; yet, something of the incalculable moral influence which Goethe forecast that he would wield may be seen in Tennyson, Dickens, Ruskin and Browning. His style, whether ruggedly colloquial or majestically eloquent, has a teeming wealth of idiom, graphic force, saturnine humour ('grisly laughter,' Meredith called it), above all, unparalleled inventiveness of phrase and imagery. Carlyle defines it himself in the chapter 'Characteristics' in *Sartor Resartus*.

Thomas Babington Macaulay 1800–59, and James Anthony Froude 1818–94, are also of the school of pictorial historians; both are modern in the wide range of research, though both are justly charged with faults, Macaulay with partisanship and advocacy, Froude with inaccuracies. Both were probably men of too strong prejudices to write impartially, if, indeed, that is ever possible. Both have added imperishable pictures to the gallery of history; Froude (who makes Henry VIII into a Carlylean hero) describes the protestant struggle with the papacy in Tudor times, with much illumination from Spanish sources; Macaulay describes the beginning of the whig supremacy in 1688. Macaulay's extraordinarily voluminous reading and tenacious memory enabled him to summon illustrative material

Macaulay and Froude

for every contingency, to fill his scenes with picturesque and convincing detail, set in relief by his brilliant, though rather metallic, expression, with short arresting sentences and antithetic clauses deftly wrought into the large fabric of the paragraph. He writes in his *History of England* 1848–55 like an orator, with strong, sometimes violent effects, splendid narrative power and fine emotional response to heroic deeds and names, just the things which, in fact, inspire his *Armada* and *The Lays of Ancient Rome*. He is rather typical of Victorian 'respectability' and contentment; he has not much subtlety or speculative gift, but he has all the sagacity and judgment which come of acquaintance with affairs. Much the same may be said of his *Essays*, which excel in the illustrative and historical aspects, though there is penetrating criticism in such an essay as that on Addison.

Mention should be made of Grote and Thirlwall, historians of Greece; of Thomas Arnold, historian of Rome; of Hallam, historian of the Middle Ages; they furthered in various ways the science of history; but we may think of Stubbs as the first representative of the modern school of history intent on minutely examining and elucidating documents before slowly and surely re-erecting—on the immovable basis of knowledge, without the loose mortar of conjecture, the false perspective of partisanship and the needless decoration of rhetoric—the edifice of man's past.

Matthew Arnold 1822–88, like Ruskin and Carlyle, is a critic of contemporary life, but his most effec-

Matthew Arnold

tive range is in the criticism of literature. He stood firmly as an opponent of 'stock romanticism' on the ground of its self-will, eccentricity, violation of restraint and proportion, want of the unity which comes of a clearly grasped central subject, its general lack of what Greece might teach us. He sought to formulate new standards; he had a keener sense of the varied beauties of literature than the *a priori* critics of the eighteenth century, but his bent is still towards ethical aspects, 'the criticism of life,' and his method is the application of preconceived tests. He is apt to make use of catchwords: 'sweetness and light,' 'higher truth and seriousness,' 'the grand style,' though he is not vague about them, never shrinking from definition. From the critic he demands disinterestedness, knowledge and justness of spirit. These sane and lofty canons are applied to many topics in his *Essays in Criticism* 1865, *Mixed Essays* 1879, *On Translating Homer* 1861, and in other books. Yet, perhaps his largest service was the suggestion of the comparative method, which should bring an enlightened knowledge of European literature to bear in judging any great work; he left it to later critics to enforce the historical point of view as well. His criticisms of the English social order were directed against its deficiencies in large ideas, and in the power (which he believed the French possessed) of applying them freshly and freely; and against philistinism and routine thinking. The wittiest of these writings is his *Friendship's Garland* 1871; his excursions in theology were less authoritative. His style has lucidity, urbanity, piquancy and, though rather full of reiteration, shows a sense of buoyancy denied to his graver verse.

John Ruskin 1819–1900 began, in his *Modern Painters* 1843–60, as critic and expositor of art.

Ruskin He was an apostle of beauty, and shared the predilection of the pre-Raphaelites for the sensitive colouring of early renascence art. He had other enthusiasms—for Turner's landscapes, for medieval architecture (the chapter in *The Stones of Venice* on 'The Nature of Gothic' sets forth his doctrine that the inspiration to work should be found in the soul of man) and for all the pageantry of sky, sea, Alps, plains, rocks and trees with their colours, surfaces and textures. He went voluminously into the abstract problems of art, and his *Seven Lamps of Architecture* 1849 (which are Sacrifice, Truth, Power, Beauty, Life, Memory, Obedience) indicates his ethical bent. About 1850, he came definitely under the influence of Carlyle, whom he revered as 'master.' Henceforth, though he never abandoned art, his criticism and thought were directed towards economics and sociology, which he sought to humanise as he sought also to stir the utilitarian and commercial age to some protest against its own ugliness and cruelty. In volumes such as *Unto this Last* 1862, *Sesame and Lilies* 1865 and the autobiographical *Fors Clavigera* and *Praeterita*, though some of his theories may be whimsical and some of his enthusiasms unbalanced, it is clear that Carlyle's prophetic mantle descended to a spirit kindred in sincerity of conviction, moral urgency, belief in the natural order as the expression of the Divine Mind—as well as in a certain imperious dogmatism of statement. His style is masterly, lucid and delightful; his long periods are marvellously harmonious and rhythmical, his diction opulent to a degree; his achievement in style is the more remarkable since he writes a modern prose; the Ciceronian tradition, in which De Quincey is still steeped, has passed away. Wherever his judgment and thought and feeling are of the quality of his craft of expression, we may hail Ruskin as the grand master of English prose of the ornate kind.

Of many critics since Ruskin we may name as a representative of scholarship Mark Pattison; and of aesthetics J. A. Symonds. Oscar Wilde illustrates the decline from aestheticism to decadence, but his *Intentions* is of worth in respect of its rare insight, witty paradox and beautifully finished prose. Walter Pater 1839–94 may stand as representative of those

Walter Pater

literary descendants of Ruskin, who are quite untouched by the ethics of Ruskin; he is a lover of strange beauty. Leonardo's *Mona Lisa*, with its baffling union of diverse qualities and remote suggestions, is the subject of a famous passage in Pater's *Studies in the History of the Renaissance*; at the close of the same book, he unfolded the ideal of being 'present always at the focus where the greatest number of vital forces unite in the purest energies,' and of 'art for its own sake.' 'For art comes to you, proposing frankly to give nothing but the highest quality to your moments as they pass, and simply for those moments' sake.' This sophisticated and over-subtle sense of beauty found its ideals less in Greece than in Rome, as we may judge from *Marius the Epicurean* 1885, and in the renascence period of Montaigne as we may

judge from *Gaston de Latour* 1896. *Appreciations*
1889 is his fullest body of critical pronouncements,
and its opening essay on 'Style' proves him a pupil
of Flaubert and a devotee of the *mot propre*. In
this spirit, he aims at writing an artist's prose, the
words pregnant by their choice and association,
delicately inlaid, suggestive by their juxtaposition of
light and shade, surprising and exciting the reader
by unexpected felicities of rhythm. In this studied
art, he has no equal. This brief survey of the
progress of criticism must close with the reminder
that criticism is constantly becoming more comprehensive and more complex. Sainte-Beuve introduced
the method of psychological estimate and minute
study of environment; other lines of its advance are
the historical method, in one direction, and, in
another, the comparative; in this last direction,
French scholars have, up to the present, led the way.

We have not much concern with these matters
except so far as they become the subjects of high and

Economics,   noble expression; we cannot do more
theology,   than note the succession of books which
science   established and developed the utilitarian philosophy (which stirred Carlyle's wrath),
from the great codifier Bentham's *Principles of
Morals and Legislation* 1780, to John Stuart Mill's
more human and sympathetic *Liberty* 1859, and
Utilitarianism 1863. His *System of Logic* 1843
touches the science of thought and is in the em-
pirical tradition of Locke and Hume. Economics is
the theme of a vast literature, from Adam Smith's
Wealth of Nations 1776 (providing a theory for
industrialism, out of which grew the *laissez-faire*

school of free competition), through Ricardo and Malthus to Ruskin and the later scientific economists. Nearly allied is Buckle's *History of Civilization* 1857, a large, stimulating, though not always convincing, study of the general laws of development of the English state.

The tractarians troubled thought much, but literature little, except in the case of John Henry Newman 1801–90; with the precise cast of his dogma and his grounds for passing over to the Roman church we are unconcerned. In his *Apologia pro Vita Sua* 1864, his intense personality sets his graceful scholarly periods aglow with an impassioned defence of principles, the fruit of long-sifted thought and acute spiritual need. Some of the finest ideals of knowledge and culture find consummate expression in his *Idea of a University* 1854, where his style, as in the best of his *Plain and Parochial Sermons,* blends precision, charm and eloquence in a fashion unparalleled in the nineteenth century.

It is inevitable that the last words of this book should deal, however briefly, with science; though science, in the main, still awaits its transmutation in the alembic of style. We can only name the direct, unpretending prose of Darwin's *Origin of Species* 1859; the solid industry and ambitious synthesis of Spencer's *First Principles* 1862, and *Principles of Biology* 1864–7; the controversial eagerness and vivid epigrammatic speech of Huxley's *Essays.* But these are enough to show that the advent of science—like the renascence three hundred years before—has shaken the whole

Y. 14

universe of thought; it admits no compromise in its pursuit of truth, and its sway is widening in all the provinces of man's endeavour. Since literature must remain firmly planted in one or another kind of experience, it is bound to take up into itself more and more of the forms and principles and ideals with which science is impregnating the soil of all human activities.

APPENDIX

The following table presents the plays of Shakespeare in approximately chronological order. Many of the dates depend upon inference and conjecture, and the whole arrangement must be regarded as provisional.

The letter M following twelve of the plays signifies that those plays are mentioned in Francis Meres's *Palladis Tamia* 1598.

The third column gives the dates of all the known quarto editions before 1623. All the plays mentioned were printed in the first folio (1623), with the exception of *Pericles* and *The Two Noble Kinsmen*. The date 1623 in the fourth column simply indicates that in those cases the earliest extant version of the play is in the first folio (1623).

The later folios are the second (1632), with Milton's verses; the third (1663) re-issued in 1664 with *Pericles*; and the fourth (1685).

Date	Play	Quartos	Folio
c. 1591–3? (revised 1597)	*Love's Labour's Lost* M	Q 1598	
c. 1591–3?	*The Two Gentlemen of Verona* M		1623
c. 1591–3? also played Gray's Inn 1594	*The Comedy of Errors* M		1623
c. 1591? revised later 1595?	*Romeo and Juliet* M	Qq surreptitious 1597, authentic 1599 and 1609	

Date	Play	Quartos	Folio
c. 1592?	*Henry VI, part i*		1623
[1] c. 1592?	*Henry VI, part ii*		1623
[2] c. 1592?	*Henry VI, part iii*		1623
1593–4?	*Richard III* M	Qq 1597, 1598, 1602, 1605, 1612, 1622	
1594?	*Richard II* M	Qq 1597, 1598, 1608 and 1615	
[3] 1593–4	*Titus Andronicus* M	Qq 1594, 1600 and 1611	
1594?	*The Merchant of Venice* M	2 quartos in 1600	
1594?	*King John* M		1623
1595?	*A Midsummer Night's Dream* M	2 quartos in 1600	
[4] 1595–6?	*The Taming of the Shrew*		1623
1596?	*All's Well that Ends Well* (if identical with Meres's *Love's Labour's Won;* but possibly later)		1623
1597	*Henry IV, part i* M	Qq 1598, 1599, 1604, 1608, 1613, 1622	
1597	*Henry IV, part ii*	Q 1600	
1598?	*The Merry Wives of Windsor*	Qq 1602 imperfect, and 1619	
1599	*Henry V*	Qq 1600 imperfect, 1602, 1608	
1599?	*Much Ado about Nothing*	Q 1600	
1600?	*As You Like It*		1623
1600–1 also acted 1602	*Twelfth Night*		1623

[1] In 1594 was printed *The first part of the Contention betwixt the two famous houses of Yorke and Lancaster.* This is not Shakespearean; but it is the basis of the play which is printed in F. 1623 as Henry VI, part ii.

[2] In 1595 was printed *The True Tragedy of Richard Duke of York and the death of Good King Henry Sixt.* This is not Shakespearean; but is the basis of F. 1623, Henry VI, part iii.

[3] Authorship disputed.

[4] Adapted from *The Taming of a Shrew* printed in 1594.

Date	Play	Quartos	Folio
1601?	*Julius Caesar*		1623
1602	*Hamlet*	Qq 1603 imperfect; also 1604 and 1611	
1603?	*Troilus and Cressida*	Q 1609	
1604	*Othello*	Q 1622	
1604	*Measure for Measure*		1623
1605–6	*King Lear*	2 quartos 1608	
1606	*Macbeth*		1623
1607	*Timon of Athens* (in part)		1623
1607	*Pericles* (in part)	Qq mangled form 1609; 1611 and 1619. In folio 1664, not in folio 1623	
1608	*Antony and Cleopatra*		1623
1608–9	*Coriolanus*		1623
1610–11	*Cymbeline*		1623
1610–11	*The Winter's Tale*		1623
1611	*The Tempest*		1623
1612	*The Two Noble Kinsmen* (in part)	Q 1634, not in folio 1623	
1613?	*Henry VIII* (in part)		1623

Recent researches seem to indicate that the following quartos in the above lists bear fictitious dates, and were actually printed in 1619. In each case the quarto affected is the one without the printer's address.

A Midsummer Night's Dream	Q	1600
The Merchant of Venice	Q	1600
Henry V	Q	1608
King Lear	Q	1608

Vide Pollard, *Shakespeare Folios and Quartos.*

INDEX

NOTE. *Italic figures indicate the principal references. Dates of the plays of Shakespeare are given in the Appendix.*

Abbot, The 1820 170

A. B. C. (Chaucer) c. 1370 27

Absalom and Achitophel 1681 118

Across the Plains 1892 198

Adam Bede 1859 194

Adam Smith 1723–90, *Wealth of Nations* 1776 208

Addison, Joseph 1672–1719 112, Essays *116*, 117, 121, 124, 129, 134, 143, 204

Adonais 1821 100, 163, 164, 165

Advancement of Learning, The 1605 67

Advice to a Dissenter 1687 113

Advice to Young Men and Young Women 1830 176

Aelfric *fl.* 1006 12, 13

Aeneid, The 20, 51, 187

Affliction of Margaret, The 1804? ptd 1807 154

Ajax and Ulysses, The Contention of 1640 94

Akenside, Mark 1721–70, *The Pleasures of Imagination* 1744 135

Alastor 1815 ptd 1816 163, 165

Albion's England 1586–1602 63

Alchemist, The 1610 ptd 1612 90

Alcuin 735–804 7, 10

Aldhelm 640?–709 10

Alexander and Campaspe 1580 ptd 1584 76

Alexander's Feast 1697 119

Alexander, Sir William 1567?–1640 53

Alfred, King 849–901 2, 6, 10, 11

Alice du Clos 1825? 158

All Fools 1599 ptd 1605 92

All for Love 1677 ptd 1678 143

Alliterative poems of the 14th century *23*

Alma 1718 120

Alphonsus 1589 ptd 1599 77

Alton Locke 1850 196

Alysoun c. 1310 23

Amazing Marriage, The 1895 200

Amelia 1751 131

American Speeches 1774–5 128

Amis and Amiloun 1275–1300 20

Amoretti 1595 53

Amyot (trans. Plutarch 1559) 72

Anacreon 96

Anatomy of Melancholy, The 1621 68

Anatomy of the World, An 1611 62

Ancient Mariner, The 1798–1817 149, 156, 157

Ancren Riwle c. 1210 *33*

Andreas 8, 22

Andrewes, Lancelot 1555–1626 107

Andrew of Wyntoun's *Cronykyl* c. 1406 39

Anelida and Arcite c. 1380 27

Anglo-Saxon Chronicle, The closes 1154 9, 11, 13, 20, 33

Annals of the Parish 1821 132

Annus Mirabilis 1666–7 118

Anselm 1033–1109 15

Anti-Jacobin, The 1797–8 134, 170

Antonio and Mellida 1599 ptd 1602 92

Antony and Cleopatra 143

Apologia pro Vita Sua 1864 209

Apology for Poetry 1581? pub. 1595 69

Appreciations 1889 208

Arbuthnot, Dr John 1667– 1735 115, 121, 131

Arcades 1633 ptd 1645 100

Arcadia pub. 1590 71

Areopagitica 1644 105

Arethusa 1820 166

Argument against abolishing Christianity, An 1708 114

Ariosto 1474–1533 (*Orlando Furioso* 1516) 52, 56, 60

Aristotle 113, 120

Armada, The 1848 204

Arnold, Matthew 1822–88 31, 100, 151, 165, 168 Poems *184*, 185, Prose *204*, 205

Arnold, Thomas 1795–1842 204

Arraignment of Paris, The c. 1581 ptd 1584 77

Art of English Poesie, The 1589 69

Artemis Prologuizes 1842 182

Arthur, King 17, 20, 21

Ascham, Roger 1515–68 44, 47, 66

Asser's *Life of Alfred* c. 900 10

Asolando 1889 183

Astrolabe, The 1391 35

Astrophel and Stella 1580–4 ptd 1591 52

As You Like It 72, 84

Atalanta in Calydon 1865 189

Atheist's Tragedy, The 1603 ptd 1611 92

Auchinleck MS c. 1320 22

Aurora Leigh 1857 184

Austen, Jane 1775–1817 132, *133*, 134, 170, 197

Autobiographic Sketches 1834 ff. 175

Autobiography (Gibbon) pub. 1796 125, 128

Ave atque Vale 1867 190

Awyntyrs of Arthur 1350–1400 19, 23

Ayenbite of Inwit, The c. 1340 33

Aytoun, William Edmond- stoune 1813–65, *Bon Gaultier Ballads* 1845 188

Bacon, Francis, Lord Verulam 1561–1626 46, 47, *67*, *68*, 69, 70, 109

Bacon, Roger 1214?–94 15, 77

Bailey's *Festus* 1839 188

Balaustion's Adventure 1871 182

Balder Dead 1855 185

Bale, John 1495–1563 75

Ballad of Agincourt 1605 64

Ballad of Charity 1770 138

Ballads and Sonnets (Rossetti) 1881 186

Ballads, The 41, 117, 136

Barbour, John 1316?–95, *Brus* c. 1376 39

Barclay, Alexander 1475?–1522, *Ship of Fools* 1509 38

Bard, The 1757 136

Barham, Richard Harris 1788– 1845, *Ingoldsby Legends* 1840 188

Barnaby Rudge 1841 192

Barnes, Barnabe 1569?–1609 53

Barons' Wars, The 1603 63

Barrow, Isaac 1630–77 107

Barry Lyndon 1846 193

Bartholomew Fair 1614 ptd 1631 90

Bartolomaeus Anglicus *fl.* 1230– 50 35

Battle of Brunanburh, The 937 11

Battle of Lewes, The 1264 23

Battle of Maldon, The 991 12

Battle of the Books, The ptd 1704 114

Baxter, Richard 1615–91, *Saints' Everlasting Rest* 1650 107

Beauchamp's Career 1875 201

Beaumont, Francis 1584–1616 59, 92, 93

Beaumont, Joseph, 1616–99, *Psyche* 1642 65

Beaux' Stratagem, The 1707 144

Becket 1884 180

Beckford, William 1759–1844, *Vathek* 1786 132

Beddoes, Thomas Lovell 1803–49 169

Bede 673–735, *Ecclesiastical History of the English Race* 731 7, 10, 11, 20

Beggar's Opera, The 1728 144

Behn, Mrs Aphra 1640-89 97

Bells and Pomegranates 1841–6 182

Benoît de Ste More *fl.* 1165 28

Bentham, Jeremy 1748–1832 208

Beowulf 1, *2*, 3, 4, 9, 12, 18, 187

Beppo 1818 162

Berkeley, George 1685–1753 123

Bermudas, The 1650-2 ptd 1681 98

Berners, Lord (John Bourchier) 1467–1533 36, 44, 70

Bestiary c. 1130 15

Bevis of Hampton 1300–25 19

Bible in Spain, The 1843 196

Bible, The 34, 35, 45

Biographia Literaria 1817 172, 173

Birthday, A 1857 186

Black Arrow, The 1888 198

Blackmore, Sir Richard d. 1729 120

Blackmore, Richard Doddridge 1825–1900, *Lorna Doone* 1869 196

Blackwood's Magazine founded 1817 147, 174

Blake, William 1757–1827 138 Poems *140*, 141

Blessed Damozel, The c. 1847 ptd 1856 and 1870 186

Blickling Homilies c. 975 12

Blind Harry's *Wallace* 1470–80 39

Bloomfield, Robert 1766–1823, *Farmer's Boy* 1800 169

Blot in the 'Scutcheon, A 1843 182

Boccaccio 1313–75 28, 29, 119

Bodel, Jean *fl.* 1200 19

Boece 1377–81 34

Boethius c. 470–525, *De Consolatione Philosophiae* 11, 34

Boileau 1636–1711, *L'Art Poétique* 1674 120

Bolingbroke, Viscount (Henry St John) 1678–1751 121, 123

Bon Gaultier Ballads 1845 188

Book of the Duchess, The 1369 27

Book of Common Prayer, The 45

Book of Philip Sparrow, The before 1508 38

Borrow, George 1803–81 196

Bossuet 1627–1704 107

Boswell, James 1740–95 *125*, 126

Bothwell 1874 190

Borough, The 1810 139

Bothie of Tober-na-Vuolich, The 1848–9 185

Bourdaloue 1632–1704 107

Breton, Nicholas 1545?–1629? 54

Bright, John 1811–89 43

Brignall Banks 160

Britain's Ida (attributed to Phineas Fletcher) 1628 *59*

Britannia 1586–1607 69

Britannia's Pastorals 1613–15 64

Broken Heart, The 1629 ptd 1633 94
Brome, Richard d. 1652? 94
Brontë, Charlotte 1816–55 195, 197
Brontë, Emily Jane 1818-48 195, 197
Brothers, The (Wordsworth) 1800 155
Brougham Castle 1807 153, 156
Browne of Tavistock, William 1591–1643? 64
Browne, Sir Thomas 1605–82 *108, 109,* 110, 111, 113
Browning, Elizabeth Barrett 1806–61 184
Browning, Robert 1812–89 147, 177 Poems *181,* 182, 183, 184, 189, 203
Bruno, Giordano 1550?–1600 47
Brut c. 1200 and c. 1250 17
Buckle, Henry Thomas 1821-62, *History of Civilisation* 1857 209
Bulwer-Lytton, Edward 1803–73 196
Bunyan, John 1628–88 43, 57, 65, 104, *108,* 110, 129
Bürger's *Lenore* 1774 160
Burke, Edmund 1729–97 115, *128,* 129, 170
Burnet, Gilbert 1643–1715, *History of my own Times* pub. 1723–34 127
Burney, Frances (Mdme D'Arblay) 1752–1840, *Journal* 125, *Evelina* 133
Burns, Robert 1759–96 40, 61, 135, 138 Poems *141,* 142, 157, 166, 201
Burton, Robert 1577–1640, *Anatomy of Melancholy* 1621 68, 131
Bussy d'Ambois 1598? ptd 1607 92
Butler, Joseph 1692–1752, *Analogy* 1736 123

Butler, Samuel 1612–80 71, *120*
Butler, Samuel 1835–1902 197
Byrd, William 1538?–1623 54
Byron, George Gordon, Lord 1788–1824 59, 134, 147, 150, 158 Poems *161,* 162, 169, 172, 185
By the North Sea 1880 187

Cadenus and Vanessa 1713 120
Caedmon *fl.* 670 7
Cain 1821 162
Caleb Williams 1794 132
Calverley, Charles Stuart 1831–84 188
Calvin's *Institutes* 1536 (trans. 1559) 48
Camden, William 1551–1623, *Britannia* 1586–1607 (trans. by Holland 1610) 69
Campaign, The 1704 134
Campbell, Thomas 1777–1844 134, 140
Campion, Thomas 1567?–1620, Poems 54, Criticism 70
Canning, George 1770–1827 170
Canterbury Tales, The begun c. 1387 27, *29,* 37
Cap and Bells, The 1819 168
Capgrave, John 1393–1464, *Chronicle* 1450 42
Captain Singleton 1720 118
Cardinal, The lic. 1641 ptd 1652 94
Carew, Thomas 1595–1639? *Poems* 1640 62, 91, 96
Carlyle, Thomas 1795–1881 170, 174, 177, 178, *201,* 202, 203, 206, 208
Casa Guidi Windows 1851 184
Castara 1634 97
Castaway, The 1798 140
Castiglione (*Il Cortegiano* 1528) 72
Castle of Indolence, The 1748 135

Castle of Otranto, The 1764 132
Castle of Perseverance, The c. 1430 74
Castle Rackrent 1800 132
Catiline 1611 90
Cato 1713 143
Catriona 1893 198
Catullus 96
Cavendish, George 1500–61? 43
Caxton, William 1421?–1491 43, 44
Cenci, The 1819 ptd 1820 143, 165
Centuries of Meditations c. 1670 ptd 1908 97
Cervantes 1547–1616 131
Chamberlayne, William 1619–89, *Pharonnida* 1659 98
Changeling, The c. 1623 ptd 1653 92
Chanson de Roland, Le 1000–1100 18
Chapman, George 1559?–1634 48, 49, 59, *60*, 61, 91, *92*, 166
Chapman's *Iliad* 1598–1611 60, 166
Chapman's *Odyssey* 1616 60
Character of a Trimmer 1685 ptd 1688 113
Characters 71
Characters of Shakespeare's Plays, The 1817 173
Charles O'Malley 1841 196
Chartism 1839 202
Chastelard 1865 190
Chatterton, Thomas 1752–70 136, 138
Chaucer, Geoffrey 1340?–1400 14, 15, 18, 20, 23 Poems *26*, 27, 28, 29, 30, 31, 33 Prose *34*, 35, 37, 38, 39, 40, 41, 42, 46, 49, 79, 114, 119, 136, 187
Cheke, Sir John 1514–57 47
Chesterfield, Earl of (Philip Dormer Stanhope 1694–1773), *Letters* 1737 ff. 124

Chester plays 1390–1420, MSS 1591–1607 74
Chettle, Henry ?–1607? 92
Chevy Chase 70
Childe Harold 1812–17 161
Childe Maurice 42
Child's Garden of Verses, A 1885 198
Chillingworth, William 1602–44, *Religion of Protestants* 1638 105
Choice, The c. 1665 97
Chrestien de Troyes *fl.* 1160–80 21
Christabel 1797 and 1800 ptd 1816 16, 139, 156, *158*
Christian Morals ptd 1716 109
Christmas Eve and Easter Day 1850 181
'Christopher North' (John Wilson 1785–1854) 174
Christ's Victory and Triumph 1610 *65*
Churchill, Charles 1731–64, *Rosciad* 1761 134
Churchyard, Thomas 1520?–1604 52
Cicero 113, 207
Cinthio 1504–73 (*Hecatommithi* 1565) 77
Citizen of the World, The 1760–2 123
City Madam, The 1619 ptd 1658 93
Civil Government 1690 106
Civil Wars, The 1595–1623 63
Clare, John 1793–1864, *Descriptive Poems* 1820 169
Clarissa Harlowe 1748 130
Cleanness c. 1350 24
Cleon 1855 182
Clerk Saunders 41
Cloister and the Hearth, The 1861 196
Cloud, The 1820 166
Clough, Arthur Hugh 1819–61 185

Cobbett, William 1762–1835 43, 176
Codlingsby (in *Punch*) 1847 194
Coeur de Lion 1275–1300 20
Coleridge, Hartley 1796–1849 156, 170
Coleridge, Samuel Taylor 1772–1834 137, 138, 139, 146, 147, 148, 149, 151, 152, 153 Poems *156*, 157, 158, 159 Criticism 172, 173, 177
Colin Clout c. 1519 38
Colin Clout's Come Home Again 1591 58, 65
Collier, Jeremy 1650–1726, *Immorality of the Stage* 1698 144
Collins, William 1721–59 135, 137
Colubriad, The 1782 pub. 1806 140
Comedy of Errors, The 82
Complaint of Buckingham 1563 56
Complaint of Rosamond 1592–1623 63
Complaint of the Black Knight, The 38
Complaint to his Empty Purse, The 1399? 30
Complaint unto Pity c. 1372 27
Complaints 1591 58
Compleat Angler, The 1653 110
Comus 1634 ptd 1637 77, 92, *100*, 103
Conduct of the Allies, The 1711 114
Confessio Amantis 1390 32
Confessions of an English Opium-Eater 1821 175
Congreve, William 1670–1729 112, 113, 115, 144
Coningsby 1844 196
Conquest of Granada, The 1669–70 143
Conscious Lovers, The 1722 144
Constable, Henry 1562–1613 53

Cooper's Hill 1642 97
Coriolanus 87, 88
Cornish dialect plays, before 1300, MS 15th cent. 74
Corn-Law Rhymes 1831 170
Coronach 160
Coryat, Thomas 1577?–1617, *Coryat's Crudities* 1611 69
County Guy 160
Court of Love, The before 1500 38, 39
Coventry plays 1416, MS 1468 74
Coverdale, Miles 1488–1568 45
Cowley, Abraham 1618–67, Poems 96, 98 *Essays* 1667 109
Cowper's Grave 1838 184
Cowper, William 1731–1800 60 Letters 125, 135, 136, 138 Poems *139*, 157
Crabbe, George 1754–1832 134, *139*, 170, 191
Cranford 1853 195, 196
Cranmer, Archbishop 1489–1556 45
Crashaw, Richard 1613?–49 97
Crist 8
Crist and Satan 7
Critic, The 1779 144, 145
Cromwell's Letters and Speeches 1845 202
Cronica Tripartita 1400 32
Crossing the Bar 1889 180
Crotchet Castle 1831 172
Cry of the Children, The 1843 184
Cuckoo and the Nightingale, The 1403–10 38
Cudworth, Ralph 1617–88, *True Intellectual System of the Universe* 1678 105
Curse of Kehama, The 1810 159
Cursor Mundi 1300 22
Cynewulf *fl.* 750 7, *8*, 9
Cypress Grove, A 1623 109

Daffodils 1804 pub. 1807 153

Dame Siriz c. 1260 23

Damon and Pythias 1564 ptd 1571 76

Daniel 7

Daniel Deronda 1877 194

Daniel, Samuel 1562–1619 Poems 53, 54, *63*, 64 Criticism 70, 91

Dante 1265–1321 50, 137

Dante and his Circle 1861 186

Dares the Phrygian 28

Dark Ladye, The 1798 ptd 1834 158

Darkness 1816 161

Darwin, Charles Robert 1809–82, *Origin of Species* 1859 209

Darwin, Erasmus 1731–1802, *Loves of the Plants* 1789 134

Davenant, Sir William 1606–68 94, 98

David and Bethsabe 1589 ptd 1599 77

David Copperfield 1849–50 192

Davideis 1656 98

Davies, Sir John 1569–1626 60

Davison's *Poetical Rhapsody* 1602 54

Day, John *fl.* 1606 92

Death of Dr Swift, The 1731 ptd 1739 120

Death of Œnone, The 1892 180

Death's Jest Book 1825–49 ptd 1850 and 1851 169

De Augmentiis Scientiarum 1623 67, 70

Decameron 1350 29

Decline and Fall of the Roman Empire, The 1766–88 *127*

De Consolatione Philosophiae 11, 34

Defence of Guenevere, The 1858 187

Defence of Poetry 1821 ptd 1840 165, 172

Defoe, Daniel 1660?–1731 112, *117, 118*, 129

Deistic controversy, The 122

Dejection 1802–17 159

Dekker, Thomas 1570?–1641? Songs 54 Prose 71, 90 Plays 92

Delia 1591 and 1592–1623 53

Deloney, Thomas 1543?–1607? 71

Denham, Sir John 1615–69 98

Dennis, John 1657–1734 114

Deor's Lament 1

De Proprietatibus Rerum c. 1231 trans. 1398 35

De Quincey, Thomas 1785–1859 148, 173, 175 Essays *175*, 207

De Regimine Principum 1413 37

Descriptive Sketches 1793 151

Deserted Village, The 1770 135

Desportes 1546–1606 52

Destruction of Britain, The c. 560 10

de Tabley, Lord 1835–95 188

Diana of the Crossways 1885 199, 200

Dialogues between Hylas and Philonous 1713 123

Dialogues of Gregory the Great 11

Dickens, Charles 1812–70 133, 178, 181 Novels *191*, 192, 194, 197, 203

Dictionary 1755 (Johnson) 126

Dictys the Cretan 28

Dirge in Cymbeline 1749 137

Discourse of English Poetry 1586 69

Discoveries 1641 70

Dispensary, The 1699 120

Disraeli, Benjamin, Lord Beaconsfield 1804–81 194, 196

Divine Poems (Donne) ptd 1633 62

Dobell, Sydney 1824–74 188

Dolores 1864 189

Don Juan 1818–22 161, 162

Donne, John 1573–1631 Poems *61* Satires 65 Influence 95, 96, 97 Sermons 107

Don Quixote 1605–15 72, 120

Dorset, Earl of (Charles Sackville) 1638–1706 97, 120

Douglas, Gavin 1474?–1522 40, 41

Dover Beach 1867 184

Dowland, John 1563?–1626 54

Dowsabel 1593–1619 64

Dr Faustus 1588 ptd 1604 78

Dramatic Idyls 1879–80 182

Dramatis Personae 1864 182

Drapier's Letters 1724 115

Drayton, Michael 1563–1631 49, 53, 54, 59 Poems *63, 64,* 71, 79, 92, 97

Dream, The 1816 161

Dream Fugue 1849 175

Dream of Fair Women, A 1833–42 180

Dream of John Ball, A 1888 188

Dream of the Rood, The 8

Dream Pedlary ptd 1851 169

Dr Jekyll and Mr Hyde 1886 198

Drummond of Hawthornden, William 1585–1649 53, 60, 90

Dryden, John 1631–1700 38, 66, 95, 96, 97, 98, 112 Prose *113* Poems *118,* 119, 120, 122, 126, 143, 144, 168, 172

Du Bartas 1544–90 60

Du Bellay 1525–60 52

Duchess of Malfi, The 1614? ptd 1623 93

Dunbar, William 1465?–1530? 34, *40,* 41, 142

Dunciad, The 1728–42 121

Duns Scotus 1265?–1308? 15

Dunstan 924–988 12

Dyer, John 1700?–58, *Grongar Hill* 1727 124, 135

Dyer, Sir Edward d. 1607 54

Earle, John 1601?–65, *Microcosmographie* 1628 71

Earth and Man 1883 188

Earthly Paradise, The 1868–70 187

Eastward Ho! 1605 92

Edgeworth, Maria 1767–1849 132

Edinburgh, The founded 1802 147, 174

Edward II 1592 ptd 1594 and 1598 78, 79

Edwards, Richard 1523?–66 76

Egoist, The 1879 201

Eikonoklastes 1649 105

Elegy in a Country Churchyard 1751 135, 136, 137

Elegy to the Memory of an Unfortunate Lady 1717 121

Elegy on Donne 1633 96

Elene 8

Eliot, George (Mary Ann Evans) 1819–80 178 Novels *193,* 194, 197

Elizabethan classical translations *59, 72*

Elizabethan lyric poetry *54*

Elizabethan patriotic poetry *63*

Elliott, Ebenezer 1781–1849 170

Ellis, George 1753–1815 170

Eloisa to Abelard 1717 121

Elyot, Sir Thomas 1499–1546 43

Emblems 1635 97

Emilia in England 1864 201

Emma 1816 133

Endymion and Phoebe 1594 59

Endymion (Keats) 1818 148, 166

Endymion (Lyly) 1585 ptd 1591 76

Eneydos 1490 40

England's Helicon 1600 54

England's Heroical Epistles 1597–1615 64

English Bards and Scotch Reviewers 1809 134, 161
English Comic Writers, The 1819 173
English Humourists, The 1851 ptd 1853 194
English Mail-Coach, The 1849 175
English Poets, The 1818 173
Enoch Arden 1864 180
Eothen 1844 196
Epipsychidion 1821 163
Epistle to the Lady Margaret 1603 63
Epistles and Satires (Pope) 1733 –39 121
Epitaphium Damonis 1639–40 100
Epithalamium 1595 53, 58
Erasmus 1466–1536 45, 47
Erechtheus 1876 189
Essay Concerning Human Understanding, An 1690 106
Essay of Dramatic Poesy, An 1668 114
Essay on Criticism, An 1711 120
Essay on Man, An 1733 121
Essay on the Comic Spirit, An 1877 pub. 1897 201
Essays in Criticism, 1865 205
Essays 1597–1625 (Bacon) 67, 69
Essays (Macaulay) 1825 ff. 204
Essays of Elia 1820–5 175
Estate, The c. 1665 97
Etherege, Sir George 1635?–91, *Man of Mode* 1676 144
Euganean Hills, The 1818 163
Eugene Aram 1829 169
Euphues 1579 70
Euphues and his England 1580 70
Euphuism 44, 70
Evan Harrington 1861 199
Evelina 1778 132
Evelyn, John 1620–1706, *Diary* 1641–1705 107

Eve of St Agnes, The 1819 pub. 1820 146, 148, 167
Eve of St Mark, The 1819 pub. 1848 167
Everyman before 1490 ptd 1509– 30 74
Every Man in his Humour 1598 ptd 1601 90
Excursion, The 1814 150, 153
Exodus 7, 8
Expostulation (Cowper) 1782 139
Expostulation and Reply 1798 153
Fables (Gay) 1727 vol. ii 1738 120
Fables of Aesop c. 1476–86 40
Fables, Ancient and Modern (Dryden) 1700 38, 119
Fabyan's Chronicle c. 1510 ptd 1516 42
Faerie Queene, The 1590–96 53, 55, 56, 58
Fair Annie 41
Fairfax, Edward d. 1635, trans. of *Gerusalemme Liberata* 1600 60
Faithful Shepherdess, The 1608 ptd c. 1610 91
Falkland, Lord (Lucius Cary) 1610?–43 105
Falls of Princes, The c. 1435 pub. 1494 37, 50
Fancy 1819 pub. 1820 168
Fancy, The 1820 169
Farewell to Norris and Drake 1589 63
Farquhar, George 1678–1707 144
Fatal Sisters, The 1768 136
Fates of the Apostles 8
Fears in Solitude 1798 158
Felix Holt 1866 194
Feltham, Owen 1602?–68, *Resolves* 1620? 69

Female Phaeton, The ptd 1722 134

Fergusson, Robert 1750–74, *Poems* 1773 141

Ficino 1433–99 55

Fielding, Henry 1707–54 129, *130*, 131, 134, 160, 170, 191, 197

Field, Nathaniel 1587–1633 94

Fifine at the Fair 1872 183

Fig for Momus, A 1589 65

Fight at Finnsburh, The 4, 12

Filmer, Sir Robert d. 1653, *Patriarcha* pub. 1680 106

Filostrato c. 1338 28

First Principles 1862 209

Fisher, Bishop 1459–1535, *Sermons* c. 1509 43

Fitzgeffrey, Charles 1575?–1638 63

FitzGerald, Edward 1809–83 180, 188, 189

Flaming Heart, The 1652 97

Flaubert 1821–80 208

Fletcher, Giles 1588?–1623 *65*

Fletcher, John 1579–1625 64, *93*

Fletcher, Phineas 1582–1650 *56*

Florio, John 1553?–1625, *Montaigne* 1603 72

Floris and Blanchefiour 1275–1300 20

Flower and the Leaf, The c. 1450 38

Flowers of Sion 1623 60

Ford, John 1586–1640? 94, 130

Forest, The 1616 91

Forsaken Garden, A 1878 189

Forsaken Merman, The 1849 185

Fors Clavigera 1871 ff. 206

Fortescue, Sir John 1394?–1476? 43

Fortunes of Nigel, The 1822 171

Four Books of Airs (Campion) 1601–17 54

Four Elements, The c. 1515 ptd 1519 74

Four Hymns (Spenser) 1596 55

Four P. P., The c. 1544 75

Fox and the Wolf, The c. 1260 23

Foxe, John 1516–87, *Book of Martyrs* 1563 48

Fragment from the Recluse 1814 153

France 1798 159

Francis, Sir Philip 1740–1818 125

Fraser's Magazine founded 1830 174

Fraunce, Abraham *fl.* 1587–1633 55

Frederick the Great 1858–65 202

French Revolution, The 1790 (Burke) 128

French Revolution, The 1837 (Carlyle) 201

Friar Bacon and Friar Bungay 1589 ptd 1594 77

Friendship's Garland 1871 205

Froissart's *Chronicles*, Berners's trans. c. 1523 36, 44

Frost at Midnight 1798 158

Froude, James Anthony 1818–94 203

Fudge Family in Paris, The 1818 169

Fulke Greville, Lord Brooke 1554–1628 61

Fuller, Thomas 1608–61 107

Gaimar, Geoffrey *fl.* 1140 15

Gallathea 1584 ptd 1592 77

Galt, John 1779–1839, *Annals of the Parish* 1821 132

Gammer Gurton's Needle c. 1550 ptd 1575 76

Gardener's Daughter, The 1842 180

Garden of Cyrus, The 1658 109

Garden of Florence, The 1821 169

Garden of Proserpine, The 1866 190

Garden, The (Marvell) c. 1651 ptd 1681 98

Garrick, David 1716–79 140, 143

Garth, Sir Samuel 1661–1719, *Dispensary* 1699 120

Gascoigne, George 1525?–77 *52*, 76

Gaskell, Mrs Elizabeth Cleghorn 1810–65 195, 196

Gaston de Latour 1896 208

Gaudeamus Igitur 42

Gawayne and the Grene Knight c. 1350 23, 24

Gay, John 1685–1732 115, 120, 121, 134, 144

Genesis 7, 8

Genesis and Exodus c. 1250 16

Geoffrey of Monmouth's *History* c. 1136 15, 21

Gesta Romanorum in English 1425–50 ptd c. 1472–5 32

Geste Historyale of Troy c. 1360 28

Giaour, The 1813 162

Gibbon, Edward 1737–94 125, *127*, 128, 170

Gifford, William 1756–1826 174

Gildas 516?–570? 10, 13, 20

Giraldus Cambrensis 1146?–1220? 15

Glaucus and Scylla 1589 59

Goblin Market 1859 ptd 1862 186

Godwin, William 1756–1836, *Caleb Williams* 1794 132 *Political Justice* 1793 152, 164

Goethe 1749–1832 185, 201, 202, 203

Golding, Arthur 1536?–1605?, *Metamorphoses* 1567 60

Goldsmith, Oliver 1728–74 Essays 123 Novel 131, 134, 135 Poems 136, 139 Plays 145

Gondibert 1651 98

Good-Natured Man, The 1768 145

Good Thoughts in Bad Times 1645 and 1646 107

Googe, Barnabe 1540–94 52

Gorboduc 1562 ptd 1565 and 1570 76

Gosson, Stephen 1554–1624, *School of Abuse* 1579 69

Governor, The 1531 43

Gower, Sir John 1325?–1408 31, *32*, 33

Grace Abounding 1666 108

Granville, George, Lord Lansdowne 1667–1735 120

Gray, Thomas 1716–71 98, Letters 124, 126, 135 *Elegy* 1751 136, 137

Great Expectations 1860–61 192

Greene, Robert 1560?–92 Songs 54 Novels 71 Plays 77, 80

Green, Matthew 1696–1737, *The Spleen* 1737 120

Greville, Fulke, Lord Brooke 1554–1628 61

Griselda (Chaucer) after 1373 42

Grocyn, William 1446?–1519 47

Grongar Hill 1727 120, 135

Grosseteste, Robert d. 1253 15

Grote, George 1794–1871 204

Guardian, The 1713 123

Guevara's *Dial of Princes* 1529, Berners's trans. 1534 70

Guido delle Colonne *fl.* 1270–87 28

Guillaume de Lorris *fl.* 1237 27

Guillaume de Machault c. 1300–77 31

Guilpin's *Skialethia* 1598 65

Gulliver's Travels 1726 *115*

Gull's Horn Book, The 1609 71

Guthlac 8

Guy Mannering 1815 171

Guy of Warwick 1300–25 19

Habington, William 1605-54 97

Hajji Baba 1824 172

Hakluyt, Richard 1552?-1616, *Principal Navigations* 1589-1600 49, 69

Hales, John 1584-1656 105

Halifax, Earl of (George Savile) 1633-95 113

Hallam, Arthur Henry 1811-33 178

Hallam's *Middle Ages* 1818 204

Hall, Joseph 1574-1656, *Virgidemiarum* 1597 65

Hall's *Chronicle* c. 1530 42

Hamlet 50, 78, 84, 88

Handlynge Sinne 1303 22

Handy Andy 1842 196

Happy Warrior, The 1807 155

Hard Cash 1863 196

Hardy, Thomas b. 1840 178, 197, 198

Harman's *Caveat for Common Corsetors* 1567 71

Harrington, James 1611-77, *Oceana* 1656 106

Harrington, Sir John 1561-1612, *Orlando Furioso* 1591 60

Harrison, William 1534-93, *Description of England* 1577 69

Harvey, Gabriel 1545-1630 47, 55

Havelok c. 1302 19

Hawes, Stephen 1475?-1530? 38

Hazlitt, William 1778-1830 124, 148 Criticism 173 Essays 174, 198

Heart of Midlothian, The 1818 171

Heart of Oak 140

Heavy Brigade, The 1882 and 1885 180

Heine's Grave 1867 185

Hekatompathia 1582 52

Hellas 1822 164

Hellenics 1846 168

Henry IV parts i and ii 86

Henry V 64, 86

Henry VI 79, 85

Henry VII (Bacon) 1622 69

Henry VIII 86, 92

Henry Esmond 1852 192, 193

Henryson, Robert 1430?-1506? 40

Herbert, George 1593-1633 22, 96, 97

Herbert of Cherbury, Lord 1583-1648 96

Hero and Leander 1593 pub. 1598 48, 59

Heroes and Hero-Worship 1840 pub. 1841 202

Heroic play, The 143

Heroic poem, The 98

Herrick, Robert 1591-1674 63, 96

Hesperides 1648 96

Heywood, John 1497-c. 1580, *Interludes* 75

Heywood, Thomas ?-1650? 92

Hickscorner c. 1509 75

Hind and the Panther, The 1687 119

History of Charles V 1769 127

History of England (Macaulay) 1848-55 204

History of John Bull 1712 115

History of Scotland (Robertson) 1759 127

History of the Great Rebellion pub. 1702-4 106

History of the World (Ralegh) 1614 69, 109

Hobbes, Thomas 1588-1679 106, 110

Hoby, Sir Thomas 1530-66, *Courtier* 1561 (from Castiglione) 72

Hogg, James 1770-1835 169

Holinshed, Raphael d. 1580, *Chronicles* 1577 and 1586-7 42, 69, 72, 85, 89

Holland, Philemon 1552–1637, translations c. 1600 72
Holy Dying 1651 109
Holy Maidenhood c. 1210 33
Holy War, The 1682 108
Holy Willie's Prayer 1785 142
Homilies of Aelfric 990–5 12
Homilies of Wulfstan c. 1010 13
Honest Whore, The 1604 92
Hood, Thomas 1799–1845 169
Hooker, Richard 1554?–1600 48, 66
Horace 96, 113, 120
Horatian Ode 1650 98
Horne, Richard Henry 1803–84 188
Hours of Idleness 1807 161
House of Fame, The 1383–4 28
House of Life, The 1847 ff., 1870, complete 1881 186
House of the Wulfings, The 1889 188
Howell, James 1594–1666, *Familiar Letters* 1645–55 107
Huchowne *fl.* 14th c. 24
Hudibras 1663, 1664 and 1678 71, 120
Hughes, Thomas *fl.* 1587 76
Humane Knowledge, Of 1633 61
Hume, David 1711–76 Empiricism 123, 177, 208 *History of England* 1762 127
Humphrey Clinker 1771 132
Hunt, Leigh 1784–1859 166, 169, 173, 174
Hunting of the Cheviot, The 41
Huon of Bordeaux ptd 1534? 44
Huxley, Thomas Henry 1825–95, *Essays* collected 1893–4 178, 209
Hyde, Edward, Earl of Clarendon 1609–74 *106*, 110, 111
Hyde Park lic. 1632 ptd 1637 94

Hydriotaphia, or *Urn Burial* 1658 109
Hymn to Proserpine 1866 190
Hymn to St Teresa, The 1652 97
Hyperion 1818–20 ptd 1820 167

Idea 1594–1619 53, 64
Idea of a University 1854 209
Idler, The 1758–60 123
Idylls of the King 1859–85 179
Iliad (Pope) 1715–20 121
Il Penseroso c. 1632 ptd 1645 100
Imaginary Conversations 1824–53 174
Imitations of Horace 1733–9 121
Induction to *The Mirror for Magistrates* 43
Inn Album, The 1875 183
Inheritance 1824 132
In Memoriam 1850 177, 179, 181
Instauratio Magna 1620 67
Intentions 1891 207
Interludes 74
In the Bay 1878 190
Ipomedon c. 1400 20
Irene 1749 143
Irish Melodies 1807–34 169
Isabella 1818 ptd 1820 167
Island, The 1823 162
Itylus 1866 190
Ivanhoe 1820 171, 172

Jack Wilton 1594 71
James I of Scotland 1394–1437 39
James IV 1590 ptd 1598 77
Jane Eyre 1847 195
Jean de Meung d. 1305 27
Jefferies, Richard 1848–87 197
Jeffrey, Francis, Lord 1773–1850 148

Jenny ptd 1870 186
Jerusalem 1804 141
Jew of Malta, The Rich 1589 ptd 1633 78
Jinny the Just (in Longleat MSS) c. 1716? 135
Jocasta 1566 52
Johan Johan 1533-4 75
John Gilpin 1782 140
John of Salisbury d. 1180 15
John of Trevisa 1326-1412 35
Johnson, Dr Samuel 1709-84 62, 96, 100 Essays 123, 125 *Lives* 126 Poems 134, 136, 143, 201
Jolly Beggars, The 1785 142
Jonathan Wild 1743 131
Jonson, Ben 1573?-1637 48, 54, 55, 65 Prose *70*, 72, 80 Plays *89*, 90, 91 Poems 95, 96, 144, 191
Joseph Andrews 1742 130
Journal of the Plague Year 1722 118
Journal to Stella 1710-13 114, 124
Journey from this World to the Next, A 1743 131
Journey to the Western Isles 1775 126
Judith 12
Juliana 8
Julian and Maddalo 1818 163
Julius Caesar 87
Juvenal 66

Keats, John 1795-1821 59, 64, 101, 137, 138, 142, 148, 149, 150, 157, 163 Poems *166*, 167, 168, 169 Letters 172, 179, 180, 181
Keble, John 1792-1866, *Christian Year* 1827 186
Keith of Ravelston 1856 188
Kenilworth 1821 171
Kidnapped 1886 198
Kilmeny 1813 169

King Alfred 849-901 2, 6, *10*, 11
King Alisaunder 1275-1300 20
King Arthur 20
King Horn c. 1250 19
Kingis Quair, The c. 1423 39
King John (Bale) c. 1548 75
King John (Shakespeare) 86
Kinglake, Alexander William 1809-91 196
King Lear 84
King's College Chapel 1820? 156
Kingsley, Charles 1819-75 196
King Stephen 1819 ptd 1848 168
King's Tragedy, The 1880 ptd 1881 186
Knight of the Burning Pestle, The 1609? ptd 1613 93
Knight's Tale, The 18, 20, 30
Kubla Khan 1797 ptd 1816 146, 156
Kyd, Thomas 1557?-95? 78

La Belle Dame sans Merci 1819 pub. 1820 148, 168
Lady of Pleasure, A 1635 ptd 1637 94
Lady of Shalott, The 1833-42 180
Lady of the Lake, The 1810 159
Lalla Rookh 1817 169
L'Allegro c. 1632 ptd 1645 100, 101
Lamb, Charles 1775-1834 78, 92, 124, 148, 170 Criticism 173 Essays *175*
Lamb, Mary Ann 1764-1847 173
Lament for the Makaris, The c. 1508 40
Lament of Tasso, The 1817 162
Lamia 1819 ptd 1820 167
Land of Cockaigne, The c. 1258 23
Landor, Walter Savage 1775-1864 111 Poems 168 Prose *174*, 189, 190

Langland, William 1332?-99? 23, *25*, 33

Laodamia 1814 pub. 1815 156

Lark Ascending, The 1881 and 1883 188

La Saisiaz 1878 177, 181

Last Days of Pompeii, The 1834 196

Last Instructions to a Painter 1667 98

Last Word, The 1867 185

Latimer, Hugh 1485?-1555 43

Latter-Day Pamphlets 1850 202

Laura 1327 ff. 52

Laus Veneris 1862 ptd 1866 189

Lavengro 1851 196

Laws of Ecclesiastical Polity bks I-IV 1594 66

Law, William 1686-1761, *Serious Call* 1728 123

Layamon's *Brut* c. 1200 and c. 1250 *17*, 18

Lay of the Last Minstrel, The 1805 158, 160

Lays of Ancient Rome 1842 204

Lee, Nathaniel 1653?-92, *Rival Queens* 1677 143

Legend of Good Women, The 1385-6? 28, 29

Leland, John 1506?-52, *Itinerary* c. 1540 42

Le Morte Arthur finished 1469 pub. 1485 21, 43

Lemprière, John 1765?-1824, *Dictionary* 1788 166

'Lenten is come with love to toune' c. 1310 23

L'Estrange, Sir Roger 1616-1704 113

Letters of Junius 1769-72 125

Letters on a Regicide Peace 1795-7 129

Letter to a Friend, A pub 1690 109

Letter to Lord Chesterfield 1755 126

Letter to Maria Gisborne 1820 163

Lewis, Matthew Gregory 1775-1818, *The Monk* 1795 132

Lewti 1798 158

Lever, Charles James 1806-72 196

Leviathan 1651 106

Liberty, On 1859 208

Liberty of Prophesying, The 1646 105

Library, The 1781 134

Life and Death of Jason, The 1867 187

Life and Death of Mr Badman, The 1680 108

Life of Alfred c. 900 10

Life of Cowley 1779 62, 96, 136

Life of Johnson (Boswell) 1791 125

Life of Nelson 1813 172

Life of Sir Walter Scott 1836-8 172

Life of Sterling 1851 177, 203

Life of Wesley 1820 172

Lillo, George 1693-1739, *George Barnwell* 1731 144

Linacre, Thomas 1460?-1524 47

Lindsay, Sir David 1490-1555 39, 41

Little Geste of Robin Hood, The 1400-1500 41

Lives of divines (Walton) 1640-78 110

Lives of the Poets 1779-81 125, 126, 136

Livy 72

Locke, John 1632-1704 105, 106, 123, 177, 208

Lockhart, John Gibson 1794-1854 72

Locksley Hall 1842 180

Lodge, Thomas 1558?-1625 Sonnets 53 Songs 54, 59, 65 Novels 71, 77

London 1738 134

London Magazine, The founded 1820 174
London Lickpenny 37
Lord of the Isles, The 1815 160
Lord Ormont and his Aminta 1894 200
Lorna Doone 1869 196
Love (Coleridge) 1799 ptd 1800 158
Lovelace, Richard 1618–58, *Lucasta* 1649 96
Love Song c. 1240 23
Lover, Samuel 1797–1868 196
Loves of the Plants, The 1789 134
Lover's Message, The 6
Lucrece 1594 59
Lucretius 1869 180
Lycidas 1637 pub. 1638 100, 101
Lydgate, John 1370?–1451? 20, *37*, 38, 50
Lyly, John 1554?–1606 Novels 70 Plays 76, 77
Lyrical Ballads 1798 2nd edition 1800 146, 152, 156

Macaulay, Thomas Babington, Lord 1800–59 126, *203*, 204
Macbeth 50, 84, 87, 92, 173
Macflecknoe 1682 119
Machiavelli 1469–1527, *The Prince* 1532 68
Mackenzie, Henry 1745–1831, *Man of Feeling* 1771 131
Macpherson, James 1736–96, *Ossian* 1762 136
Madoc 1805 159
Magnificence 1516? 74
Maid Marian 1822 172
Maid's Tragedy, The 1611? ptd 1619 93
Male Règle, La c. 1406 37
Malory, Sir Thomas *fl.* 1470 21, *43*, 44, 56, 179
Malthus, Thomas Robert 1766–1834 209

Man 1633 97
Mandeville, Bernard 1670?–1733, *Fable of the Bees* 1714–23 123
Mandeville's *Travels* French MS 1371 36
Manfred 1817 161, 162
Mannynge, Robert, of Brunne *fl.* 1288–1338 22
Man of Feeling, The 1771 131
Man of Mode, The 1676 144
Mansfield Park 1814 133
Mantuanus d. 1516 55
Map, Walter *fl.* 1200 15
Marie de France *fl.* 1180 15
Marino Faliero 1820 162
Marius the Epicurean 1885 207
Marlowe, Christopher 1564–93 34, 47, 48, 50, 54 Poems *59* Plays *78*, 79, 86
Marmion 1808 146, 160
Marot, Clément 1496–1544 55
Marryat, Frederic 1792–1848 196
Marston, John 1575?–1634 48 Satires 65, 90 Plays 92
Martial 96
Martin Chuzzlewit 1843 192
Martin Marprelate 1588–90 48, 71
Mary Barton 1848 196
Mary Stuart 1881 190
Marvell, Andrew 1621–78 98
Masque, The *91*
Masque of Anarchy, The 1819 164
Masque of Queens, The 1609 91
Massinger, Philip 1583–1640 93
Maud 1855 179, 180
May, Thomas 1595–1650, *History of the Long Parliament* 1647 107
Medieval survivals 49
Melibeus and Prudence 34
Memorial Verses 1850 ptd 1852 and 1855 185

Memories and Portraits 1887 198

Men and Women 1855 182

Meredith, George 1828–1909 133 Poems 188, 197, 198 Novels *199*, 200, 201, 203

Merlin and the Gleam 1889 179

Merope 1858 185

Merry Beggars, The 1641 ptd 1659 94

Merry Wives of Windsor, The 82, 90

'Metaphysical' poets 62, 96

Michael 1800 146, 154

Midas 1589 ptd 1592 77

Middlemarch 1871–2 194

Middleton, Conyers 1683–1750 123

Middleton, Thomas 1570?–1627 92

Midsummer Fairies, The 1827 169

Midsummer Night's Dream, A 77, 83

Mill, John Stuart 1806–73 208

Mill on the Floss, The 1860 194

Milton (Blake) 1804 141

Milton, John 1608–74 21, 50, 60, 65, 77, 79, 93, 95, 96, 98 Poems *99*, 100, 101, 102, 103, 104 Prose *105*, 106, 110, 111, 112, 126, 135, 141, 151, 155, 167, 181, 183

Minot, Laurence 1300?–52 23

Minstrelsy of the Scottish Border, The 1802–3 160

Miracle plays 12th century ff. *73*, 101

Mirror for Magistrates, The 1559–63 37, 50

Mirrour de l'Omme c. 1376 32

Misfortunes of Arthur, The 1587 76

Miss Ferrier 1782–1854, *Inheritance* 1824 132

Mitford, Mary Russell 1787–1855 195

Mixed Essays 1879 205

Modern Love 1862 188

Modern Painters 1843–60 206

Modest Proposal, A 1729 115

Molière 1622–73 144, 145

Moll Flanders 1721 ptd 1722 118

Monarchy, Of 1633 61

Monk's Tale, The 29, 37

Montaigne 1533–92, *Essays* 1580–3 68, 72, 87, 207

Mont Blanc 1816 ptd 1817 165

Moore, Thomas 1779–1852 169, 170

Morality plays *74*

Moral Ode, The c. 1170 16

More, Hannah 1745–1833 132

More, Henry 1614–87, *Philosophical Poems* 1647 65

More's *History of Richard III* ptd 1543–57 69

More, Sir Thomas 1478–1535 66, 69

Morning Post, The founded 1772 124

Morris, William 1834–96 31, 178, 185 Poems *186*

Mort Arthur 19

Morte Arthur, Le 1469 ptd 1485 21, 43

Morte d'Arthure c. 1400 23

Morte D'Arthur (Tennyson) 1835 ptd 1842 179, 181

Much Ado about Nothing 84

Mother Bombie 1590 ptd 1594 and 1598 76

Munday, Anthony 1553–1633 92

Muses' Elizium, The 1630 64

Music's Duel 1648 97

Musophilus 1599 63

Mysteries of Udolpho, The 1794 132

Narrenschiff (Brant) ptd 1494 38

Nashe, Thomas 1567–1601 71, 78, 118

Natural History of Selborne 1789 196

Nennius *fl.* 796 10

New Atlantis, The pub. 1627 68

Newcomes, The 1854–5 192, 193

Newman, John Henry, Cardinal 1801–90 178 *Dream of Gerontius* pub. 1865 186 Prose 209

New Way to pay old Debts, A 1626? ptd 1633 93

Nibelungenlied c. 1150 4

Nicholas of Hereford c. 1250 34

Nightingale, The 1798 (Coleridge) 158

Night Thoughts 1742–4 135

Nimphidia 1627 63

Noble Numbers 1647–8 96

Noctes Ambrosianae 1822–35 174

Northanger Abbey ptd 1818 132, 133

Northern Farmer: Old Style 1864 180

North, Sir Thomas 1535?–1601?, *Plutarch* 1579 72

Norton, Thomas 1532–84 76

Nosce Teipsum 1598 ptd 1599 60

Notes of Instruction 1575 52

Novel, The, 70, 71, 129–134, 170, 191–201

Novum Organum 1620 67

Nun's Priest's Tale, The 23, 30

Nut-Browne Maid, The ptd 1503 40, 42

Occleve, Thomas 1368?–1450? 37

Ode on a distant prospect of Eton College 1742–8 137

Ode on a Grecian Urn 1819 pub. 1820 167

Ode on Melancholy 1819 ptd 1820 149, 168

Ode on the Intimations of Immortality 1803–6 ptd 1807 154

Ode on the Nativity 1629 ptd 1645 99

Odes (Drayton) 1606–19 64

Ode to Duty 1805 ptd 1807 153

Ode to Evening 1747 135, 137

Ode to Liberty (Shelley) 1820 164

Ode to Mistress Anne Killigrew 1686 119

Ode to Naples 1820 164

Ode to Simplicity 1747 137

Ode to the Nightingale 1819 149, 168

Ode to the West Wind 1820 164

Odyssey (Morris) 1887 187

Old Curiosity Shop, The 1840 192

Old Fortunatus 1596 ptd 1600 92

Oldham, John, 1653–83 98

Old Mortality 1816–7 170

Old Wives' Tale, The 1590 ptd 1595 77

Oliver Twist 1837–9 191

One of Our Conquerors 1891 200

On Indolence 1819 pub. 1848 168

On the Loss of the Royal George 1782 pub. 1803 140

On the Receipt of my Mother's Picture 1790 pub. 1798 140

On Translating Homer 1861 205

Orchestra 1594 60

Ordeal of Richard Feverel, The 1859 199

Origins of drama *73*

Orion 1843 188

Orison of Our Lady, The c. 1210 16

Ormulum c. 1200 16

Orosius *fl.* 416 11

Osborne, Dorothy 1627–95, *Letters* 1652–4 107

O'Shaughnessy, Arthur 1844–81 188

Ossian 1762 136

Otho the Great 1819 pub. 1848 168

Otway, Thomas 1652–85, *Venice Preserved* 1682 143

Our Village 1824–32 195

Overbury's? *Characters* 1614 71

Ovid 19, 28, 60, 64

Owl and the Nightingale, The c. 1220 17

Oxford movement, The 177, 178

Pains of Sleep, The 1803 ptd 1817 159

Palace of Art, The 1832 and 1842 181

Pamela 1740 130

Pandosto 1588 71, 72

Paracelsus 1835 182

Paradise Lost 1650–63 ptd 1667 in ten books, 2nd edn 1674 in twelve books 7, 99, *101*, *102*, 103, 104, 117

Paradise Regained 1671 65, 99, *103*

Parcy Reed 41

Pardoner's Tale, The 30

Paris, Matthew d. 1259 15

Parker, Archbishop 1504–75 45

Parliament of Fowls, The 1382 28

Parnell, Thomas 1679–1718, *Night-Piece* pub. 1721 120, 135

Parochial Sermons 1836–42, *Parochial and Plain Sermons* 1868 209

Parson's Tale, The 34

Past and Present 1843 202

Pastime of Pleasure, The 1505–6 38

Paston *Letters* 1424–1506 42

Pastoral Care 10, 11

Pater, Walter Horatio 1839–94 123, *207*, 209

Patience c. 1350 24

Patmore, Coventry 1823–96, *Odes* 1877 188

Pattison, Mark 1813–84 207

Peacock, Thomas Love 1785–1866 172, 199

Pearl c. 1350 24

Pecock, Reginald 1395?–1460? 42

Peele Castle 1805 pub. 1807 154

Peele, George 1558?–97? Poems 54, 63 Plays 77

Pendennis 1849–50 192

Pentameron, The 1837 174

Pepys, Samuel 1633–1703, *Diary* 1660–9 107, 113

Percy folio MS c. 1650 41

Percy, Thomas 1729–1811, *Reliques* 1765 136

Peregrine Pickle 1751 132

Pericles and Aspasia 1836 174

Persius 66

Persuasion 1816 133

Petrarch 1304–74 49, 51, 52, 61

Pettie's *Petite Palace of Pleasure* lic. 1576 70

Phaer, Thomas 1510?–60, *Vergil* 1560 59

Pharonnida 1659 98

Philarete 1622 64

Philaster 1610? ptd 1620 93

Philips, John 1676–1709, *Splendid Shilling* 1701 135

Philobiblon 1345 15

Phoenix, The 8

Physiologus 9

Pibroch, The 160

Pickwick Papers, The 1837–9 192

Piers the Plowman's Creed c. 1393 26

Pilgrimage of the Life of Man, The 1426 37

Pilgrim's Progress, The 1678–84 108

Pindaric ode, The 98, 119, 137
Pippa Passes 1841 182
Piscatory Eclogues ptd 1633 64
Pistil of Susan, The in Vernon
MS c. 1380 24
Plain Dealer, The 1674 ptd
1677 144
Plautus 76
Pleasures of Hope, The 1799
134
Pleasures of Imagination, The
1744 135
Pleasures of Memory, The 1792
134
Pléiade, The 1549 52
Plutarch's *Lives* 72, 89
Plutarch's *Morals* 72
Poems and Ballads 1866 189
Poems and Ballads 1878 2nd
series 190
Poems and Ballads 1889 3rd
series 190
Poetaster, The 1601 ptd 1602 90
Poetical Sketches 1783 141
Poetic Mirror, The 1816 169
Political Justice 1793 152
Polychronicon c. 1350 trans.
1387 35
Poly-Olbion 1613–22 49, 63
Pope, Alexander 1688–1744
60, 66, 112, 115, 119 Poems
120, 121, 122 Letters 124,
126, 134, 135, 136, 138, 139,
161, 181
Praed, Winthrop Mackworth
1802–39 188
Praeterita 1885–89 206
Preface to *The Fables* 1700 114
Prelude, The 1799–1805 pub.
1850 151
Pre-Raphaelites, The 138, 149,
177, 178, *185*, 206
Pricke of Conscience 1349? 22
Pride and Prejudice 1813 133
Princess, The 1847 180
Principles of Biology 1864–7
209

*Principles of Morals and Legis-
lation* 1780 208
Prior, Matthew 1664–1721 120,
134, 140, 188
Prisoner of Chillon, The 1816
161
Progress of Poesy, The 1757
136
Progress of the Soul, The (*Me-
tempsychosis*) 1601 ptd 1633
62
*Prologue to the Canterbury
Tales, The* c. 1387 29
Prometheus Unbound 1820 146,
150, 164
Prophecy of Dante, The 1821
162
Prophetic Books 1793–1804 141
Prosopopoia or *Mother Hubberd's
Tale* 1591 58, 65
Prothalamium 1596 58
Proud Maisie 160
Proverbs of Alfred c. 1250 16
Proverbs of Hendyng c. 1270
16
Pseudodoxia or *Vulgar Errors*
1646 109
Pulley, The 1633 97
Purchas his Pilgrimage 1613 69
Purple Island, The 1610 pub.
1633 64
Purvey, John 1353?–1428? 34
Puttenham's *Art of English
Poesie* 1589 69

Quarles, Francis 1592–1644 97
Quarterly, The founded 1809
147, 174
Queen's Wake, The 1813 169
Quentin Durward 1823 171

Rabbi Ben Ezra 1864 182
Rabelais c. 1500–53 40, 72,
131
Ralegh, Sir Walter 1552?–1618
47, 53 Poems 54, 55 Prose
69, 109

Ralph Roister Doister 1553? ptd 1566 76

Rambler, The 1750-2 123

Ramsay, Allan 1686-1758, *Gentle Shepherd* 1725 135 *Poems* 1721 141

Randolph, Thomas 1605-35 94

Rape of the Lock, The 1712-4 120, 146

Rasselas 1759 123

Rastell, John d. 1536 75

Reade, Charles 1814-84 196, 197

Reason of Church Government, The 1641 105

Red Cotton Night-Cap Country, 1873 183

Reformation, The 48

Rehearsal, The 1671 144

Rejected Addresses 1812 170

Relapse, The 1697 144

Religio Laici 1682 119

Religio Medici 1642 and 1643 108

Religious Musings 1794 pub. 1796 151

Renascence, The *46*

Resolution and Independence 1802 pub. 1807 155

Resolves 1620? 69

Retaliation 1774 136

Revenger's Tragedy, The 1606-7 ptd 1607 92

Revenge, The 1880 180

Review, The (Defoe) 1704-13 117

Revolt of Islam, The 1817 ptd 1818 164

Revolt of the Tartars, The 1837 175

Reynard the Fox ptd Caxton 1481 23

Reynolds, John Hamilton 1796-1852 169

Reynolds, Sir Joshua 1723-92 123

Rhoda Fleming 1865 200

Rhyme of the Duchess May, The 1844 184

Ricardo, David 1772-1823 209

Richard II 79, 85, 86

Richard III 79, 85

Richard Cœur de Lion 1275-1300 14

Richard of Bury's *Philobiblon* 1345 15

Richardson, Samuel 1689-1761 *130*, 131, 197

Richard the Redeless c. 1400 26

Riddles, Old English 9

Ring and the Book, The 1868-9 183

Rivals, The 1775 145

Roaring Girl, The 1610 ptd 1611 92

Robene and Makyne 40

Robert de Borron c. 1215 21

Robert of Gloucester c. 1300 22

Robertson, William. *History of Scotland* 1759 127

Robin Hood 1400-1500 42

Robin Hood plays 74

Robinson Crusoe 1719 118

Rochester, Earl of (John Wilmot) 1647-80 97

Roderick Random 1748 132

Roderick, the last of the Goths 1814 159

Rogers, Samuel 1763-1855, *Pleasures of Memory* 1792 134

Rolle, Richard, of Hampole c. 1300-49? 22, 34

Roman Actor, The 1626 ptd 1629 93

Romances of chivalry *18*

Roman de la Rose, Le c. 1237 and c. 1278, Chaucer's? translation c. 1360-5 *27*, 32, 38

Romantic and classic *150*

Romantic drama *95*

Romantic revival, The *146*

Romany Rye, The 1857 196

Romaunt of Margret, The 1835 184

Romeo and Juliet 87

Romola 1863 194

Ronsard 1524–85 52

Rosalynde 1590 71, 72

Rose Aylmer 1806–31 169

Rosciad, The 1761 134

Rossetti, Christina Georgina 1830–94 186

Rossetti, Dante Gabriel 1828–82 185, 186, 187

Roundabout Papers 1860–3 194

Rousseau 1712–78 132, *147*, 178

Rowley poems, The 1765 ff. pub. 1777 136

Rowley, William, 1585?–1642? 92

Rubáiyát of Omar Khayyám 1859 188

Rugby Chapel 1857 ptd 1869 185

Ruins of Time, The 1591 58

Ruin, The 6

Rule Britannia 1740 140

Rural Rides collected and pub. 1830 176

Ruskin, John 1819–1900 123, 178, 203, 204, *206*

Ruth 1799 pub. 1800 154

Rymer, Thomas 1641–1713 114

Sackville, Thomas, Lord Buckhurst 1536–1608 *49*, 76

Sad Shepherd, The 1614 ptd 1641 91

Sainte-Beuve 1804–69 208

Saint-Évremond 1613?–1703 114

Saint Peter's Complaint 1615 61

Salmacis and Hermaphroditus 1602 59

Salomon and Saturn 9

Samson Agonistes 1671 103

Sandford and Merton 1783–9 132

Sandys, George 1578–1644, *Metamorphoses* 1621–26 60, 97, 166

Sannazaro (*Arcadia* 1490) 55

Sartor Resartus 1834 177, 201, 203

Satire of the Three Estates 1535 ptd 1602 39

Satires upon the Jesuits 1679 98

Schlegel, A. W. von 1767–1845 172

Scholar Gypsy, The 1853 185

School for Scandal, The 1777 145

Schoolmaster, The pub. 1570 66

Schoolmistress, The 1742 135

School of Abuse, The 1579 69

Scots poets *39*, 141

Scott, Sir Walter 1771–1832 132, 150, 158 Poems *159*, 160, 169 Novels *170*, 171, 172, 173, 178, 179, 197

Sea-farer, The 6

Seasons, The 1726–30 135

Second Defence of the English People (in Latin) 1654 105

Sedley, Sir Charles 1639?–1701 97

Sejanus 1603 ptd 1605 89

Selden, John 1584–1654 63

Senecan drama 70, 76, 78

Sennacherib 1815 161

Sense and Sensibility 1811 133

Sensitive Plant, The 1820 163

Sentimental Journey, A 1768 131

Sesame and Lilies 1865 206

Settle, Elkanah 1648–1724 119

Seven Deadly Sins, The c. 1512 40

Seven Lamps of Architecture, The 1849 206

Seven Sages of Rome, The 20

Shadwell, Thomas 1642?-92 90, 119, 144

Shaftesbury, Earl of (Antony Ashley Cooper 1671-1713), *Characteristics* 1711 123

Shakespeare, William 1564-1616 (*vide* list of plays pp. 81, 82 and Appendix) 46, 50 Sonnets *53* Poems *54*, *59*, 70 Prose 72, 73, 75, 78 Plays *79-89*, 91, 93, 94, 96, 121, 126, 136, 143, 149, 166, 171, 173, 185, 200

Shelley, Percy Bysshe 1792-1822 59, 100, 137, 141, 143, 147, 148, 149, 150, 159, 161, 162 Poems *163*, 164, 165, 166, 167, 168, 169 Criticism 172, 179, 189

Shelton's *Don Quixote* 1612 and 1620? 72

Shenstone, William 1714-63, *Schoolmistress* 1742 135

Shepherd's Calendar, The 1579 55, 70

Shepherd's Hunting, The 1615 64

Sheridan, Richard Brinsley 1751-1816 144, 145

She Stoops to Conquer 1773 145

Ship of Fools, The 1509 38

Shirley 1849 195

Shirley, James 1596-1666 91, 94

Shooting Niagara 1867 202

Sidney, Algernon 1622-83 106

Sidney, Sir Philip 1554-86 47, 50, *52*, 55, 58, *69*, 70, 71, 72

Siege of Corinth, The 1816 158

Siege of Rhodes, The 1656 94

Sigurd the Volsung 1876 187

Silas Marner 1861 194

Silent Woman, The 1609 ptd 1616 90

Silex Scintillans 1650 97

Sir Charles Grandison 1753 130

Sir Ferumbras c. 1400 19

Sir Galahad 1842 180

Sir Gowther c. 1400 19

Sir Joshua Reynolds' *Discourses* 1759-90 123

Sir Martin Mar-All 1667 ptd 1668 144

Sir Orfeo 1330-40 19

Sir Thopas c. 1390? 20, 22

Sir Tristrem 1275-1300 19

Sister Helen 1853, 1870 and 1881 186

Skelton, John 1460-1529 38, 74

Sleep and Poetry 1817 166

Smart, Christopher 1722-71, *Song to David* 1763 136

Smith, Horace 1779-1849 170

Smith, James 1775-1839 170

Smith, Sydney 1771-1845 174

Smollett, Tobias George 1721-71 127, *132*, 170, 196, 197

Sohrab and Rustum 1853 185

Solitary Reaper, The 1803-5 pub. 1807 156

Somnour's Tale, The 30

Song of Italy, A 1867 189

Song of the Shirt, The 1843 170

Songs before Sunrise 1871 189

Songs of Innocence 1789 141

Songs of Experience 1794 141

Sonneteers, Elizabethan *52*

Sonnets from the Portuguese 1850 184

Sonnets of Milton 101

Sophonisba 1730 143

Sordello 1840 182

Soul's Ward c. 1210 33

South, Robert 1634-1716 107

Southey, Robert 1774-1843 147 Poems *159*, 163, 169 Prose 172, 174

Southwell, Robert 1561?-95 61

Spanish Friar, The 1681 144

Spanish Military Nun, The 1847 175

Spanish Tragedy, The 1586 ptd 1594 78

Specimens of the Dramatic Poets 1808 173

Spectator, The 1711-2 *116*, 117, 123

Speed, John 1552?-1629, *History of Great Britain* 1611 69

Spencer, Herbert 1820-1903 209

Spenser, Edmund 1552-99 38, 46, 48, 50, 52 Sonnets *53* Poems *55*, 56, 58, 62, 64, 65, 79, 97, 135, 136, 166, 174

Spirit of the Age, The 1825 174

Splendid Shilling, The 1701 135

Sprat, Bishop 1635-1713 113

Squire of Low Degree, The 20

Squire's Tale, The 20, 30

Stanyhurst, Richard 1547-1618, *Vergil* 1582 59

Stanzas from the Grande Chartreuse 1855-67 185

Stanzas written in Dejection near Naples 1818 163

Staple of News, The 1625 ptd 1631 90

Steele, Sir Richard 1672-1729 112 Essays *116*, *117*, 123, 129 Plays 144

Steel Glass, The 1576 52

Stepping Westward 1803-5 pub. 1807 153

Stevenson, Robert Louis 1850-94 196, 197, *198*, 199

Stevenson, William d. 1575 76

Stones of Venice, The 1851-3 206

Story of Rimini, The 1816 169

Story of Thebes, The c. 1420 20, 37

Stow, John 1525?-1605, *Survey of London* 1598 and 1603 42, 69

St Ronan's Well 1824 171

Stubbs, Bishop 1825-1901 204

Studies in the History of the Renaissance 1873 207

Suckling, Sir John 1609-42 64, 96

' Sumer is i-cumen in ' c. 1310 23

Supposes, The 1566 32

Surrey, Earl of (Henry Howard) 1517?-47 *51*, 52

Suspiria de Profundis 1845 149, 175

Swift, Jonathan 1667-1745 112 Prose *114* Poems 120, 121, 124, 129, 131, 172

Swimmer's Dream, A 1894 189

Swinburne, Algernon Charles 1837-1909 137, 139, 150, 174, 185, 188 Poems *189*, 190, 195

Sybil 1845 196

Sylvester, Joshua 1563-1618, *Divine Weeks and Days* 1592-1605 60

Sylvia's Lovers 1863 196

Symonds, John Addington 1840-93 207

Symposium of Plato 163

Synge, J. M. 1871-1909 145

System of Logic 1843 208

Tables Turned, The 1798 153

Table Talk (Cowper) 1782 139

Tacitus 4

Tale of a Tub, A 1704 114

Tale of Balen, The 1896 190

Tale of Two Cities, A 1859 192

Tales from Shakespear 1807 173

Tales in Verse 1812 139

Tales of the Hall 1819 134, 139

Talisman, The 1825 171

Tamburlaine 1587? ptd 1590 77, 78

Taming of the Shrew, The 82

Tam o' Shanter 1785 142

Tancred 1847 196

Task, The 1785 135, 140

Tasso 1544–95, *Gerusalemme Liberata* 1581 56, 60
Tatler, The 1709–11 116, 117, 118
Taylor, Jeremy 1613–67 105, *107*, 110, 111
Tears of Peace 1609 61
Tempest, The 50, 91
Temple, Sir William 1628–99 107, 113
Temple, The (Herbert) 1633 96
Tennyson, Alfred, Lord 1809–92 11, 21, 177 Poems *178*, 179, 180, 181, 187, 203
Terence 76
Testament of Cressid, The 40
Tethys' Festival 1610 63
Thackeray, William Makepeace 1811–63 *178* Novels *192*, 193, 194, 197
Thalaba 1801 159
Theobald, Lewis 1688–1744, *Shakespeare* 1734 121, 136
Theocritus 55
Theophrastus 71
Thirlwall, Connop 1797–1875 204
Thistle and the Rose, The 1503 40
Thomas de Hales *fl.* 1250 23
Thomas of Ercildoune 41
Thompson, Francis 1859–1907 188
Thomson, James 1700–48 135, 140, 137 *Sophonisba* 143
Thoughts on the Present Discontents 1770 128
Thyrsis 1861 100, 185
Tickell, Thomas 1686–1740, *Elegy on Addison* 1721 134
Tiger, The 1794 141
Tillotson, Archbishop 1630–94 112
Times, The founded 1788 124
Tindal, Matthew 1657–1733 123
Tintern Abbey 1798 149, 153, 154

Tithonus ptd 1860 181
Titus Andronicus 79
To a Child of Quality 135
To a Skylark (Shelley) 1820 166
To Autumn 1819 pub. 1820 168
Toland, John 1670–1722 123
Toleration, On 1689 ff. 105
To Maia 1818 pub. 1848 167
To Mary Unwin 1793 pub. 1803 140
Tom Jones 1749 130, 131
Tom Thumb 1730 144
To Psyche 1819 ptd 1820 167, 168
To the Departing Year 1796 159
To the Men of Kent 155
Tottel's *Miscellany* 1557 52
Tourneur, Cyril 1575?–1626 92
To Venice 1818 162
Towneley mysteries c. 1350 MS 15th century 74
Toxophilus 1545 66
Tractate on Education 1644 106
Traherne, Thomas 1634?–74 97
Traitor, The lic. 1631 ptd 1635 94
Traveller, The 1764 134
Treasure Island 1882 198
Trick to catch the old one, A 1606 ptd 1608 92
Tristram of Lyonesse 1882 190
Tristram Shandy 1760–7 131
Triumph of Life, The 1822 165
Triumphs of Owen, The 1768 136
Trivia 1716 134
Troilus and Criseyde c. 1383 20, 28, 40, 70
Trollope, Anthony 1815–82 196
Troy Book 1412–20 ptd 1513 37
Turbervile, George 1540?–1610? 52
Tusser, Thomas 1524–80 52

Twa Dogs, The 1786 142
Two Foscari, The 1821 162
Two Married Women, The c. 1512 40
Two Noble Kinsmen, The 1612 ptd 1634 92
Twopenny Post-Bag, The 1812 169
Tyndale, William d. 1536 45
Tyrwhitt, Thomas 1730–86, *Chaucer* 1775 136

Udall, Nicholas 1505–56 76
Ulysses 1842 180, 181
Ulysses and the Siren 1605 63
Underwoods 1616 91
Universal History (Orosius) 416 King Alfred's trans. c. 890 11
Universal Passion, The 1725–8 134
University wits, The 76
Unto this Last 1862 206
Urquhart, Sir Thomas 1611–60, *Rabelais* 1653 72
Utilitarianism 1863 208
Utopia 1515 and 1516, in English 1551 66

Vanbrugh, Sir John 1664–1726 144, 145
Vanity Fair 1847–8 192, 193
Vanity of Human Wishes, The 1749 134, 136, 146
Vathek 1786 132
Vaughan, Henry 1622–95 97, 186
Venetian Republic, The 1802 155
Venus and Adonis 1593 59
Vicar of Wakefield, The 1766 131
Victorian Age, The 177
View of Ireland (Spenser) 1596 58
Village, The 1783 139
Villette 1852 195
Virginibus Puerisque 1881 28

Virgin Martyr, The lic. 1620 ptd 1622 93
Vision of Judgment, The 1822 162
Vision of William concerning Piers the Plowman 1362, 1377 and 1398? 25
Vittoria 1866 201
Volpone 1605-6 ptd 1607 90
Voltaire 1694–1778 128, 201
Vox Clamantis 1382 32
Voyage and Travel of Sir John Mandeville French MS 1371 36

Wace *fl.* 1170, *Brut.* c. 1155 15, 17, 21
Wallace 1470–80 39
Wallenstein 1800 159
Waller, Edmund 1606–87 96, 97
Walpole, Horace 1717–97 *Letters* 124 Novels 132, 148
Walton, Izaak 1593–1683 110
Wanderer, The 5
Wandering Willie's Tale in Redgauntlet 1824 171
Warburton, William 1698–1779, *Shakespeare* 1749 136
Warner, William 1558?–1609, *Albion's England* 63
Warton, Thomas 1728–90, *History of Poetry* 1774–81 136
Watson, Thomas 1557?–92, *Hekatompathia* 1582 52
Waverley 1814 170
Way of the World, The 1700 144
Weather, The c. 1533 75
Webbe's *Discourse of English Poetry* 1586 69
Webster, John 1580?–1625? 93
Weekly Political Register 1802–35 176
Weir of Hermiston 1896 198
Werferth, Bishop d. 915 11
Wesley, John 1703–91 124, 136

Westward Ho! 1855 196

Whetstone, George 1544–87 52, 76

White Devil, The 1611 ptd 1612 93

White Doe, The 1807 ptd 1815 156

White Ship, The 1880 ptd 1881 186

Widsith 1

Wife of Usher's Well, The 41

Wife's Complaint, The 6

Wilbye, John *fl.* 1600 54

Wilde, Oscar 1856–1900 145, 207

Wild Life in a Southern County 1879 196

William of Malmesbury d. 1143? 15

William of Ockham d. 1349 15

William of Palerne c. 1350 23

William of Shoreham *fl.* 1320 22

Wilson, John ('Christopher North') 1785–1854 174

Winter Evening, The 1785 140

Winter's Tale, The 72

Wishes to his (supposed) Mistress 1648 97

Wit and Science end of Henry VIII's reign 74

Witch of Atlas, The 1820 165

Witch, The 1610? pub. 1778 92

Wither, George 1588–1667 Poems 64 Songs 96

Wives and Daughters 1865 195

Wolfe, Charles 1791–1823 170

Woman Killed with Kindness, A 1603 ptd 1607 92

Woods of Westermain, The 1883 188

Woodstock 1826 171

Wordsworth, Dorothy 1771–1855 152

Wordsworth, William 1770–1850 97, 104, 120, 122, 137, 139, 142, 146 Criticism 147, 148, 149 Poems *151–156*, 158, 159, 164, 169, 172, 173, 179, 181, 183, 185

Worthies of England, The 1662 107

Wortley Montagu, Lady Mary 1687–1762, *Letters* 1763 124

Wotton, Sir Henry 1568–1639 54

Wounds of Civil War, The 1587 ptd 1594 78

Wulfstan's *Address to the English* c. 1010 13

Wuthering Heights 1848 195

Wyatt, Sir Thomas 1503?–1542 23, 50, *51*, 65, 95

Wycherley, William 1640?–1716 144

Wyclif, John 1320?–84 34, 48

Yardley Oak 1791 140

Yeast 1848 196

Yellow-Plush Papers, The 1838–40 193

Yew-Trees 1803 pub. 1815 156

York mysteries c. 1340–50, MS 15th century 74

Young, Edward 1683–1765, *Night Thoughts* 1742–44 135 Satires 134 *Revenge* 143

Ywain and Gawain 1330–40 19

For EU product safety concerns, contact us at Calle de José Abascal, 56–1°, 28003 Madrid, Spain or eugpsr@cambridge.org.

www.ingramcontent.com/pod-product-compliance
Ingram Content Group UK Ltd.
Pitfield, Milton Keynes, MK11 3LW, UK
UKHW012330130625
459647UK00009B/195